# High Achiever:

## The Shocking True Story of One Addict's Double Life

## Tiffany Jenkins

# Copyright

Some names and identifying details have been changed to protect the privacy of certain individuals.

This book or any portion thereof may not be reproduced or used in any manner whatsoever without the express written permission of the publisher except for the use of brief quotations in a book review.

Www.Jugglingthejenkins.com
www.facebook.com/jugglingthejenkinsblog
www.youtube.com/jugglingthejenkins

Cover: SelfPubBookCovers.com/INeedABookCover

## Dedication

For my parents, Tina & Freddy. If it wasn't for you two, I wouldn't be here today. Literally and figuratively. I miss you both, and hope I'm making you proud.

Chapter One

"One, two, three."

The light from the flash was blinding. I hadn't washed my hair in three days, and since I was arrested directly from my bed where I'd been sleeping, the mugshot about to be plastered all over the headlines was most likely just as horrendous as the crimes that started this whole ordeal.

"I am going to uncuff you, briefly, so that you can remove your jewelry and place it in this bag. Once you do that, you will head to that holding cell right there," the officer said pointing, "and change out of your clothes. You look to be a large, so here, take these," she said, handing me a polyester jumpsuit. She reached into a nearby bin and pulled out a pair of rubber flip flops.

"These are your new shoes. You will wear them at all times –including when you take a shower. Don't lose them." She thrust the shoes into my already full hands and nudged me toward the cell. I tried my best not to think about all the different feet that had already worn these rubber shoes, but despite my best efforts; I was haunted by the thought of how many different species of bacteria would soon be inhabiting my toes.

I jumped when the metal door slammed behind me. The room was dark, and the acidic smell of urine was overwhelming. I held my breath and quickly stripped off my clothes, before slipping into the jumpsuit. It felt like I was wearing cardboard. The female deputy had been observing me through the window and opened the door once I was dressed.

"Put your stuff in here." She held out a brown paper bag and I stared at my belongings as I dropped them in. My heart sank when she folded up the bag and handed it to another deputy. My clothes were no longer my own, they belonged to them now. "C'mon, you gotta see the nurse for some blood work and a pregnancy test." For a moment, I secretly prayed I was pregnant, maybe then they would let me go home.

Home. I wasn't even sure where that was anymore. I certainly couldn't go back to my home. In fact, by now, my belongings were most likely packed and sitting outside.

As I sat down on the cold metal chair across from the nurse, I suddenly realized how shitty I felt, physically. The chair was freezing yet somehow, I was sweating. My bones began aching and my eyes watered uncontrollably. I was sick.

"Okay, Miss Johnson. I'm going to do a couple of tests but first I'd like to ask you a series of questions," she said, grabbing a nearby clipboard.

"Name?"

"Tiffany Johnson."

"Age?"

"Twenty-seven."

"Weight?"

"Um, like 160 I think?"

"Currently taking any medication?"

I hesitated. She glanced up at me and repeated the question. "Are you currently taking any medication? Yes or no."

"Yes."

"What medication?"

I took a deep breath, and began. "Dilaudid, Roxicodone, Oxycoton, Xanax, Percocet, Loritab, Vicodin and Marijuana. I'm not sure if that last one counts as medication but-"

"Okay. And would you describe the crimes you have been charged with as 'shocking in nature'?"

"Yes. Yes, I would."

She looked up at me over the brim of her glasses as she set her pen down and leaned back in her seat. "Okay, I don't usually do this, but you have piqued my interest. Would you mind telling me why you consider it to be shocking in nature?"

As I proceeded to tell her what happened, I watched her expression morph from confusion, to shock, to disgust, then back as she leaned forward to check something off on her clipboard. "Okay, yes, I would say that counts as shocking in nature, definitely," she said, attempting to regain focus.

She cleared her throat and nervously glanced up at me as she made some notes. "Alright, since you are obviously going to be experiencing a severe withdrawal from opiates, we are going to keep you in Medical for a few days before bringing you to general population. There we will be able to monitor you to make sure you have a safe detox. I am just going to quickly get a few samples from you and then they will take you down."

I watched intently as she prepared her syringe and my stomach doubled over on itself at the sight. My palms began to perspire and suddenly I felt as if I might explode. My skin crawled and my legs were restless. It had only been about 20 hours since I'd last gotten high and I already felt like shit. This was going to fucking suck.

Once the nurse was finished, she motioned for an officer who, upon entering the room, placed me back in handcuffs. He didn't say a word as he led me down a long hallway. He led me to a cell in Medical and slid the heavy metal door open, and slamming it shut behind me the moment I entered. I turned to ask him when I would be getting my phone call – as I'd seen this in movies—but he was gone. I turned back around and took inventory of my tiny room. There was a metal toilet, a metal sink, a roll of toilet paper and a large plastic tub on the floor; I was assuming I was supposed to put this plastic mat I was holding inside the tub to sleep.

Suddenly, I felt something brush against my foot, and I let out a scream that sounded like someone being murdered. It was then that I noticed I wasn't alone. On the floor to my left, there was another tub, and it was occupied. The person was wrapped from head to toe in a wool blanket, completely covered, all I could see was the outline of their body.

I quietly placed my mat into the tub on the floor next to this mystery person and laid down. My withdrawal was going to take place in jail, and the realization that I was an actual inmate, began settling in. I stared at my cellmate's shape for what seemed like an eternity, trying to imagine what kind of criminal I was trapped in a tiny room with. My thought process was interrupted by a loud 'click', as the door to our cell was opened. An inmate in a red striped jumpsuit slid two trays across the floor, then promptly shut the door. Before I could even process the contents of the tray, the wool blanket went flying and my cellmate sat straight up and stared at me.

*Oh shit, it's awake. Don't panic*, I thought, giving her an awkward smile.

"You finna eat cho dinner?" she asked, burning a hole into my soul with her angry gaze.

"Oh, um hi. I'm Tiffany, I'm not sur–, I mean I'm not that hung- I hadn't really thought about it, how come?" I said, trying to keep it cool and hide the fact that I was terrified.

"Cuz Im'a eat it if you ain't," she said, never breaking eye contact. My heart began racing as I noticed a tattoo on her neck. It looked like a symbol, probably from a gang. Shit, I was trapped with a gang member. This was too much!

"Oh, okay," I said nervously. "Sure, go right ahead, I'm not hungry anyway. Actually, I don't even really like food, so..."

Without hesitation, she lunged for the trays and snatched them back to her bed like a wild animal. Not wanting to awkwardly stare at her while she ate, I laid down in my plastic boat and closed my eyes. I knew I wouldn't be able to sleep, I was feeling way too sick. I didn't know what else to do with myself, so I just stared at the ceiling. I was listening to the disgusting sound of her gorging on my dinner when suddenly it stopped. "Let me see them boobs."

My eyes popped open and I looked over at her to see who she was talking to. She was staring at me. "I'm sorry?" I asked. Perhaps I didn't hear her correctly—maybe she said books— were there books in here? Please let there be books in here.

"Your boobs, let me see them," she said with a straight face, her eyes locked on mine.

Now, if you were in my shoes what would you have said? "Screw you? No way. You're crazy, leave me alone?" Any of those responses would have been appropriate. However, I was terrified, and I had seen enough movies to know that jail fights are as common as dirt and I was not about to get my ass kicked my first day in.

"Are you being serious or no? I can't tell," I said nervously.

"Does it look like I'm being serious?" she said, looking serious.

"Okay, is that a thing? Is that what people do? Is this like initiation or something, I don't really want to be in a gang. I jus-"

"Goddamnit, show me your tits, I don't know how many times I gotta ask you, girl."

My hands shook as I grabbed the bottom of my shirt and pulled it up. I kept my breasts exposed for about three seconds, then slowly pulled it back down. I settled back into my cot, awaiting further instruction, but she didn't say a word. She just kept peeling her orange. I sat in silence, trying to read her face for clues as to what the hell was going on around here, but she was stone-faced. Watching me as if she were watching a commercial on TV—expressionless. She finished her orange and slid the empty trays back to the door then continued staring at me for a moment. I smiled, because I didn't know what else to do. "Breakfast is at 6 a.m., let me know if you want it or not." She pulled the blanket over her head and flopped back down into her cot...

I sat there in silence, staring at the outline of her body once again. Is this what I have to look forward to? I've only been here three hours and I've already given up a meal and flashed my tits. My drug withdrawal had only just begun, and I still hadn't gotten to make a phone call. I was stuck in an 8ft x 10ft cell with a lesbian woman-beast, and no one had told me anything about what my charges were, when I was getting out, or what happens next. Tears started rolling down my cheeks as the uncertainty of everything overwhelmed me. I was alone, confused, and I realized right then and there that I better get some thicker skin, and quick. I had many strange, uncomfortable, scary situations in store for me, and this was only the beginning.

Chapter Two

As the warm sun enveloped me in its comforting rays, I wiggled my toes deeper into the fine, powdery sand. I closed my eyes and inhaled a deep breath of salty ocean air as the waves lapped at the shore. I listened as they fizzled and dissipated, then returned once again to greet the sand in a loving embrace. This was my happy place. I had never taken advantage of the fact that I lived five minutes from this paradise. I was always "too busy" or "too tired." I am going to make a habit of spending more time here, this is the only place my soul feels at peace.

As I filled my lungs once again with the warm ocean air, my moment of serenity was suddenly interrupted by a loud 'bang.' I snapped my eyes open and attempted to locate its origins, but saw nothing, just the sparkling sand, water and bright blue skies. Maybe someone in the distance had slammed their trunk shut? I thought as I closed my eyes once more and reached for a handful of sand. The second 'bang' was deafening.

I sat straight up and opened my eyes to find I wasn't on a beach at all. The realization of where I was, hit me hard. I was in a cold, dark jail cell – I was an inmate. A wave of shame, embarrassment and guilt rose up from the depths of my being and consumed me. I felt as though an anaconda had coiled itself around my body, and each moment that passed, it clenched tighter and tighter.

The emotional pain I felt in that moment was matched only by the physical pain I suddenly realized. I desperately needed to get up and use the toilet, but I couldn't bring myself out from under the warmth of my covers. It felt as if each of the bones in my body were in a vice grip, moments away from being snapped. It was unbearable. This was usually the point I would do anything and everything to get my drugs, but that was no longer an option. I was trapped—and surrounded by guards. I had no choice but to feel every ounce of pain this addiction could unleash.

I was trapped. Trapped in this cell, in this broken body and this warped mind—I had nowhere to go. There were no clocks, so I had no idea how long I'd been here. My world had become gray, completely void of color. It was as if the warden wanted to strip us of any reminder of the outside world.

Yesterday I was watching Dr. Phil and eating ice cream on my couch with my puppy. Today, I am locked in a dark room with a stranger whom I will have to—at some point very soon—take a shit in front of. Each moment that dragged on felt like a century, so I decided to try and sleep to help pass the time. I managed to drift off somehow, but it was short lived.

The pain within my body was crippling, a constant reminder of the horrific reality I'd created for myself. I wondered if I'd made the news yet.

I peeked my head out from under the covers to scan my room, and was shocked to find my cell-mate's legs an inch away from my face. What the hell? My eyes followed her legs all the way up and as I got up to her face, she was peering down at me and smiling. She was trying to kill me in my sleep.

"Yo, my bad dude, your bed is right under the window, I didn't want to wake you, but my boyfriend just got back from work," she said. My eyebrows furrowed as I tried to process what she had just said.

"Um, I'm sorry, what?" I asked, feeling as if I were in the twilight zone. Boyfriend? Work?

I sat up and wiggled my way out from under her, stepping back to get a better look at what was going on. She was standing at the window, doing what I can only assume was sign language to someone. Her hands moved at lightning speed. She would pause—start laughing, say something like, "Boy, you crazy," then start flipping her hands around again.

"Love you too!" she said, kissing the window.

She turned around and noticed me wrapped in my blanket like a burrito, staring at her like she was nuts. "Das my man right there," she said cheerfully, clapping her hands together.

"Where?" I asked.

She pointed out the window. "Right there! You don't see that building right there?" I leaned right up to the window to see what the hell she was talking about. I squinted and stood on my tippy toes and finally located the building, just as the door to our cell flew open. "INMATE JOHNSON!"

I spun around and stared wide eyed at the guard, wondering why he was yelling. "Get away from that window, RIGHT NOW. The hell do you think you're doing?" he asked, stepping into our cell. I looked at my cellmate for back-up, but she apparently got a sudden urge to make her bed and she now had her back to us.

"Oh, I was, um, I just... I was just checking out the view...I guess...because it's nice outside—, I'm sorry, is that bad? Should I not look out the window? I thought that's what windows were fo..."-

"Enough!" he interrupted, "do not look out the windows. You are new here, so I'll give you a warning, but only one. Stay away from the windows," he said angrily, turning to exit the room.

When the door slammed shut I turned to look at this traitor in my cell. "Um, thanks for leaving me hanging, and why the hell are there windows if we can't look out of them?"

She turned and sat on her bed, letting out a heavy sigh. "Look, my bad. I'm doing 11-29 as it is, I can't risk no more time. My man and I got locked up together, and that's the only time I get to see him, when he gets back from work. He's in the work pod. So, we talk through sign language. You ain't allowed to do it tho, so you gotta be careful."

"What is 11-29?" I asked. "11-29, its 11 months, 29 days. If you get sentenced to a year or more, you go to prison, sometimes they will give you one day less than a year, so you gotta serve your time in county," she said.

What the hell. A year? I began to wonder what this woman had done, when our cell door opened again.

"Put your mat on the floor until we can get you a cot," the guard said, ushering another inmate into our already cramped cell.

"Don't bother getting me a damn cot, Pig. I'll be outta here in ten fucking minutes!" the woman yelled over her shoulder at the closed door, obviously drunk. I noticed she had crutches, and as I looked down to her legs to see if she had a broken bone, I noticed something was missing. Her jumpsuit was dangling in the wind where her leg was supposed to be, and she caught me staring.

"The fuck are you starin' at, four-eyes." She leaned up against the wall attempting to regain her balance. "I have diabetes, and you need to keep your eyes to your damn self."

"Hey! 'Scuse me, girl. Not you, four-eyes, the other one." She was pointing at my cellmate.

"My name is Destiny, what do you want?" my roommate replied.

"Can I tell you a secret?" Ilene asked, (We will call her Ilene, I don't know her name.)

"What?" Destiny snapped.

"Well, I'm asking you, because I know that nerdy girl with the glasses will probably snitch, but you look like you can keep a secret, come here." She waved Destiny towards her. Destiny stood up and walked to Ilene, who motioned for her to lean down then whispered something into her ear.

"Are you serious?" Destiny said looking surprised.

"As a heart attack, I just need some help."

"If you fuck me over, I will cut off your other leg—do you understand me?"

"Loud and clear," Ilene said as a smile crept across her face. They both looked at me and my heart started pounding. I'm going to die. This is it. They have just planned my murder.

"Hey, Johnson, we need you to keep a lookout. If you see someone coming we need you to cough, okay?" Destiny said.

"A lookout? For what? I don't want to get in trouble," I replied, sounding like a pussy.

"I know, man, that's why we aren't involving you, if you don't see nothin' you don't know nothin'. Just face the door and don't turn around until we say. If you see someone coming, let us know—aight?"

"I...guess," I said, getting up to stand and face the door like a five-year-old in time out.

I heard Destiny say, "Ready?"

Ilene said, "Go." Ilene let out a groan, and the curiosity of what the hell was going on behind me was overwhelming. I had to look.

I slowly turned my head until my eyes reached the women. What I saw next will haunt me for a lifetime.

I snapped my head forward in shock and stared out into the hallway to process what I'd just witnessed. Life didn't make sense anymore. This had to be a joke. A test. I was on a hidden camera show, it was the only explanation that made any sense. Destiny had her entire fist shoved into this one-legged woman's ass.

I have seen a lot of messed up things in my life, but for some reason, witnessing two complete strangers—whom had met less than five minutes before, fishing around in one another's bowels was on the top of my "Things I Want Permanently Erased from My Memory" List.

"Got it," Destiny whispered excitedly as Ilene began laughing.

"Hell yeah. Good girl. Hurry up and rinse it."

"Can I turn around now, please?" I asked. I was asking permission to turn around, what the hell had my life come to?

"Yes, but if you say anything to anyone, I will beat the brakes off you. You hear me?" Destiny said sounding scary again.

"Got it," I said, on the verge of vomiting.

I went and sat down at my bed, trying to catch a glimpse of what was going on. The two women were sitting across from each other on the bed, hurriedly spreading into two lines whatever the hell just came out of that woman's asshole. They each took turns sniffing whatever it was, and I was suddenly overcome with jealousy. "What is that?" I asked. Destiny looked over at me as she sniffed whatever remnants were left in her nose—-deep into her nasal cavity.

"It's meth," she replied. "You want some?"

Chapter Three

I had only tried meth once in my life. One little puff – and I hated it. However, as an addict, if someone offers you drugs—regardless of the brand—you do them. Before I could open my mouth to say, "Hell yes," pain in the ass (pun intended) Ilene threw a fit.

She snarled, "These ain't your drugs to offer to anyone. I only gave you some because you went in and got em. I don't have enough to keep sharing—sorry, four-eyes."

To say I was disappointed would be an understatement. There is nothing worse than anticipating a high, then something taking that promise away-especially if you are on day three of detoxing. I was consumed with rage. I contemplated murdering them and taking the drugs for myself, but there were no weapons available, so I had to come up with another plan. I had a few ideas—all equally absurd. One involved rappelling down from the ceiling while they napped and grabbing them out of her pocket. However, I was not Tom Cruise and this was not *Mission Impossible* so I scrapped that one. Suddenly a voice over the intercom interrupted my scheming. "Johnson—roll it up, you are going to Gen Pop."

I glanced over at my cellmates looking perplexed. "So, was that English or...-? What the hell did thing just say?" Destiny laughed at my ignorance and let me know that the woman basically said to gather my belongings, because they are moving me to general population—another word for, "one big room filled with a shit ton of criminals."

I tried to act cool, like it was no big deal that I was about to enter a den of ravenous animals in various stages of drug withdrawal, many suffering from undiagnosed mental problems and rage issues—but inside I was freaking out.

I gathered my mat and sheet and stood by the gate, waiting to be let out. When the guard slid the door open, I turned around and smiled at my roommates. "It was nice meeting you guys!" I said cheerfully, but they were too busy trying to avoid eye contact with the guard to even look up to bid me farewell. They should really teach etiquette classes here, I think I'm going to write someone a letter about that.

The guard led me down a long corridor with my hands and ankles shackled. The metal was digging into my Achilles tendon and it was incredibly painful. "Um, excuse me, officer?" I whispered.

"Quiet in the hallways," he grumbled.

"Okay, it's just that..."

"NO TALKING IN THE HALLWAYS!"

"Kay," I replied sharply. I was immediately brought back to my elementary school days. Walking quietly in a straight line and following orders. I felt like a fucking child. Last week I was managing a restaurant, and today I'm getting screamed at for speaking.

"Alright, I'm going to undo these shackles and send you in with Deputy Flower," the guard said. Aww, Deputy Flower, she sounds nice. He unlocked my chains and my ankles immediately felt better. He nudged me into the dark room where I was met by a female deputy, staring at me with her hand on her gun. "Take your clothes off, please," Miss Flower demanded.

"Whoa, whoa, whoa. We just met, it's a little soon, don't you thi-,"

She interrupted before I could finish my joke. "Jesus Christ, you are literally the millionth person to say that shit to me. Take your goddamn clothes off and put your hands on the wall. Now!" Apparently, Deputy Flower wasn't the joking kind. Noted.

I felt very uncomfortable showering in front of a complete stranger, but after the shower when she told me to 'bend over and spread,' I reached a whole new level of humiliation.

"Put these on," she said sternly, tossing me a new outfit. She then handed me a roll of toilet paper and a toothbrush. "We are out of soap, tell the night guards, they will bring you one."

"No problem," I said, not realizing it would be four more days until my soap would arrive. Turns out my comfort wasn't their main priority. I came to learn this—and many other fun facts about the guards as time went on.

She led me to a large door and said, "Ready, " into her walkie talkie to the person in charge of opening the doors remotely.

I wanted to grab her walkie and yell, "Wait! I'm not ready!" into it, but I figured it would probably get me tased.

As the door clicked she pulled it open and said, "You're in cell five," shutting it behind me.

The loud roar of wild women suddenly stopped short. There was complete silence as hundreds of women suddenly were eyeing me. I wasn't sure what to do so I awkwardly smiled. Some of them laughed, some started yelling inappropriate comments, and one person yelled, "Police-ass hoe!"

I didn't know what that meant, but later found out that if you look like you don't belong in jail, they think you are an undercover cop. So, that's good.

I found cell #5 and hesitantly stepped in. There were four mats occupying six of the metal bunk beds, so I headed toward one of the empty spots. "Hello, I'm Tiffany. Would it be okay if I put my mat here?" I asked the toothless woman picking her toenails on the bunk above.

"I don't give a flying fuck," she said, never taking her eyes off her foot. *Well, she seems nice*, I thought as I slapped my mat down and began making my bed.

I remained in bed for most of the day. My body was in so much pain from the withdrawal that I was finding it hard to breathe. I watched through the bars of my cell as women were running around, laughing and having a good time. How the hell could they laugh at a time like this? Do they not realize they are in jail? A lot of them seemed...happy. I don't think I'll ever be happy again.

Depression and despair weighed down on me so heavily that I felt paralyzed. I realized that I was going to spend a very long time in jail, and even when I did get out, I was going to spend the rest of my life being despised by everyone, and I would certainly never be respected again. Dark thoughts of what my future would look like came crashing into my mind. I would be homeless. No one would ever want to love a horrible person like me, especially after they find out what I did to my last boyfriend.

Living with the choices I had made became impossible to imagine. I didn't have it in me to keep going. I suddenly wanted out. The anticipation of the unexpected, the waiting and worrying – I just couldn't do it. I had already been locked up for what seemed like a lifetime, and I hadn't even learned what my charges were. I wasn't cut out to be an adult, I wasn't meant to live a full life. I am a junkie loser and that's all I'm ever going to be. I have no choice, there is no other way. Tonight, after everyone falls asleep... I'm going to kill myself.

Chapter Four

I was staring out the window of my cell as everyone else was eating dinner in the Mess Hall. I didn't have much of an appetite, I didn't see any point in eating either, as I knew I was only a few hours away from the end of my time here on earth.

I had spent some time deliberating how I was going to carry out my plan—which was difficult, seeing as how I didn't have many options. They didn't make it easy for anyone contemplating suicide here, I'm assuming it's because the number of people who would take advantage of it would be astronomical. Detoxing from drugs alone is enough to make any civilized person contemplate jumping off a building. But when you add the mess I'd left in the wake of my destruction, death was my only option.

Drops of rain began peppering the window as my mind started to drift. I thought about my sisters, and how heartbroken they would be when they got the news tomorrow. I immediately forced those thoughts out of mind, because my will to die was much stronger than any concern I had for anyone else's emotions. I was afraid that giving my family too much thought would change that. I thought about how unfortunate it was that I wasn't going to experience having children, or being married. I would make a shitty wife and mom anyway, so I was doing the world a service, really.

I was hoping to somehow see my mom. If for some crazy reason heaven did end up being real (which, to me, was preposterous) then I knew that's where she was. But if that was in fact the case, we would most likely never cross paths again. They say suicide is a sin, and chances are you are going to hell, but if hell was real, I had already purchased a one-way ticket there, anyway, regardless of my exit strategy. So, fuck it.

I stayed in the same position for the next few hours, until "lights-out." My cellmates hadn't bothered me because they could tell I was severely withdrawing, and I had glared angrily at anyone who attempted to make eye contact or approach me.

I waited patiently, quietly, anxiously for each of them to drift off, each making a different sound as they breathed in the night air. Some women snored, some breathed quietly, but I waited until I was sure that every one of them was asleep. When the last woman tossed and turned until finally settling in to the perfect position; I knew it was time.

I sat up in my bunk, and delicately set my feet on the cold concrete floor. As I stood up, I glanced around to ensure that no one had stirred. My hands found their way to the corner of my sheet and I gently began removing it from my mat. Sheet in hand, my fingers began moving automatically, almost as if they were programmed to tie this knot. There was no thought, just mindless twisting and pulling. I wasn't thinking of anything other than how desperate I was for this to be over. I didn't want to spend another moment here on this earth, I needed to go, and I needed to go now.

I nervously glanced around the room one last time—making sure everyone was still fast asleep, and I carefully tied one end of the sheet to the corner of the bunk above me. I braced for the girl above me to wake up, as I had tied the knot about two inches from her foot—but she didn't budge. I took one last, deep breath in as I wrapped the other end of the sheet around my neck... And pulled it as tight as I possibly could. There were no tears and no second thoughts as I took in one last breath, and pushed myself off the bed.

There was no place high enough in my cell to completely hang from, so I let my legs go limp, and allowed my body weight and gravity to do the work. I was hanging from my neck, my legs outstretched in front of me. The pressure around my throat was overwhelming, it felt as though my spine was separating from my skull. I could feel my face getting hot, it felt like it was swelling with blood. I had to fight my natural instincts, which desperately sought air. My physical body was aching to stand up and breathe, but my mind was stronger. There was no going back now.

The sounds of the world around me began to grow faint and my peripheral vision started to darken; it was as if I was looking down the length of a tunnel. The walls of darkness were closing in and the world had gone silent. The pressure was causing the blood vessels inside my eyes to burst and at any moment I was certain that my eyes were going to pop free of their sockets completely. Everything had gone black and I knew this was it, it was almost over. For the first time, in a very long time, I felt...free.

I was startled by a bright light beaming down on me, and I realized I was passing through another dimension. I smiled, anxious to be free of my damaged earthly body, now a part of the universe. The light continued to grow brighter—almost blinding and I gasped as air suddenly filled my lungs with a "whoosh." What the hell? I was choking, I couldn't catch my breath. I began to see flashes of light and hear intermittent yelling as my hearing slowly returned. I blinked a few times, and a blurry image began taking shape above me. It was a face. But not the face of God—or the devil—it was Officer Cache. "Johnson! Can you hear me? Tiffany! Wake up."

Anger began coursing through every vein in my body once I realized what was happening. I began violently throwing my arms and kicking, desperate to get everyone the hell away from me.

"Why!!?" I screamed. "Why the fuck did you wake me up? Why? Why didn't you let me go!"

I began sobbing uncontrollably out of anger and frustration. I had been so close. Close to being home, with my mother and grandparents - and now, I was right back in hell. Right back into the reality from which I had so desperately tried to escape.

Chapter Five

I glanced around the room at my cellmates who looked
shocked and horrified. I wanted to scream at them for being
so dramatic. I wanted to find out who the hell foiled my plan,
ruining any hope of me being free from this shitty planet. Before I could say another word to anyone, a deputy pulled my
wrists behind my back and handcuffed me. She said, "Come
on, we gotta take you to medical."

I stood up and she pulled me toward the dayroom. I
wanted to run, I wanted to slam my head into the fucking wall
and finish the job. Instead, I went quietly, because the moment I exited my cell I realized all the lights in the pod had
been turned on, and every inmate in Female West was standing at their gates—watching me be dragged out, the sheet still
hanging loosely from my neck.

My body remained limp as the guards dragged me into a
room and I noticed instead of walls, there were Plexiglass windows. I had seen one of these rooms in a movie once, it was
known as an Observation Cell. These cells were specifically
designed for inmates who were suicidal, therefore, it was
made to be "death proof." Someone who wants to end their life
can become quite crafty, so they take special precautions to

ensure that it would be virtually impossible for any inmate to do so.

All protrusions from the room had been removed such as: sprinkler heads, bunk bed rails and windows. My jumpsuit had been replaced with what I can only describe as a large, bulky, Velcro potato sack. There was no loose fabric, so even if I wanted to attempt to twist my new attire into a death weapon—my efforts would be futile.

"I need to take your glasses as well, ma'am," the guard said, sticking out her hand.

"I can't see without my glasses, I need them," I pleaded.

"It is our job to make sure you are safe while in our custody, your glasses could easily be fashioned into a weapon and we are not going to take any chances, I have to take them."

As she slipped off my glasses, the world around me became a blur. My vision is terrible and without my glasses I couldn't tell how many fingers you would be holding up—even if they were an inch from my face.

She removed the handcuffs from my wrists and a moment later I heard the cell door slam behind her. I could only assume she had left, because I sure as hell wasn't able to see her leave.

I was barefoot and blind. I felt naked. Anyone passing by would be able to peer in at me and check to make sure that I was still breathing, everyone had a complete 360-degree view of everything I did in the cell, including using the restroom.

I felt like an animal at the zoo. I could see the silhouettes of officers in uniform passing by, occasionally stopping at the glass and making snide comments. Most of the correctional officers knew why I was in there; they had access to the entire report which detailed the things I had done to their brother in blue. Needless to say, each of them wanted to ensure I was fully aware of what a piece of shit I was. I could hear them say, "I don't blame her for trying to kill herself, I would too. She's looking at a lot of time. She's blind as a bat, serves her right."

I was embarrassed, ashamed and there was nowhere for me to hide.

After about seven hours in my aquarium, I started to lose my fucking mind. I was already feeling mentally unstable; and the current conditions certainly didn't help. The longer I sat here—blinded and stripped down to nothing—the more my grip on reality seemed to slip away. I walked into the jail as "Tiffany" but in this moment—I was something else. An animal in a cage, a suicidal maniac, a thieving liar, an inmate. The old me was gone, and I was fairly certain she'd never be seen again.

I'd been vomiting repeatedly as the drugs made their way out of my system. I spent most of my time hunched over the toilet, heaving as I desperately tried to get the poison out of my body. I had my head resting on the cold metal of the toilet seat and suddenly had an idea. They had all these measures in place for suicide prevention—but I was smarter, and I was going to finish the job.

I pulled my potato sack up over my head to conceal the upper half of my body. Once hidden, I crossed my arms, placing both of my thumbs onto the boney part of the front of my throat and began pushing and squeezing as hard as I could. I wanted to break the bones in my throat in hopes that it would cause me to suffocate to death. I wanted death more than I had ever wanted anything before in my life. I needed it. I knew that if I succeeded, I would be free. My earthly body had malfunctioned, and I didn't want to carry on inside of it.

The bones in my throat were more malleable than I had anticipated. Instead of breaking beneath my strong grip, they shifted backwards, causing me to choke loudly. I dug my fingers into my flesh and twisted the bones and muscles around, but it wasn't fucking working.

In the distance, I heard someone calmly say, "Here she goes, open #4." Seconds later the door clicked open. I felt the heavy hands of the guard on my shoulders, pulling me back away from the toilet. I landed flat on my back and he held me down with his elbow to my chest. "Stop this—right now," he growled.

"Just fucking let me go!" I shrieked. "Goddamnit. Why the hell won't you people just leave me alone?! It's my fucking life!" I twisted and writhed about the floor as they attempted to restrain me. I couldn't see anything, making it difficult to fight back. "It's none of your business, just stop. Let me finish, please!" I howled. Despite the cold floor on my legs and back, I was hot with rage. "Please just beat me over the head with your night stick. Please, please, please just kill me. I'm begging you. Shoot me with your taser please. Please," I pleaded, "I want to die."

"I'm not going to kill you, Johnson. That's a lot of damn paperwork and I've got a date with my wife when I get home. I'm going to stand up and exit the cell, you have one more chance," he said. "If you pull some bullshit like this again, we won't hesitate to shackle your hands and feet. It will be a lot more uncomfortable for you if we have to do that so knock it off." The lack of compassion in his voice was startling. The worst day of my life was just another day on the job for him.

In that moment I came to terms with the reality of my current living situation. These people didn't give a shit about me. They were just waiting for their shifts to end, hoping things remained quiet in the meantime. They didn't care that I was once captain of the cheerleading squad, or voted class clown by my peers. They didn't care that I was a sister and a daughter or that I once did roller derby. They didn't care that I was voted queen at the Valentine's Dance in high school or that I was a restaurant manager for three years. None of that mattered, I was no longer that person- I was inmate 4012342, and nothing more.

After what felt like an eternity in isolation—there was a small knock on my cell door. "May I come in?" I heard a kind sounding voice say from the other side.

"I don't give a shit," I said, huddled in the corner of my cell with my knees pressed to my chest. I heard the door click open, but I couldn't see the person standing there. I could tell by her silhouette, however, that she wasn't a guard.

"I would like to come closer, but I need to know that you won't hurt me... Can I trust you not to hurt me?" she said calmly.

"Hurt you? Why would I hurt you? I wouldn't do that, I don't even know who the hell you are, I can't see shit," I said.

"Well my name is Dr. LaChance and I would like to speak with you."

I took a deep breath and stared down at the floor. "I don't really feel like talking right now, no offense."

"Well I certainly don't blame you, you are in a glass box, near nude without sight. I'll tell you what. If I could convince the guards to get your glasses for you, could you make a promise to me that you wouldn't try to harm yourself with them?" she said.

My heart skipped a beat. Being able to see what was happening around me would certainly help me to comprehend my surroundings, and I would feel better equipped to handle my current situation. "Oh my God yes. Please. I promise on my mother's life I will not use them for anything other than looking at things. Please, can you do that? Can you get them?" I asked eagerly.

I could hear that she was smiling as she spoke. "My, you certainly perked up didn't you. Give me just a moment." She exited the cell and a spark of hope ignited somewhere deep inside me.

I had taken my sight for granted and once I no longer had it, I realized how important it was to me. I waited with anticipation for what seemed like hours for her to return and I began pacing back and forth in my cell. Suddenly, doubt crept in. I realized she wasn't coming back. I knew this was too good to be true. I hadn't encountered one employee whom had talked to me as if I was a person since I had been here. Why would a sweet stranger whisk in and reward me with my glasses out of nowhere? I had officially lost my damn mind-I was hallucinating now.

I sat back down in the corner, defeated, and pressed my chin to me knees. A click of the door and my head snapped back up. "Hello, Tiffany, it's me. May I come in?" Dr. LaChance asked.

"Yes, of course," I said. I heard her heels click on the concrete floor as she entered the cell, but then they suddenly stopped. It had grown silent.

She giggled. "Oh, I forgot. You probably can't see me. I'm handing you your glasses," she said as she slid them into my right hand. Tears of gratitude and relief rolled down my cheeks as I slid my glasses onto the bridge of my nose. My jaw dropped when my guardian angel came into focus. I knew her. How did I not recognize her voice? My face suddenly flushed with embarrassment once I realized this was Katie. I used to be her cheerleading coach.

Chapter Six

I instantly felt embarrassed at the condition she had found me in. The last time she'd seen me, I was the bright, bubbly blonde cheerleading coach whom she looked up to as a role model for many years, and now... I was a thin, pale, sweaty, junkie cowering in the corner of a jail cell.

She must have noticed the various emotions I was going through, because she gently placed her hand on my knee and smiled. "I know what you are thinking and I want you to know – that the person you are today, in this moment – is not you. I know you, I know the real you. You are the funniest girl I have ever met, still to this day. I have always looked up to you, and that hasn't changed." She ushered me to the wall and we both sat on the concrete floor, our backs to the wall. "Your path in life seems to have taken a detour; but I am not here to judge you, Tiffany, I am here to help. I'm the Therapist here at the jail, and I just want to talk to you. Will you talk to me?" she asked.

Katie and I spent the next two hours talking about everything. I told her all the things that had happened in my life since I became addicted to drugs and she sat quietly and listened. She would occasionally speak up but only to ask questions which caused me to probe deeper into my thoughts, as if she was trying to get me to think of things from a different perspective. In a weird way – for a moment it felt like we were back in high school. This was the first time I had felt human since I had arrived.

I felt free after speaking with her, as if I had been lugging around a giant sack of rocks for a very long time and Katie gently took my bag from me, freeing me up to focus on the journey ahead, instead of worrying about how I could possibly make it while toting around this heavy load.

"I am proud of you for being so honest with me. I know you don't want to die, and I think now you realize it too." She leaned her head down until her eyes met mine. "I would like to see you a week from today, would that be possible, you think?"

I knew what she was doing, she was trying to hold me accountable. If I had a date set up with her a week from now, I would have to be alive for it – she was ensuring I didn't off myself in the meantime. "I would love that," I said, and I meant it.

"I will tell the guards you are ready to go back to general population, okay?" she said standing up from the floor and dusting the back of her skirt off.

"I don't know," I replied, "everyone saw what happened, and I feel really awkward walking back in there."

"Can I give you some advice – off the record? Screw them. I mean, not literally of course." She walked towards me laughing with her arms outstretched and gave me a tight hug. It felt so good to be embraced, I had been moments away from shattering into a thousand pieces before she entered my cell, and her presence gave me a flicker of hope. She reminded me that I was in fact still human, even though it didn't feel like it lately.

I was standing outside of general population waiting to be let in and my heart was pounding at lightning speed. My sweaty hands were trying to keep a firm grip on the sleeping mat I'd been carrying, and I was shaking uncontrollably. The guard looked me up and down and the corner of his mouth lifted into a smirk. It was as if he got some sort of enjoyment out of seeing me squirm.

The door clicked loudly and swung open and when it did, the familiar sounds of screaming and complete chaos filled the hallway. "Go on," the guard said nodding toward the door. I stepped into the pod and the room fell silent, you could hear a pin drop. I visually located the cell I had been designated to and made a beeline for it with my head down.

As I entered, a petite, kind-looking blonde girl looked up at me from her notepad. I began to introduce myself but was interrupted by her jumping to her feet and throwing her hands up. "Oh hell naw!" she yelled marching out of the cell. I leaned back to peer outside the door to see where the hell she was going and noticed she was stomping toward "The Button" at the entrance of the pod.

"The Button" was used to contact guards in an emergency. No one was to push it unless shit was hitting the fan. I watched in confusion as she pushed the button twice and crossed her arms, a look of defiance on her little face. "What's the emergency?" the guard said over the intercom.

"Um yeah, hi, uh so somebody put that suicidal undercover cop in my cell, and I need ya'll to reassign her somewhere else. I'm gonna end up fighting her, and I don't want to go to lock," she said staring me in the face the entire time she spoke.

What...in the actual HELL was she talking about?

"Daniels, you know damn well we don't take requests. This line is for emergencies only, press the button again and you will end up in lock anyway," the guard said, agitated.

Fuck my life, this was going to be awkward. I watched as "Daniels" marched up to a group of girls and angrily began speaking. She was throwing her arms up and occasionally punching her fists while they all took turns glaring at me. *Why did this chick want to fight me?* I didn't want to make my bed just yet because I didn't know what the hell to expect from this little psycho. I was afraid she might rip my mat off the bunk and beat me with it, so I just carried it out to the dayroom with me and sat at an empty table.

You know that dorky loser kid in movies who has no friends and awkwardly sits at the lunch table by himself? That was me. Except I was surrounded by felons, not high school students.

I felt a hand on the small of my back and I jumped because I thought I was about to get shanked. "Hi, I'm Brandi," a girl said, sticking her hand out for me to shake. I reluctantly shook it, noting how beautiful she was. "I heard you tried to kill yourself, that sucks I've been there. I also heard what that whore said to the guard about you and I'm sorry. I figured you could use a friend, do you want to bunk with me?" She smiled.

My heart almost exploded with gratitude. "Oh my God yes, please," I said desperately.

"Come on, we are over here." She took my hand and led me to the very last cell in the row. My bed was right next to hers, and I felt relief the instant I sat down. The vibe in this cell was awesome, and it was because Brandi had such a beautiful soul.

We spent the rest of the day talking about life. I did most of the talking and she just listened for the most part. She would periodically tell me stories about crazy things she had done, and I think she was trying to make me feel better about some of the choices I had made. She showed me how to order shampoo and shared her dinner with me. I even laughed out loud for the first time in what seemed like years.

When it came time to go to sleep she came over and gave me a hug. "I'm really glad to have met you, sleep with the angels and I'll see you tomorrow," she said then skipped back to her bunk.

Brandi was the first friend I'd made since I'd been in jail. I watched her snuggle into a comfortable position and smiled realizing that someone cared about me. Had I known that she would be dead a week later, I might have hugged her a little tighter that night.

Chapter Seven

After spending two days back in general population, I began to get a feel for how things worked around here. There was a schedule – and it sucked.

Six a.m. The lights turn on, the doors click open and we're allowed to exit our cell and line up for breakfast. Inmates from the Working Pod set up at the entrance of our pod and quickly begin to serve the food. I learned that when it was my turn, I was to say my last name and cell number to the guard and he would put a checkmark by my name. This was a way for them to keep track of who was eating and who wasn't. If you skip too many meals, they take you to medical, assuming you are trying to kill yourself by starvation.

There are technically no assigned seats for meals. However, certain people claimed certain seats, and should an innocent new inmate ignorantly sit in one of those spots, they were verbally assaulted until they voluntarily moved to another place (I learned that the hard way.)

Six thirty a.m. Breakfast is over and we all go back to our cells—with the exception of the inmates whose cell was on cleaning duty that week. We were locked in the cell until 7:15 a.m., so that the guards could go around and count. Evidently, this was to make sure no one had hidden in a garbage can and got wheeled the hell outta there and escaped during breakfast.

Seven thirty a.m. The doors click open and we are free! The women usually fly out of their cells, desperate to escape the confined space. The first two days back I basically used to observe my surroundings. I noticed that jail was kind of like a weird summer camp for the outcasts of society. At one table, you had a 46-year-old woman and a 19-year-old girl coloring pictures of hearts and animals. In the corner of the day room, three women were seated with their backs to each other braiding the hair of the one in front of them. Another table would have two grown ass women playing patty cake and giggling like seven-year-olds. It really gave me the creeps.

The middle table had girls yelling and laughing while playing cards, while two others would be making up a dance routine at the top of the stairs. I glanced around in amazement at how these women were acting. It was as if either they had forgotten where they were—or they were very good at adapting. I really think a lot of these women loved the idea of not having any responsibility other than making their bed and exchanging their clothes on laundry day.

It was fascinating and terrifying all at once. I tried to imagine myself being that carefree and having fun here, and it seemed impossible to me. I didn't belong here. This wasn't my idea of "fun." I missed hot coffee, and sunshine and Taco Bell and watching Dr. Phil, and sleeping in a comfy bed. I missed freedom – and it hadn't even been a week.

Nine a.m. The fun would be interrupted by guards barging in and ordering everyone back to their cells. It was time for another lockdown, so they could make sure no one escaped through a toilet bowl or the shower drain. (Because literally those were the only two exits and it would be physically impossible to do so.) The fact they had 100 counts a day started to really piss me off. We were locked in the cells for another hour.

Ten a.m. Lunchtime! Once again, the women sprang out of their cells like wild animals the moment the doors clicked open. Last name, cell number, bologna sandwiches, assigned seats, 15 minutes to eat – back in cell for an hour for the "after lunch" count. Fuck, this was getting annoying.

Eleven a.m. – 3:30 p.m. Free time. The moment the doors clicked open it was like a stampede. The women trampled each other to get to a phone. There were six phones and about 100 women who wanted to call their loved ones, so you can imagine the drama that ensued the minute the beasts were freed from their cages. This was the longest time between lockdowns, and the first time we permitted to use the phones. This was when I considered our "day" to really begin. There wasn't much to do while stuck in one giant room with nothing but time, so people had to get creative. I spent the first two days napping and lying in bed. I was still detoxing – but it had gotten better.

Three p.m. Lockdown, and another motherfucking count.

Four p.m. Dinner. This was the last meal of the day, and I had previously discovered that by 8 o'clock p.m. – I was starving again. The only way to eat outside of chow time was to purchase commissary. Our loved ones can put money on our accounts, enabling us to buy shampoo, conditioner and snacks. My family hated me currently, so I was shit-out-of-luck there.

Four thirty p.m. You guessed it—lockdown and count.

Five thirty p.m. - 8:30 p.m. Free time. This is when things usually got wild. Women would take jelly packets and instant coffee to make "whips." You whip the jelly and coffee together until it forms this...goo. Then you dab a bit on the top of your hand and lick it off, over and over until it's gone. I shit you not, this is a real thing, and everyone was doing it. I suppose this was the jailhouse equivalent to partying and getting wild. Girls would be snorting headache medicine in their cells and flashing their tits to each other across the day room. It was a madhouse. There was an observation room with eight giant windows on top of the dayroom, and guards were stationed there to watch our every move. Occasionally they would yell over the loudspeaker for us to "calm the hell down," but for the most part, it was a free-for-all.

Eight thirty p.m. Final lockdown. We are confined to our cells until the next morning. They do a final count and shut the lights out. From that point on, we are required to be silent. If we are caught talking—the entire cell has to go to "lock," which is slang for Solitary Confinement.

We are supposed to sleep at this point, but sleeping is impossible in this place. Toilets are flushing loudly all night, my cellmates snore like bears and the lights never really go off. They stay on all night long, which was really going to take some getting used to.

That night, before lights out, Brandi and I were talking about our high school experience. I brought up the fact that I used to be a cheerleader and she began laughing hysterically, saying she could never imagine me doing that. I was about to stand up and show her some of my moves when suddenly her expression turned serious. "Tiff, if you don't mind me asking... What did you do to get in here?"

There it was. I knew it was coming eventually and I swore to myself that I wasn't going to tell anyone what my charges were, because my case was still pending. I had heard rumors that you've got to be careful what you say in here, because people will do just about anything to get their sentences reduced—

including running to the cops with inside information about your case.

But I trusted Brandi, I was very good at reading people and could tell she had a good soul. She befriended me when I needed it most and I felt as if I owed her. I looked into her eyes and hesitated for just a moment, I was trying to read her to see if she really wanted to know, or if she was just using me to find out the gossip. I took a long, hesitant breath—and began to tell her everything.

Chapter Eight

Brandi was sitting on the edge of her bunk and I noticed her foot was tapping the floor rapidly as she waited for me to begin my story.

"When I was arrested, I was arrested at my home," I began. "I shared that home with my boyfriend, and he is a deputy for this county." Her jaw dropped open as she inched closer to the edge of her bed. "I had been doing pills every day behind his back—for two and a half years."

"When it got really ba-" My story was abruptly interrupted by a sudden flurry of movement in the corner of my eye. I looked to my left and noticed that all the girls were running back to their cells.

Our cellmates ran in where Brandi and I had been seated and swiftly began making their beds, a look of horror on their faces. "What the hell is going on?" I asked, standing up and glancing down at my bed—wondering if I should fix mine up too for some reason. Brandi looked out into the dayroom and I watched as the realization of what was happening washed over her face.

"Um, hello? Can someone please tell me what is happening? Why is everyone freaking out?" I asked straightening the edges of my sheets. Brandi dropped to the floor and began straightening up the contents of her bin. She didn't even look up at me to answer:

"Riggins."

"Huh? Riggins? What the hell is a Riggins?" I asked.

"No one told you?!"

"No one told me what? Is my life in danger? Like, what the fuck is going on?" I asked, a mixture of terror and confusion in my voice.

Before she could answer I heard the door of the dayroom slam shut, and our entire pod fell silent. I could hear a set of keys jingling and a pair of sneakers tapping the floor as the person wearing them jogged up the stairs. I sat on the edge of my bed observing my cellmates. They were frozen in place, a look of fear on their faces – it was as if the President of the United States had just walked in and was hand selecting people to go to war.

"You nasty hoes wash your pussies today?!" someone yelled from the top tier. "I know some ah ya'll stank bitches is on day two of no shower, witcho nasty asses."

Wait...What?

"Ay! Da fuck I tell you about making sure deez beds was made when I came in? Ohhhh ya'll thought Deputy Flower was on tonight, huh? That's why you just said, 'fuck it', and let ya shit stay messy. Well surprise, mothafuckers, Riggins is in the house tonight!"

The guard was making her rounds across the top tier when she suddenly came into view across from our cell. I expected a man beast of a woman to come bounding around the corner. This lady was 5 ft 2 in. tall, but something told me her size was irrelevant.

I watched her move quickly past the cells, analyzing the appearance of each one. She began jogging down the stairs and heading straight for our cell, a look of determination in her eyes. For some reason, I suddenly felt like I was about to shit my pants.

She glanced into our cell and continued walking, but then I heard her sneakers 'squeak' as she stopped short and backed up. She looked in our cell again and began laughing as she unhooked her keys from her belt and opened our door.

She was laughing and shaking her head as she entered and then she stopped. She stared into my eyes with a look I can only describe as the look your mother gives you when she's about to beat your ass.

"Well, well, well—what we got here? You must be new. Man, that's messed up, ya'll didn't give her the heads up? Ya'll didn't educate her bout Riggins didja?" she said, looking at my cellmates. "Well I'll just have to introduce myself then. What's up, crack head, I'm Riggins, and I'm gonna make you wish you never stepped foot in my jail."

She walked toward me and bumped me as she headed toward my bed. She proceeded to rip the entire mat off my bunk and throw it into the middle of the dayroom. I could feel everyone's eyes on me, and my face began burning with embarrassment. "Im'a teach you how to make your bed right. Come on." She bounded out to the dayroom and stood with her arms crossed, waiting for me to exit my cell.

I walked toward her and stood above my mat, unsure of what exactly was going on. "So, should I make my-" Before I could finish she lunged over to where I was standing, got about an inch from my face, and began screaming at the top of her lungs while looking me dead in the eyes.

"Did I motherfucking ask you to talk, motherfucker? No, I don't think so. Don't say another motherfucking word unless you want me to throw your nasty ass in lock. Now close your mouth, and make your Goddamn bed, hoe," she said, stepping back to give me room.

I could feel the tears forming in my eyes and tried with everything in me to not let them fall. I couldn't help it, I had never been so humiliated in my life.

I began sobbing as I dropped to my hands and knees in front of every woman in my pod—and began making my bed.

It was incredibly demeaning to have to get down on the floor like a child and make my bed in front of my peers. I secretly hoped she would realize that I was new here, and give me a break...She did the opposite.

"Oh my God. Look at this. Hey ya'll, hey! Look down here right quick. This girl over here cryin' bout makin' her damn bed." I heard a few snickers from the women and I cringed, thinking about how I was trapped with these people for God knows how long, and now they were completely aware of what a pussy I am. "This bitch here probably ain't used to havin' to do chores. She been too busy getting high and suckin' dick on the streets to worry 'bout making her damn bed at home." She leaned down and placed her hands on her knees, getting eye level with me and stared menacingly into my soul. "You're in my house now, bitch," she whispered.

"I would like this whiney little junkie to be an example to all ya'll. You bitches wanna act hard out on them streets, but when you're in here, you ain't shit. Right now, I want all ya'll to take your sheets off your bed and make them damn beds perfectly – you know how I like it. When you're done, take the sheets off again and remake them. You can stop when Inmate Johnson here makes her bed correctly. I'll be back to check on ya'll in a few, don't be comin' out them cells till you're done."

The women began groaning and pulling their sheets off, cursing and talking about how they were going to beat my ass when the doors unlocked. Deputy Riggins had almost made it out of the pod before she stopped abruptly. She turned back around and began walking toward me as silence once again fell upon the pod. I felt myself tense up as she leaned close to me, putting her mouth right next to my ear.

"I know what you did, Johnson, Chuck is a good friend of mine. You shouldn't have done him like that when he loved you. Best believe I'm going to make sure that while you are here, you pay for what you did." She roughly patted me on the back and once again headed toward the door. "One more thing!" she yelled over her shoulder as she exited the pod. "Make sure the minute those cells unlock for you to come out, ya'll let this girl know how much you appreciate her for making ya'll do your beds over and over." She laughed as the door slammed shut behind her.

Chapter Nine

I spent the next 45 minutes making—then re-making my bed. I could see Mrs. Riggins standing in the observatory platform watching, from the corner of my eye. Each time I finished making what I thought was the perfect bed, I would look up at her pleadingly in hopes she was satisfied. My fate rested on what she would say, because each time I had to remake mine, the rest of the pod did too.

A terse "Nope" over the intercom would echo through the dayroom and all the females would collectively groan. I began to perspire from the pressure I was experiencing while performing this task.

When I finally somehow managed to do it correctly (which, I'm pretty sure it looked the exact same every time; she was just fucking with me at this point), the entire pod sarcastically applauded. I breathed a sigh of relief and began walking back to my cell, accompanied by random outbursts such as: "Finally!" "I was about to snap." "One dumbass bitch can't make a bed and the rest of us have to suffer." "Four-eyes is lucky I ain't tryin' to go to lock or I'd smack dem glasses off her ugly face."

I stood outside the cell for what seemed like an eternity waiting for them to pop it open. I wanted to crawl into my perfectly made bed and sleep the rest of my time here away. I didn't know what was going to happen once the doors opened, but imagined it would mostly involve nasty looks and hateful comments.

"Those girls aren't gonna do shit," Brandi said noticing my expression of concern. "They talk a lot of shit, but they're pussies when it comes to going to lock. The worst they'll do is talk shit. I promise, and if they do try anything else, I'll shank 'em in their fucking throats."

"With what?" I laughed.

"With this," she replied whipping out a sanitary pad from her bin. We both began laughing hysterically. I needed something to take my mind off the mix of emotions I was experiencing, it was a nice reprieve from the past drama-filled hour.

Usually whenever any type of negative emotion began creeping in I ran as fast as I could to my drugs. I numbed my feelings the moment they tried to make themselves known. Now I had no choice but to feel them and I found I was incapable of handling them very well.

I pulled the sheet up over my head and snuggled into my bed. Just as I was dozing off I heard the doors pop open. I ignored it. If someone wanted to beat my ass – so be it. Hopefully they would knock me unconscious and I wouldn't have to deal with this shit. Brandi, along with my butch lesbian "bunkie" (apparently this is what you call a roommate in jail, it's edgier) Sharon, promised to keep an eye on the cell while I napped.

I was awoken a short time later by my name being called. My eyes sprang open and I jumped out of bed instinctively. I looked out into the dayroom where everyone was and realized they all were staring at me. I made eye contact with one chick who had to be in a gang of some kind, because she had tattoos on her face and looked like she wanted to murder me.

"You got mail, Puta," she said. Now I don't speak Spanish, but I have a pretty good idea of what she called me just then. Most people would probably challenge her, I however, am a big wuss.

"Oh, thank you so much." I smiled, while sprinting with my head down toward the guard to get my mail.

I studied the envelope on my way back to my cell and it appeared to be from a lawyer. I was assuming it was from my lawyer. I had spent all my money on drugs and cigarettes, so affording a fancy attorney was not in my budget. If you can't afford an attorney, the state appoints you a Public Defender.

We had something in the jail that was referred to as the "Public Defender Phone." It was the only phone in the pod that made incoming calls and when it rang, the women turned into ravenous animals, knocking one another down to answer.

The reason being, if you answer and it happens to be your attorney on the lineeven if he's calling for someone else, you are allowed to ask him questions about your case. I hadn't received my first call from mine yet so, I was eager to see what the letter was about.

"Brandi!" I said running up to her with the letter, "I just got this, what the hell does it mean?" I asked, shoving it into her hands.

It only took her a glance to realize what it was (apparently, she had received plenty of these). "Oh, it's just saying who your attorney is and—ewwww—oh, man, Thomas-he's the worst. That sucks, dude," she said handing it back to me. "Wait!" she said, pulling it back out of my hands and examining it. "Holy shit, you have court tomorrow."

The next morning, I was lying on the cold cement floor for what had to be three hours. My hands and feet had been shackled to my waist and I was using a toilet paper roll as a pillow. Seven other women and I had been crammed into a holding cell, waiting for them to call each of us out before the judge.

All but two of us had gone and pleaded; only myself and another woman remained. The anticipation of the unknown had wreaked havoc on my body and mind. I was utterly exhausted from all the worrying I had done since I found out I was coming here today. The girls gave me an idea of what to expect but it didn't help. Every case and every judge was different. I had finally met my attorney briefly in the hallway on the way in. He apologized for not calling and told me that he thought he had. Essentially, I was going into this blind, with no instruction from him or anyone else.

"Johnson, you're up," the deputy said, peeking her head in the door. I recognized her. Her name was Tara and I had been to her wedding. As I sat up, I'd wondered for a moment if she remembered me puking all over the dance for during the "Cha, Cha Slide." Hopefully not.

I rolled around on the floor with my hands and feet shackled trying to get my footing. I looked like a walrus and the girl in the cell with me was pretending not to watch. I finally stood up and headed toward the door where Tara was waiting, and I gave her a sheepish smile—because I wasn't sure exactly how to act in this situation. She didn't even look at me. She just said, "Let's go" and grabbed the chain between my wrists, and walked me toward the courtroom. Super awkward.

As we stood outside the door, waiting for them to give her the go ahead to bring me in, my heart felt like it was punching dents into my ribcage. My hands were sweating and my teeth were chattering, I couldn't stop myself from shaking. "You gonna be aright?" she asked while looking me up and down with disdain.

"I'm fine," I lied, trying to play it cool.

Someone said something inaudible into her radio and she opened the door. The cold air of the courtroom hit me in the face as she pulled the door open and I realized the seats were packed full of onlookers.

I wanted to turn and run, I wished I could disappear, a million things were racing through my mind at that moment, but I knew I had no choice. It was time to answer for the things that I'd done. I could hear a pin drop in that room. The only sound I heard were the chains of my shackles jingling with each step as I approached the podium in front of the judge. As I stepped up to the podium, Tara placed her hand over the microphone and whispered in my ear, "Don't speak until spoken to" and walked away. It had been so strange having a friend talk to me that way. It was as if she just flipped a switch that erased any memory she'd had of the times we'd shared. And I was now just another no name criminal she was transporting.

I watched as a young woman with blonde hair and high heels crossed in front of me and handed the judge a folder. She then turned to face me and the rest of the courtroom, and swore me in. "Do you swear to tell the truth, the whole truth, and nothing but the truth – so help you God?"

"I do," I said into the microphone, and for a split second wondered if I was supposed to say that or if you only said that at your wedding.

"Then let's begin. The charges against Tiffany Johnson are as follows:

(8) Counts of Dealing in stolen property

(8) Counts of Defrauding a pawn broker

(1) Count of Grand Theft

(3) Counts of Grand Theft – Stolen Firearms.

"The victims of the above stated crimes were her boyfriend at the time, a Deputy for the Marco County Sheriff's Office, as well as his mother and father, Linda and Darryl Henlin. Over the course of a year, the defendant stole—then pawned numerous items belonging to the victims at various pawn shops around the city. She then allegedly staged a burglary at the home they shared and stole his wallet containing $200 and his badge. We deployed numerous officers to investigate the crime. Miss Johnson was present at the home during the investigation and was interviewed about the robbery that occurred after she had left for work.

"During her interrogation, she also admitted to stealing three of his firearms, one being his off- duty weapon, and exchanging them with a local drug dealer for narcotics."

The judge, attempting to remain straight faced, slammed the file down in front of him and took off his glasses.

"Miss Johnson, how do you plead to these charges?"

"Guilty, your Honor."

"Were you forced into this plea by your Public Defender, or anyone else?"

"No, your Honor."

"And why are you pleading guilty today?"

"Because I did it."

Chapter Ten

There was an audible gasp from the occupants of the courtroom once I had admitted to committing these crimes.

I was careful not to look around at the officers surrounding
me, but I didn't have to see them to know they were glaring at
me – I could feel it.

People shuffled around in their seats and whispered to one
another as the judge thumbed through his file. That file contained all the information pertaining to my case. The person I
was before this all happened no longer mattered. Nowhere in
that file did it say: "Defendant once saved her best friend from
drowning at the beach." "Miss Johnson had straight A's at one
point and was president of Student Government," or "Defendant once stopped traffic for ten minutes to rescue a turtle."

None of the good things I had ever done mattered. The person I had become; was reduced to a few pages in a folder on
the judge's desk.

I wasn't sure how any of this worked. I had seen "Law and
Order" countless times and I assumed this was the part where
he banged his gavel down and sentenced me to life in prison.

He looked at me once more and said, "Next," then slid my
folder to the side and clasped his hands together.

A guard suddenly grabbed my shackles. "Come on," he said gruffly, ushering me to the same door I had entered.

"What the...? That's it? 'scuse me, sir. Um, am I done? I mean wasn't he supposed to sentence me or something?" I asked.

"Nope," the guard said, his gaze fixed straight ahead. By now I had learned that my mere existence annoyed the police, therefore I knew when to shut up. I realized that they viewed me as scum—the equivalent of a mangy dog with rabies. They never made eye contact and had a constant look of disdain on their faces any time they were forced to acknowledge me. It was like pulling teeth to get them to answer even the simplest of questions, so I stopped trying.

It would be seven more hours until I made it back to the jail. I was exhausted, and starving. They hadn't fed us a single thing the entire time we were gone and by the time we got back we had missed dinner.

I couldn't wait to talk to Brandi. I had questions that I knew she could answer and I could also use some cheering up – as the uncertainty of everything had made me feel 100 pounds heavier. It was as if a brick had been placed onto my chest and I couldn't remove it, making it hard to breathe.

When I entered my cell, my eyes swept the room and landed on Brandi's bunk—it was empty.

"Where the hell is Brandi?" I asked Charlotte, a prostitute that had been brought in two days before. She was detoxing bad and barely came out from beneath her covers. When she did it was for food or to use the bathroom – and I couldn't help but notice the staggering amount of scabs covering her entire body. It was apparent that she was a "picker."

"She gone," Charlotte said peeking out to see my reaction.

"What do you mean... she's gone?!" I asked, panic in my voice.

"I don't know, man, they told her to roll it up. Someone bonded her out." She pulled the covers over her head and laid back down to face the wall.

I began sobbing.

Uncontrollably, gut-wrenching crying. I dropped onto my bed and covered my face. I had only known Brandi a short time – but friendships are so different in jail. You spend every minute of every day with these people. One day in here is like a month's worth of quality friend time outside.

I was heartbroken by her sudden absence.

I heard the familiar click of the main lights shutting down. It was time for bed, and we were no longer allowed to speak. I sat in the dark quietly breaking down at the realization that my only real friend in here was suddenly, and unexpectedly... Gone. I was alone, I was hungry, and nobody gave a shit. In jail, people don't care about your feelings. We are all in the same boat. It's the only place I've ever been where tears get ignored and you are expected to handle your emotions on your own. Emotions were new to me. I didn't know what to do when I felt sad or angry. I felt I was losing control, like my body had been consumed by thoughts and feelings, and I had no coping mechanisms whatsoever. I'd been too busy getting high and feeling numb to process shit like this.

When the doors opened for breakfast, I tried to open my eyes and found they were swollen from crying myself to sleep the night before. It had been such a long time since I'd actually felt something real, that once the tears started flowing, they didn't stop.

"You look like shit," a voice I didn't recognize pointed out. I looked to my left and realized there was a new person occupying Brandi's bunk. She must have come in the middle of the night. I couldn't believe I didn't hear it.

I sat up in bed and stared at this girl. She had straggly blonde hair and bright green eyes. I was trying to get a read on her, because if she was seriously insulting me right out of the gate, I was going to punch her in the throat. I had hoped she was trying to be funny, because I was too exhausted to get into my first jail fight even though I currently felt I was capable of murdering someone with all the anger I had built up inside of me.

"I'm just fucking with you, dude, I'm Nicki," she said smiling. Her smile was sweet, her eyes crinkled and her perfectly white teeth were beautiful.

"You alright? Seems like you had a rough night."

"Yeah, I did. My best friend left when I was gone, and I didn't have a chance to say goodbye. I will probably never see her again and it's really fucking depressing."

She pouted and hopped off her bunk. She surprised me by sitting down right next to me, so close that our hips were touching. Once she was closer I realized the sides of her head were shaved and she had a tattoo of brass knuckles behind her ear.

"Aw, that sucks, man. I remember my first friend leaving jail. It gets easier. Come on, let's get some food. Crying always makes me hungry. Also – I'm pretty sure it's French toast and that shit is delicious." She stood up energetically and held her arm out to help me up. I paused for a moment, because as desperately as I wanted to stay in bed, French toast was the bomb and I was starving. I grabbed her arm and pulled myself up.

As I followed her into the dayroom I noticed the way she walked. It wasn't a normal girl walk. It was almost manly.

When she got to the back of the line she turned to make sure I was behind her and grinned.

"What's your favorite animal?" she asked as we inched forward toward the chow line.

"What?" I asked.

"What's your favorite animal? Mine is a monkey. Sometimes I wish I was a monkey, bro. You know how cool it would be to like, swing from trees and shit, just eating bananas all day?" She bounced back and forth as she spoke, imitating a monkey.

"Okay, first of all—monkeys eating bananas is a myth. They mainly eat leaves and flowers and bird eggs. Some eat bananas but that's not like, all they eat. And secondly, why the hell are you asking me this?"

"Whoa, Encyclopedia Brown, pump your brakes. I'm just trying to make conversation – cheer you up a bit. It makes me sad to see you sad and besides, we are gonna be sleeping next to each other for a while. I figured it would be nice to get to know each other." She did a little hair flip and it reminded me of Justin Bieber. I couldn't help but laugh.

"What's so funny?" she asked, poking me in my side teasingly. "Hey!" I was the most ticklish person on earth.

"No, it's nothing. You just did a little...you flipped your hair. It reminded me of—"

"NEXT!" the guard yelled at Nicki, interrupting our conversation.

Once she got her tray, she stood off to the side and waited for me. Apparently, I was sitting with her. Brandi and I used to sit together, and it really annoyed me that this chick was trying to take her place to make me feel better or something.

She sat down at a table in the corner and I reluctantly slid into the seat across from her. I began poking at my French toast when suddenly a gorgeous girl I didn't recognize came up to the table and touched Nicki's shoulder. She had shiny black hair – which was weird because most of the girls in here had raggedy sweat hair from detoxing and lack of good hygiene. This girl looked like a damn supermodel.

"Hey, Nicki, long time no see. You just can't stay away from this place, can you?" she said smiling. She sounded like a freaking sex-phone operator. I tried to ignore the conversation, but Nicki introduced me to Angelina Jolie, just as I shoved a giant piece of bread into my mouth.

"Shawna, this is...Wait, shit, I haven't even asked your name yet! What is it?" Nicki asked me. "Tiffermy," I said with my mouth full.

Nicki laughed. "This is my new friend Tiffany." She smiled and gestured towards me. I smiled with cheeks full of food like a damn chipmunk and Shawna's face fell into a look of annoyance.

She forced out a smile and quickly said, "Hi," as she looked me up and down. "Anyway, Nicki... come by my cell later. I have something I wanna show you," she said winking as she walked away.

I looked up at Nicki with my eyebrows raised.

"I know she's rude. Pay no attention to her – she always gets jealous when I talk to girls."

I watched Nicki as she sucked the orange juice from her cup, feeling incredibly confused. "Why would she get jealous? That's weird," I said.

"Yeah. She's my ex. We dated a long time ago and she's never been able to let it go. I have that effect on the ladies," she said giving me a wink.

That wink... sent a vibration through my entire body. "Oh. Okay. You're a lesbian. Gotcha. No, that's cool. I totally support the gays. I have gay friends, so... yeah, awesome." I shoved my egg into my mouth as fast as I could so that I'd no longer have to say words. I looked like a real fucking idiot. But I didn't know what the hell else to say.

Nicki froze, then began laughing hysterically at me.

"Screw you, dude." I laughed.

"Oh my God. That's the greatest thing I've ever heard. 'I have gay friends' ha ha. Oh man. I'm sorry. Whew. Yes, I'm a lesbian. I think females are the most gorgeous creatures on earth. Their eyes, their breasts, their laughs, everything about them drives me crazy." I awkwardly nodded along as she spoke, trying my best to appear supportive. "Don't worry, though, I'm not going to jump on you when you're sleeping or anything. I mean...unless you want me to," she said with a devilish smile. There it was again, that tingle inside me. What the hell was wrong with me?

I began subconsciously fixing my hair and sitting up straighter. I don't know what had gotten into me but suddenly, my feelings towards Nicki were...shifting. I watched as she ate her French toast and couldn't help but feel a little, I don't know. Interested? I can't explain what I was feeling – as all feelings were new to me. All I knew was that once I found out she was attracted to women and after she had been so caring and kind to me, I felt flattered.

She caught me staring at her and I quickly glanced down at my plate. "What?" she asked with a smirk. Jesus. My inner thighs were tingling. What is happening right now?

"Giraffe," I said, gazing across the table at her.

"Huh?" she replied, looking confused.

"Giraffe. Giraffes are my favorite animal." I felt my cheeks flush and realized...I suddenly had my first girl crush.

Chapter Eleven

"Good morning, Beautiful. Merry Christmas."

I flinched as she said the words. I had been lying awake for hours, staring at the bottom of my bunkie's bed. Depression had coiled around me like a snake this morning, I felt paralyzed.

Christmas had always been my very favorite holiday, but this year—it was a heartbreaking reminder that life as I knew it no longer existed. I closed my eyes and brought myself back to last Christmas. Chuck, my boyfriend at the time, had woken me up with a hot cup of coffee. He was supposed to be on duty, but said he had a surprise for me and couldn't wait until tonight. He placed a small square box next to my head on the pillow and smiled with satisfaction.

"Open it," he said, sitting down next to me.

I smiled sleepily and pulled myself up into a seated position. I rubbed the sleep from my eyes and began removing the shiny silver wrapping paper. My brain finally woke up and stopped suddenly before opening the box. "Hang on, let me go pee really quick," I said pulling the covers off me and tip-toeing to the bathroom.

I had realized that I would have to act excited and grateful for whatever was in that box, which seemed exhausting to me.

I ran the faucet and quickly pulled my bag of pills and a syringe from the tampon box underneath the counter.

I would have to do this faster than normal, as he was virtually on the other side of the door waiting for me. I scrambled to get everything ready, careful not to make the spoon 'clang' on the counter as I set it down. "Hurry up, babe, I gotta go back to work," he said.

"Coming! I'm brushing my teeth, I don't want to kiss you with morning breath!" I yelled as I wrapped the belt around my biceps, pulling it tight. I knew I was going to hell for this. I couldn't even begin interacting with other humans until I shot myself up with drugs. I hated myself and what I had become – but I couldn't stop. I didn't know how.

"Helllllllo? Earth to Tiffany, I said Merry Christmas," Nicki said, waving her hand back and forth in front of my face – ripping me from my daydream.

"Oh, hey. Yeah, I'm sorry. Today is a little weird for me," I said.

"I bet. Christmas in jail sucks. But there is an upside," she began, in her usual optimistic way, "the church ladies should be here any minute, and they give us socks and chocolate. So, it's not a total loss." She smiled and leaned in to give me a kiss. I grabbed the back of her head and pulled her closer. I needed love today. Even though I was surrounded by people, I felt so...

alone. My heart skipped a beat as she swirled her tongue around mine and gently squeezed the back of my neck.

We had only been seeing each other for a week or so, but a week in jail felt like a lifetime.

She briefly pulled her lips away from mine and stared deep into my eyes. My heart immediately started beating out of control and when she grabbed the back of my head to pull me in for another kiss, I noticed her breathing had gotten much heavier.

She slid her hand out from behind my neck and slowly lowered it down to my breast. My inner thighs began tingling as she started rubbing and gently kneading it in the palm of her hand. She pushed me back onto the bed and laid down on top of me completely. I was aching for her to touch me between my legs.

She must have read my mind, because she pressed her chest to mine and lifted her pelvis, allowing room for her to glide her hand underneath my pants. Before she could touch me, a metal 'bang' caused her to push off me with lightning speed and stand straight up. I was panting as I peered out the door to see that a guard had entered the pod.

Fuck. I don't know if it was because it was a holiday, or because I was overly emotional, but I was hornier than I'd ever been in my life. And frankly, I was pretty pissed at that cock-blocking cop.

Let me clear something up real quick. I am not a lesbian. I had never been in a relationship with a girl before. I mean, I'd been attracted to them because, well obviously women are beautiful beings. I'd never acted on those feelings before though, they were usually fleeting thoughts while passing someone on the street. When Nicki had kissed me, my stomach did a somersault. My friend Trina said that I was "gay for the stay" and that it was common for 'straight' girls to become interested in other women after being away from the male species for so long. But this felt different, we had a real connection, on a deeper level.

The guards locked the doors for count, and Nicki wanted to finish what we had started. Aside from the fact there were now three other people in the room, I was no longer in the mood. I was really sad. I couldn't help but wonder what my family was doing today.

I had no money on my books so I hadn't been able to make any calls, I had been closed off completely from the outside world. I was sure my sister would go visit my father today. Our mother had passed three years ago and my dad is the only other family we have here in town.

A girl in the cell above us began singing 'Silent Night.' Her voice was angelic as it echoed through the pod. Without warning, the tears began flowing from my eyes, as if someone had left a faucet running. We weren't allowed to have radios in here, so after a month of no music, her voice was the most beautifully moving sound I had ever heard.

I'd never been this heartbroken in my entire life. I missed my mom. I missed my sister, and my dad. I missed my childhood and all the wonderful Christmases we had celebrated as a family of four; before divorce, death, addiction and alcoholism had ravaged us and torn us all apart.

I closed my eyes as the beautifully nostalgic melody carried through the room. I imagined my sister and I waking up together Christmas morning and giggling with excitement as we ran down the stairs and we would both gasp in disbelief at the beautifully colorful display of gifts that Santa had left for us. I would give anything to go back to that moment. I would have done everything so differently.

My trip down memory lane had been interrupted by the voice of my arch nemesis. "Ay, somebody tell that police ass hoe she got a visitor. It's probably another cop. He's here to get the latest report!" Daniels said, as a group of girls erupted in laughter.

Daniels had had it in for me ever since the day they tried to put me in her pod and she stormed out and pushed the button. She had threatened to 'beat my ass' on several different occasions—but never did.

"Johnson, your visitation has already started. You better get in there, you only have 20 minutes," Deputy Flower said into the intercom of my cell.

What the hell? Did she say visitation?

The jail visitation room was on the opposite side of the pod. It consisted of three TVs which linked to a room in a separate building where our loved ones had to check in. Visitation had to be scheduled ahead of time online. Who the hell was here?

I ran full speed to the visitation room, ignoring the comments from the other girls regarding my weight and 'the building shaking' as I ran. I swung the door open and tried to catch my breath. There was a figure on the furthest TV from the door and the moment I registered who it was I placed my hand over my mouth and began sobbing. It was my father.

My daddy had come to visit me on Christmas. My hands trembled as I picked up the phone and placed it to my ear. "Hi, Dad," I said, breaking down into uncontrollable sobs. There are no words to describe how amazing it was to see my father's face.

"Hello, my baby," Dad said, his voice cracking as he tried not to cry. He started to say something and stopped himself. His chin began quivering as he held up one finger, telling me to hold on.

I wiped the tears from my face and hiccupped as I tried catching my breath while I waited. "My baby girl. It is so... hard... to talk to you through a screen. I am so, so sorry," he said, his voice trembling. I couldn't speak. I was drowning in emotions, he was so close, but so far away.

"No, I'm sorry, Dad. I'm sorry you have to visit me in jail. I'm sorry I lied to you, to everyone. I'm sorry that I am such a fuck up. I love you so much and I wish more than anything in the world I could hug you right now," I said, putting my hand up onto the screen.

"Your sister is in the car, she drove me here. She isn't ready to come in yet," he said.

I nodded. "I understand, please tell her that I love her and pray that one day she can forgive me. Please tell her I said Merry Christmas, Dad," I said glancing at the timer. "We only have ten minutes left Dad. God, how is this going by so quickly?"

"Listen, baby, there are a few things I want to say before the time runs out, okay?" he said. "Sure," I said.

"Chuck has written a letter to the judge to get your charges reduced," he began, his voice cracking again. "He doesn't want you in here. He has been in touch with your sister and gave her all of your belongings, he's in pretty bad shape," he said. His words cut through me like a knife. I destroyed Chuck. I took his heart and ripped it to shreds, and all of his co-workers on the force know all of the gory details. That poor man.

"Five Minute Warning," a robotic voice said into the receiver.

"Also, I thought you should know that as of today I have 45 days sober," he said.

"What? Are you serious?" My father had been an alcoholic all my life. I spent weekends with him as a child, and most of the weekend was spent at the bar. At the time, I thought it was great. My sister and I would play the jukebox and sip cherry Cokes out of wine glasses. It wasn't until much later that I realized how fucked up it is to bring your six and seven-year old children to the bar with you.

"Oh my God, Dad, that's amazing!"

He smiled and nodded, but I could tell something was off. He wasn't beaming with pride as someone with 45 days sober would.

"Well yes, it is a good thing. I feel really good for the first time in as long as I can remember. Maybe when you get out of there we can go to some meetings together," he said.

"Aw, Dad, that would be amazing. I am so, so proud of you. I've been feeling so down, but having you visit has literally changed everything for me. To know that you still love me—in spite of all the shit I did, has honestly breathed new life into me today. I really needed this."

"Babe, there is nothing you could ever do to make me stop loving you. I held you the moment you came into this world and carried you for years after; I will carry you until you are able to walk on your own again and even then, I will be holding your hand to make sure you don't fall," he said. The tears began flowing from my eyes once again.

"One Minute Remaining."

"Tiff, before we get disconnected I have to say one more thing. It's important."

"Okay? What is it?" I asked.

"I really hate to give you bad news while you're in there, but you need to know what's going on. The reason I stopped drinking was because-" He paused. Almost as if he was still debating whether to tell me. "I stopped drinking because the doctor told me I had to. I've got cancer, Tiff. It's spread to my liver and -"

"Time is up. Goodbye."

His face disappeared from the screen...

Chapter Twelve

I stared at the blank screen in disbelief for what seemed like an eternity. He had probably gathered up his belongings and was headed through the parking lot by now. I pictured his walk, his face, the joke he was going to make when he got into the car with my sister to ease whatever tension she may have been experiencing.

His words replayed over and over as I continued to stare at the screen, the phone still pressed to my ear. "I have cancer, it has spread to my liver and..." Like a CD skipping it played again and again. I was afraid to hang up the phone, because hanging up the phone meant I had to get up, walk out, and carry on as if I hadn't just received the most earth-shattering news of my life.

Cancer had taken three of my four grandparents. I'd lost my mother to cancer three years back—now this fucking disease had circled back around to snuff out the life of my father. The man who held me in his arms and rocked me to sleep at night. Who put our mattresses against the wall so we could use them as a slide. The man who carried my sister and I down the stairs each morning on his back and plopped us in front of a Disney movie while he brushed our hair and got us ready for school.

That man has this horrific condition ravaging his insides and I can't do a fucking thing about it. I'm stuck. Stuck in a cage with a hundred other heartless women who couldn't care less that my heart was breaking and my world was slowly crumbling around me. I needed a hug. I needed someone to tell me everything is going to be okay. I needed to get high. I slammed the phone into the receiver and let out a primal scream.

Why. Why had I gotten myself in a position where I couldn't be with my dad when he needed me most? I hated myself for this, for this and for so many other things. Why the hell couldn't I just be normal? Why couldn't I go to college like all my old friends, enjoying sorority life and getting an education. Why did I have to take that first pill?

I stood up from my chair and my knees buckled. I hit the floor and wailed, my voice taking up every inch of the room. No one came, no one cared and I could hear giggles and see shadows as everyone came to see what the suicidal psycho was up to this time. I took a deep breath, collecting myself and headed toward the door. I kept my head down and walked briskly back to my cell. I didn't want to inadvertently make eye contact with anyone and be forced to converse with them.

Evidently, the universe had other plans for me. I was two feet away from my cell when I heard inmate Daniels call me a "police ass hoe" in the distance. I saw red. I stopped short and immediately began heading in her direction. My legs were moving before my mind caught up, I didn't even know where I was heading at this point. I was marching toward her voice like a lion about to attack its prey. I was going to find her – and I was going to rip her fucking face off.

I spotted her when she stood up from her chair at the table where her and two other girls had been playing cards. She'd seen me bounding across the dayroom and decided to take a defensive position – to prepare for what was coming. I didn't even know what was coming, I had lost all control. My mind was merely a helpless passenger and my anger was at the helm.

The words shot from my mouth like missiles as I approached her. "YOU REALLY WANNA FUCK WITH ME TODAY, BITCH? I SWEAR TO GOD I WILL FUCKING KILL YOU!" I screamed, an inch from her face. I wrapped my hands around the fabric of her collar and twisted it as I jerked her closer to me. I watched her expression turn to fear and I could tell she was shocked and unsure of what to do. "Call me a fucking police ass hoe now, bitch. SAY IT NOW!" I spit into her face.

Had it not been for Trina yanking me off her and my glasses flying off my face, I would have slammed my fist into her face until she stopped moving.

The pain and anguish that came along with being stuck in jail combined with the news of my father had pushed me to the boiling point. Her name calling popped the lid right off – releasing weeks of anxiety and stress in the form of violent rage.

I scrambled across the floor until I located my glasses, throwing them onto my face as quickly as possible and spinning around to my back in preparation for whatever blow she was about to throw. But she was gone. I sat up and looked around the room. Everyone was staring at me, their faces a mixture of shock and amusement. I couldn't see Daniels anywhere.

"You better get your ass up and go in your cell before the guards get in here," Trina said over the brim of her glasses. "You're lucky I got you off her before they came in here and hit you wit dat taser." I jumped up to my feet glancing around nervously and headed for my cell. Daniels' bunkies must have pulled her into her cell, probably to keep her from going to lock.

Nicki was standing at the entrance to our cell, her head following me as I whisked past her and hopped into my bed. "Are you serious right now?" she said, her jaw hanging open.

"What? Am I serious about what?" I said.

"Um, about snatching Daniels up by the shirt and threatening to murder her? Like, what? It was sexy, don't get me wrong, but...I didn't know you had that in you. What just happened?" Nicki asked.

I stood up and began pacing the cell, I couldn't stay still.

"Dude, I got some real bad news in visitation and..."

"Aright, ladies! Back to your cells!" Deputy Cash yelled entering the pod.

"Shit. Am I in trouble? I'm gonna have to go to lock, huh? I should have at least throat punched her. That would've been worth going for," I said, peering through the gate to see if she-was headed my way. She was holding the pod door open with her foot and I watched as a girl came through the door holding a mat.

"Fresh meat!" one of the inmates yelled from the top tier.

Hell yes, they aren't here for me, there are new girls coming in from holding. Thank you, Jesus. "Damn, I didn't know they did a prostitution sting in the graveyard today! You bitches are looking rough!" an inmate called Cookie yelled out, causing the entire pod to erupt in laughter. When I saw the final girl enter – my heart soared.

"Brandi!" I screamed, running up to the gate and clasping the metal bars with my hands. My best friend. She was back. Seeing her face had made me momentarily forget all the drama that had just occurred. It was like the universe knew I needed a friend right now.

"Brandi! Over here!" I yelled, waving like a school girl.

"Johnson! Shut the hell up and sit down, this ain't a damn reunion," Deputy Cash yelled from the entrance. Deputy Cash was a tall lesbian. All the girls in here had crushes on her. Most of them whistled and cat-called as she passed their cells during count. They never got in trouble for it – I think she liked the attention.

I rolled my eyes and sighed as I headed back to my bed. They liked everyone to be in their room and settled as they brought new inmates in, that way they could get an accurate count.

The moment they finished the count and the doors popped open, I ran straight over to Brandi's cell. It was unfortunately located next to Daniels' cell, but I didn't give a shit. I needed to see my friend.

"Brandi!" I called as I entered her room, but once I caught a glimpse of her face – I stopped dead in my tracks. She had only been out a week or two and she looked like a completely different person. She had lost a ton of weight and her face was covered in fresh scabs. When I got closer I could tell from her gigantic pupils that she was high as a kite.

"Oh my God, Tiff! I missed you!" she said, throwing her arms around my neck. "Dude, I can't motherfucking believe I'm back in this shithole. They are tryn'a say some bullshit about me soliciting sex or some shit." She was speaking so fast I could barely make out the words. "Tiff, oh my God, I got some important shit to tell you real quick," she said, pacing back and forth while scratching her head.

I seriously couldn't believe this was the same beautiful girl I'd met when I first got here. She looked ten years older. Her eyes had sunken in and she had dark circles underneath both. "Are you okay?" I asked, looking at her intently. I knew she wasn't.

"I'm good, I'm reallly good. I was banging a hit of meth when the cops rolled up so I – boop – did it real quick." She motioned the act of shooting up. I didn't even know you could bang meth. "I knew they were taking me to jail anyway, right, and I figured what the hell, if I'm going down I'm going down with a bang," She laughed. I stared in disbelief as she continued spewing words out like a sprinkler, random bursts of clustered sentences. "But holy shit, I'm freaking out kinda," she said, glancing around nervously and bopping onto her tippy-toes as she spoke. Jealousy and longing washed over me as I imagined what the hit must have felt like. Seeing her feeling so good made every cell in my body ache. I wanted to feel that. I tightened up with anxiety knowing it was impossible. I needed to get out of this room as quickly as possible before I exploded.

"Hey, did you want to tell me something? Because I'm tired, I need to take a nap," I said, standing up preparing to exit.

"Yes! Shhh, come sit. I have to be quiet," she whispered. I reluctantly sat back down on her unmade bunk. It felt as though all the blood in my body had been replaced with little ants. My skin was crawling. I wanted to get high so bad that it physically hurt.

"Hey, so listen, you know how you told me about how you got charged with, um... selling to that drug dealer... uh... Lazarus, the guns or whatever?" she asked.

"Um, yeah, can you please shut the hell up. You are the only one who knows about that," I said, glancing around furtively.

"Okay, I know, sorry, shhh. Okay listen. Well I saw his homeboy Tre, and he said that Lazarus is really mad that you snitched on him. Cuz, um, his you know, his house got raided and stuff. So, anyway, I guess Lazarus wants to kill you. Well, not like 'kill you' but like, hurt you or your family or something really bad and – "

"Hold up," I interrupted. "Slow down. Are you fucking kidding me right now? They raided his house?" I stood up and started pacing back and forth with her. "Son of a bitch." Things had obviously gotten worse after my arrest.

"Yeah, no, it's bad like, three people got arrested and all his drugs were taken and stuff. Luckily, he wasn't home."

Yeah, luckily. Now he's free to murder my family.

"Okay so, anyway, guess what the craziest part is?" she said, her eyes looking like they were about to pop out of her head. "Lazarus has a wife, it's his son's momma and –," she lowered her voice to a whisper, "she is sitting right over there." She was pointing somewhere behind me. I slowly turned my head to follow her finger and when I saw where she was pointing my blood ran cold.

It was Daniels...

I turned back around to face Brandi and before I could say anything I watched her face suddenly twist into confusion. Her hand reached up to her heart and she muttered something, but I couldn't make out what she'd said. It all happened so quickly. Her eyes rolled back into her head and she crumbled into a pile on the floor. Her head made a 'thud' as it bounced off the ground. Brandi began convulsing and I instinctively fell to my knees next to her to hold her. When I realized I should call for help, I hopped back to my feet and ran toward the intercom. I quickly looked back as I slammed the metal button on the wall and realized she had stopped seizing.

Her arms fell limp, her legs were twisted into an unnatural position and her eyelids relaxed down onto her open eyes. They were staring straight at me, but there was no life behind them. I was shaking in panic as I jammed the emergency button on the wall to alert the correctional officers. "Yes?" the woman on the other end said calmly.

"Please hurry, I need help! My friend...I think she just fucking died."

## Chapter Thirteen

"Babe, wake up, the detectives want to talk to you," my boyfriend said, waking me from a glorious sleep. He was supposed to be on duty that day, why the hell was he waking me up? He knew better. I hated mornings, and I hated when he got me up before my alarm went off.

"What the hell? I already talked to the detectives yesterday when they were here," I grumbled from beneath the covers.

My boyfriend was a deputy for the Marco County Sheriff's Office. There had been a break-in at our home a few days ago. Someone came into the back door and had stolen his wallet—containing his badge—and $200. They also took three guns from the gun safe, including his off-duty weapon. The police had been here all day yesterday, dusting for fingerprints and asking us a bunch of questions. So why the hell were they here again at the crack of dawn?

"Please, you need to get up and get dressed, they just have a couple more questions," he said, gently placing his hand on my back. I could feel the anger rising from the depths of my soul.

I was suddenly very hot with rage. "God damnit what is going on?" I said kicking the covers off me and storming to the closet. "Why do they have to question me again? I already gave them all the information I have," I said, ripping a shirt off the hanger and angrily pulling it over my head.

Something was off. He wasn't responding to me. "Hello? I'm talking to you? I have work in four hours and I hardly slept last night, it would have been nice to have some kind of warning that they were coming. Why are you being so weird?" I asked, pulling the pants up over my hips. He didn't say a word. I watched a single tear stream down his cheek and I froze.

A wave of panic swept over me. "Are you crying?" I asked, stepping closer to him. He put his hands up to keep me at a distance. "What the hell, Chuck?" I said. "Why aren't you responding to me –," I was interrupted by our bedroom door flying open. There was a man suddenly in the doorway.

He held his badge up to show me and his other hand was rested on his gun. He was staring into my eyes and I immediately knew something was wrong. This wasn't the way my boyfriend's friends from the Sheriff's Department usually looked at me. This was different. "I need you to step into the living room, Miss Johnson. Now," he said, holding the door open and stepping back to make room for me.

I looked at Chuck and he was staring at the floor, avoiding me. What the fuck? I stepped out of the bedroom and into our living room, and our puppy bounded toward me with her tail wagging to greet me. Chuck intercepted her path and scooped her up, taking her into the room and shutting the door behind them. He just... left me out here?

I noticed there were five deputies in our house in addition to the man at our door, and they were all staring at me. "Please, have a seat," the man said, ushering toward the couch. "I'm Detective Kallin. I have a few questions I'd like to ask you, if you don't mind."

"Shoot," I said casually, not immediately recognizing my inappropriate choice of words.

"Actually, if you don't mind, I'd like to do it out front. It's gorgeous outside today and you have a beautiful porch." He smiled at me. Why the hell would he care about my porch? I wondered, slowly standing up from the couch.

"Uh...yeah, okay. We can do that," I said reluctantly.

I stepped onto my porch and in my peripheral vision I noticed a man standing at the side of my front door. He lunged at me the moment my foot hit the ground outside and grabbed my arms, pulling them behind me. I felt the heavy metal handcuffs wrap around my wrists and looked around at everyone in horror. "You have GOT to be fucking kidding me."

I had replayed the day of my arrest over and over a thousand times since I'd been here. I would think about the moment I was handcuffed, and how the natural manipulator within me believed even then, that I could con my way out of this.

I had hidden my addiction for so long. I had done so many unbelievable things day in and day out – and I'd gotten away with all of it. I thought that I was invincible, that because my boyfriend was a cop – I was untouchable.

This morning we had gotten the call that Brandi died after spending two days in the hospital. One minute she was here, walking and talking, and the next...she was a lifeless pile of skin and bones, dying of a heart attack. She was only 29 years old, the same age as me and her heart just... stopped.

The fact that it could have just as easily been me had been haunting me all day. Looking back on the day of my arrest, for the first time I began to wonder if it may have actually been a good thing. I had spent countless hours stewing about how unfair it is that I was humiliated and thrown in a cage when what I really needed was psychological help.

But today, part of me was thinking that maybe, being arrested might have been exactly what I needed to save my life. I had never looked at it that way until today. Life is fleeting, and maybe the universe knew I was headed toward being a crumpled pile on the floor – and sent the Sheriff's department to save me that day.

I had been laying in my bed most of the day, questioning my entire existence and wondering what the future held – when the public defender phone rang. As per usual, the girls trampled one another in hopes of it being their attorney.

"Yeah, hold on a sec," I heard Gemma – allegedly a member of some female Mexican mafia—say in frustration, "Johnson, it's for you."

"Hello, this is Tiffany."

"Yeah, listen. I don't got a lot of time. I'll do the talking – you do the listening."

"Oh, okay um-"

"So, I talked to the State Attorney's office. They added up your scoresheet and they wanna give you 15 years."

I sucked in all the air around me.

"That's a joke, right?"

"Quiet. We go before the judge next Monday where you will be sentenced. You have the right to refuse their offer. Just to warn you though, they don't like it when you refuse their offer, it's more paperwork. There's a good chance the offer will be even higher the second time so, just something to think about. Okay?"

"Um, yeah. Okay, so what you are saying is if I-"

"Listen, I got a meeting. I gotta go, talk to you next week."

– Click.

A crowd of girls had gathered around, evidently bored and hoping to catch up with the latest gossip from the outside world. They must have been able to tell from my expression that the call had not gone well.

"What did he say?" my friend Rebecca asked. It felt like my brain had been put into a blender. Despite my best efforts to piece together what he had just said – I was having trouble processing it. "Who's your attorney?" a girl named Stephanie asked.

"Williams," I said, staring off into the distance trying to imagine how old I would be when I got out of prison. 42. I would be 42 years old.

"Ugh, I fucking hate Williams. I had him last time I was here."

Trying to have a conversation with him is like pulling teeth," Rebecca said. "So, what did he say?"

I didn't answer. I couldn't. If I said it out loud it would make it real. I ignored the 20 eager eyes staring at me and I walked away. I needed Nicki to hug me and tell me everything was going to be okay. She had a way of making even the darkest days seem a bit brighter.

"What's the matter, babe?" she asked, sitting down next to me on the bed and putting her arm around me. "Is it Brandi?"

I shook my head and tearfully filled her in on what my asshole attorney had said. When I finished, she grabbed the sides of my face with both hands and stared deep into my eyes.

"Listen to me. You will not go to prison for 15 years. Do you hear me? You won't. The first offer is always ridiculous – they try to scare you. I promise. Worrying about what is gonna happen next week won't do a damn thing. Okay? It won't lessen your time, it won't change the outcome, it will just make you fucking crazy. So, stop. You are going to be fine," she said smiling. I believed her. I hugged her tighter than I ever had. I was so grateful to have her in here with me. To help me through the hard shit.

"Thank you, that actually makes me feel better," I said sniffling, my rigid muscles loosening a bit. "You are welcome, Tiff. I mean it. I want you to know something," she began, as she took a deep breath and continued, "I love you, like, a lot okay? And, I really want to make you my wife when we get out of here."

My face twisted in confusion and I subconsciously pulled away. "Listen, don't be scared. I know you've never been with a woman before, so this is probably overwhelming for you. But this feels...Real. And I know you feel it, too," she said pulling my arms back.

I snatched them out of her grasp and stood up. "Um, hold up. I need you to pump your brakes here, Nicki, okay. I mean, for Christ's sake. I just found out I'm gonna be in prison until I'm 104 years old – and you are picking out wedding cakes and trying to name our children? Like...What?"

How the hell could she love me anyway? She doesn't know what I look like in normal clothes. She's never seen me with make up on. She doesn't know what shows I like or the music I blast when I'm in the car. Love?

"Baby, come here. Sit."

I crossed my arms suddenly feeling very uncomfortable. I mean, I liked her – don't get me wrong. I liked her a lot. But marriage? "I'm good. I'm gonna just stand here for a minute and process this," I said.

She stood up and I noticed her face was suddenly flushed. "Tiff, I know you are having a bad day, okay. You found out the wife of the man who wants you dead is two cells over, we just found out about Brandi, then your attorney scared you – so I know you are under a lot of stress, baby. Don't let all of that distract you from what's real. You need me now more than ever," she stepped closer, "I know that I have loved you since the moment I saw you, alright, and I know you love me too so –", she stopped speaking and leaned in to kiss me. I did a move from The Matrix and swooped backwards to dodge the kiss.

This enraged her. She reached out and grabbed the back of my head and forced me to kiss her. She held my face to hers so tightly that our teeth were mashing together. I pushed her away from me in stunned disgust and watched as she smiled and wiped her lips. "I'm gonna give you some time to get your damn mind right," she said, exiting the room.

I stood there shocked for a moment feeling completely violated and fairly certain that what she had done was somehow a form of rape. I suddenly decided I no longer wanted her in my room. I didn't want to be trapped in here with a creepy violent lesbian rapist. With a sudden rush of adrenaline, I decided to push the button and tell the guards what she had done.

I turned around to head toward the button and bumped into someone who had been standing an inch behind me. I couldn't believe this psycho was back already. I looked down expecting to see Nicki staring back at me.

Instead I found myself face to face with Daniels. "Hey, bitch," she said, before sucker-punching me square in the jaw.

Chapter Fourteen

I had only been in one fight in my entire life (unless you count the knock-down drag-out fights my little sister and I would have every day of our childhood). But as far as being in a physical altercation with a stranger, it only happened once, I was hammered, and I was defending my little sister's honor at a bar – long story.

Anyway, even though Daniels was an itty-bitty nugget of a person, that shit hurt! In fact, she hit me so hard that everything suddenly went black. I could hear everything around me, but for a split second I couldn't see a damn thing. She didn't just hit me once either, she took advantage of my momentary blindness and got three hits in before my sight returned and I snapped into action.

Here's the thing. When I say, "snapped into action," what I really mean is – pushed her onto the floor and grabbed the closest thing to me to use as a weapon to beat her with. My arms were moving before my brain could catch up; and unfortunately for me, my weapon of choice was – a pillow.

I shit you not. Unbeknownst to me, my body made an executive decision to grab a mother effing pillow, and hit her with it. I turned an MMA fight into a pillow fight in two seconds flat. Halfway into her pillow beating I realized how ridiculous this was, and how confused she must have been. But it was too late, I was already going to town. I'm pretty sure I also yelled out things like: "Yeah, bitch, this will teach you to sucker-punch me!"

She suddenly wiggled out from under me and stood up. I didn't move a muscle. I clutched my pillow with all my might preparing for her retaliation. "What the fuck is wrong with you?" she asked, breathing heavily before turning and running out of the room.

That was a very good question.

I was out of breath like I'd just run a marathon and my hands were shaking uncontrollably. I sat down on my bed trying to process everything and once my adrenaline had subsided, the pain began creeping in. Above my right eyebrow I felt a dull, stinging ache. I reached my hand up to the spot and sure enough there was a lump beginning to form. Suddenly, I was overcome with the realization of what I'd just done.

I hit this girl repeatedly – with a pillow. A friggin' pillow. Like, how the hell can I even attempt to brag about this shit later like, "Yo, dawg, you shoulda seen me, I swung that pillow so hard. Feathers were flying and the cotton on the pillowcase ain't soft bro, she's hurtin' for sure. Ain't nobody wanna come around me, I'll pillow swipe em so fast, dude."

Damnit.

"Everybody to your bunks, NOW!" Miss Riggins came flying into the dayroom followed by four other CO's with a determined bound in their steps. I laid down in my bunk and slowly pulled the blanket up to my neck and pretended to be sleeping. (I used to do this all the time when my mom would angrily storm up the stairs to me and my sister's room after we'd done something stupid. So, naturally, this seemed like a good idea now).

I could hear their sneakers squeaking on the floor as their keys jingled on their hips. I tried to listen and see which direction they were headed, but my head had begun pounding at this point and it hurt to concentrate that hard.

"Who the fuck was just fighting in here?" Riggins yelled from the center of the pod.

Shit, shit, shit. I'm screwed. I listened and waited for someone to rat me out. There was silence. "I said who, the hell was fighting. Ya'll do not wanna try me tonight."

Silence.

"Okay, this how ya'll wanna do it? That's fine. Open cell five!" she yelled.

My cell.

The door popped open and I heard her getting closer and closer. I was afraid she was going to see my heart pounding through the blanket. Her footsteps suddenly stopped, and I could feel her demonic presence in our cell. I thought I might shit my pants.

"Now ya'll hoes wanna play dumb, huh?" The hair on the back of my neck stood up. "See y'all wanna sit up in here, keep quiet, pretend you sleepin', but what ya'll don't realize is I been doin' this for a long time. Now see- AY! You under the blanket, wake yo ass up before I taze you awake, hoe." Okay, she was definitely talking to me. I slowly pulled the blanket down and my eyes locked with hers. "Why you hiding?"

"I'm not, I, I wasn't. I just-"

"Shut the fuck up and stand up."

"Kay," I said, flying to my feet.

"Who was fighting?" She stared into my soul as she asked.

"Ummm, fighting? I don't think -"

"I swear to God if you lie to me it will be the last thing you do," she said through gritted teeth, stepping closer.

"A crowd was gathered outside your cell. A crowd only gathers when there's a fight. So, I'll ask you again – WHO THE FUCK WAS FIGHTING?!"

As I opened my mouth to tell on myself, Nicki spoke up. "Miss Riggins, nobody was fighting. Tiffany was showing us how she does the worm, and everyone gathered around be-cause...it was hilarious."

Miss Riggins tilted her head to the side with a confused expression on her face while I debated on whether or not to punch Nicki in the face, or give her a kiss.

"What, the hell is a worm Goddamnit? And who the hell is Tiffany?" she asked.

I took a deep breath, unsure of where this was going. I could hear a few girls chuckling, and waited nervously for someone to call Nicki out for lying to Riggins' face. No one did. No one wanted to be labeled as a snitch and apparently Daniels' posse didn't want her going to lock. Holy shit. No one said a thing.

"Well, that's Tiffany," she said pointing, "and the worm is...a dance move," she said matter-of-factly. Sheila, one of our roommates was trying her best to hide her laughter, but I could hear her wheezing as she covered her mouth.

Miss Riggins turned to face me, and my face suddenly felt hot with embarrassment. "What the hell you think this is? *'America's Best Dance Crew'*? You just gone show off your dance moves whenever you feel like it? This is not the Soul Train auditions, this is jail."

I nodded.

"Matter of fact, since you like dancin' so much. Why don't you show me? Yeah, come here," she said, walking into the dayroom.

You have got to be fucking kidding me. She was not about to do this. I would rather go to lock. I would rather be tased. I would rather get sucker punched in the face ten more times by Daniels. Please God, this is not happening.

"Come here," she said, waving me to the day room. If looks could kill, Nicki would have been a corpse. I hated her before and I hated her even more now. As soon as Riggins leaves here I'm taking my pillow of death, and smothering her with it.

"Show us whatchu got," she said as she crossed her arms. I had never done the worm a day in my life. I really wanted to die. This was something you would see on a movie. I couldn't believe this was happening.

I gave myself a quick mental pep talk. "Sixty days in isolation for fighting, or the worm, in front of everyone. Just do it. It will be over before you know it."

I took a deep breath and slowly lowered my hands to the ground while simultaneously kicking off with my legs and rolling downwards. Laughter erupted all around me as my breasts smashed into the concrete followed by my stomach and pelvis. I pushed off with my arms and continued the cycle of rolling and pushing.

I'm not gonna lie, I did better than I thought I would. Like, it was pretty good.

When I had wormed back a good twenty feet, I stood up and dusted myself off. I slowly began walking back to Riggins who was shaking her head and trying not to laugh. "Get back in your damn cell, and don't let me catch you doing that shit ever again, it was terrible."

Oh.

"White people, man." She said, exiting the cell.

Chapter Fifteen

"Will you just talk to me, please?" Nicki asked, following me around the room as I tried to get ready.

"No, I'd rather not." I yanked the cheap plastic jail comb through my hair, attempting to look somewhat presentable.

"Why though? Is it because of the kiss thing?" I rolled my eyes and walked to the opposite side of the cell. Aside from the fact that she almost broke my teeth then embarrassed me in front of the whole pod, that was not the reason I was stressing.

The trouble with being in jail is, if you happen to be trapped in a room with a psycho girl who won't leave you alone, there's really no escape. You can only walk in small circles for so long.

"Look, Tiff, I'm sorry. They switched my meds and I've been feeling a little crazy, I didn't mean –"

Her voice made me nauseous.

"Okay listen Nicki, I'm getting sentenced to fifteen years in prison in less than an hour, and I have to walk in there with a black eye, so, with all due respect – you are the least of my worries right now."

I finished getting ready and headed out of the cell to line up for court. I stopped at the door and swiveled on my heels to face Nicki. "And by the way, I saw you snort the Xanax that the nasty prostitute with no teeth brought in here. You're an idiot," I walked away before she could reply.

I overheard the girls talking about how some girl smuggled Xanax in, in her, um, Lady parts. It happened all the time and honestly, had I known how simple it was I probably would have done it myself. I had a whole bag of pills sitting at my house the day I got arrested. I thought about that bag often, filled with longing and anger at how it is going to waste just sitting there. I wonder if Chuck ever found it?

"Johnson, Durbick, Smith, Langdon, line up – you got court," Deputy Flower yelled the names off her clipboard and one by one the girls lined up behind me. Some of them were excited, some of them were quiet, and I was basically shitting my pants.

We all lined up facing the wall with our legs spread and hands up. They shackled our hands together in front of us, our feet together, then attached a chain from our waist to our arms and legs.

As we jingle-jangled down the hallway toward the van, I couldn't help but think about all the times I'd watched movies with shackled prisoners. Never in a million years did I ever think I'd be one.

As I stepped up into the van, my eyes grew wide as I realized the back four rows were filled with prisoners—and they were male. Holy shit, I hadn't seen a man in about sixty days. The guys began smiling as we entered the bus, and I immediately reached up to fix my hair, suddenly feeling self-conscious. I looked real stupid when my hand got jerked back down to my waist... I forgot I was shackled. *Damnit.*

"Aright, we got a fifteen-minute ride. If anyone talks, you're going to lock. Ladies, if you turn around, you're going to lock. Am I clear?" Deputy Flower said as the bus lurched forward.

I stared out the window and watched as the trees blurred by. I took in every sight, every color, every sound I could. Because I didn't know if I would ever have a chance to see the outside world again.

You don't realize how many things you take for granted, until you no longer have them. We passed a McDonalds and I remembered all the times my parents had taken my sister and I to eat there. I would trade my soul for a Big Mac right now.

We entered the courthouse in a straight line, and everyone in that building stopped what they were doing to take in the sight of the chained criminals.

I could tell they were studying us, sizing us up, imagining the kind of people we were and the terrible things we must have done. I stared straight ahead, careful not to make eye contact.

I used to wear fancy clothes like these people, I used to carry a briefcase and have a real job. Drugs had taken me from their side -to this side, the dark side, in an instant.

"Aright, everybody, in here. Except you, Johnson, you're up first."

Well, shit.

I was led to the courtroom, same as last time. My public defender was already waiting at the podium for me, which meant we weren't going to be able to talk about what the hell was happening.

As I approached the podium, he leaned in. "They have two options for you, six months jail, three years-probation. Or, four months jail, six months residential treatment, three years-probation. Which do you want?"

I'm fairly certain that he is supposed to tell me this shit ahead of time, so that I could have time to ponder, but I was just relieved that somehow, the courts dropped it from fifteen years, to this.

"You have about thirty seconds," he said, glancing up from his watch.

I didn't need thirty seconds. I knew what I wanted to do. I could be free from jail in four more months. I could be back out in the real world, living life again. The thing is, if I didn't take the rehab, I would be right back here in no time. Wearing this same jumpsuit, being told when to eat, what to eat. Going to the bathroom in front of six girls. I couldn't do it again.

I needed to get my brain fixed. I needed help. There were two paths laid out before me and depending on which I chose, would result in a completely different future.

"I want to go to rehab."

"Are you sure?"

"I'm sure, I want to go. I'm going."

My attorney looked surprised. I'm assuming it's because most people would have chosen to be out of jail as soon as possible, they would have chosen freedom. But even though this meant eight more months of being told what to do and when to do it, to me, this was freedom. It was my only hope of freeing myself from this addiction.

The court presented my two options, just as my attorney had said. He told them my choice, the judge responded, "Very well, then," and I was ushered out of the courtroom. That was it. It was final. I no longer had to worry about my fate.

For the first time in a long time, I would now be able to just – relax. I no longer had to obsess about the future, pray for my attorney to call, question other girls about their experience and what I should expect.

I could just be present in the moment, and ride out these last sixty days in jail. I had nothing but time on my hands now.

## Chapter Sixteen

Today was a new day. The countdown to my release began and it was an incredible feeling. When I first arrived, there were so many unanswered questions. I had no clue how anything worked, including court proceedings, so I had to rely on the experience of the other women regarding what I could expect to happen to me.

The women in there weren't necessarily what one would consider – reliable, so it was hard to take any advice they had given me to heart. In the end, things turned out better than I could have hoped and I'm sure, to many, it seemed I got off easy.

At least that's what Deputy Burns felt, and she made sure to let me know every chance she got. On the way back from court I had been feeling grateful and relieved. That all changed when Deputy Burns began unshackling me.

"Hands on the wall, Johnson," she said, kicking my ankles apart. She began frisking me to ensure I hadn't smuggled any paper clips or staplers out of the courthouse.

"Heard about your sentence," she said as her hands moved along the sides of my waist. I didn't respond, because it wasn't a question. I've learned it's better if you only speak when spoken to, and since I didn't know what to say, I didn't say anything.

"A hundred and twenty and rehab, huh?"

"Yes, Ma'am."

"Geez, you put an arsenal of weapons into the hands of known drug dealers, pieces of shit who only care about money, and will do just about anything to stay out of trouble – including shooting me or an innocent civilian, and you basically get a slap on the wrist," she whispered.

She was right, I wasn't thinking about the potential outcome of giving him those guns, I was only thinking about getting high. It wasn't until I was in the interrogation room and a member of the SWAT team who was on his way to retrieve those guns, got an inch away from my face and said, "If I die today, the blood is on your hands," that I realized the severity of what I'd done.

I didn't respond to Burns, I decided to let her vent. He was her friend after all, and I could understand why she was taking this personally.

"I hope you realize that once you are out of here, you won't be free. Once you are out of rehab, you won't be free and if you do happen to successfully complete your probation – which is highly unlikely, you won't be free then, either. The entire Sheriff's Department knows what you did to Chuck, and I'm not just talking about the stealing." She turned me around and began feeling the front of my legs. I rolled my eyes, and I'm pretty sure she'd frisked me better than I've ever been frisked, she just wanted to finish her point.

"They have had to pat his back at the bar when he breaks down in tears at the thought of you. We have all had to help him pick himself up and if it was up to us, your punishment would be much worse. That's our friend, our brother, and you broke him. You have to live with that for the rest of your life."

She pulled me away from the wall forcefully and nudged me toward the entrance of the pod. My teeth were clenched so hard my gums hurt. I wanted desperately to lash out, snap back at her about how she couldn't possibly understand my life, because she had never had an addiction. I didn't want to hurt him. I didn't want to lie, and steal and manipulate. I had to. At least, I felt like I had. I knew any attempt at responding would be futile. She had all the power, and I was nothing.

I entered the pod and was met with a hundred anticipated stares. Girls who had been following my journey and helping guide me, and nosey bitches who just wanted to know if I was spending life in prison.

My friend Sarah ran up to me and gave me a hug – which was immediately reprimanded via the intercom. "No touching, ladies, you know the rules."

"Fuck you," Sarah said under her breath as she smiled at me with curious eyes. "Well?" I nodded toward my cell and she followed me. I didn't want to entertain the curiosity of girls who really didn't care. I needed privacy and to talk with a real friend.

I filled Sarah in on everything, including my interaction with Burns. "Okay, first, yay! That's such great news, Tiff, you thought you were going away forever. And secondly, fuck Burns, she's a stupid cunt and needs to get a damn life. She was probably picked on for her fat ass in high school and she's taking that aggression out on you, don't you dare let that bitch rain on your parade. I love you, I'm so happy!"

Her happiness was rubbing off on me, and I could feel the gratitude swelling within me again. I wanted to call my dad and tell him the news. Clearly that wasn't an option. I knew he would be proud of me for choosing rehab. That man sent me a postcard every single day. Sometimes they would be informative, things that were happening in the outside world, on a few he just drew random pictures and at times, he would send childhood photos of me. Those always made me emotional. They were a reminder of the person I was before addiction, the person I wanted to be again.

"Let's celebrate!" Sarah said, jumping up from the bunk and snapping me out of my daydream. "I have an idea, let's do our hair all cute, pluck our eyebrows, put make up on and make a cake! I'll be right back," she said, skipping off to her cell.

She hadn't even waited for my response, probably because she knew the answer would be hell no. None of that sounded fun, at all. The cake maybe. But not the hair and make- up.

Sarah returned with all her supplies and laid them out on the bed. "Okay, we have twenty-four minutes until lockdown, we gotta hurry." She reached down, pulled her sock off and began stabbing it with a pencil. I knew where this was going, and I was dreading it.

She created a small hole in the sock and began ripping it until she was able to free a piece of thread. She took the ends of the long thread and tied them together. "Lean back," she said, pushing my forehead to the pillow. She began plucking the hairs from my eyebrows by slowly twisting the thread in a "figure 8" motion. I know this was supposed to be "fun girly time," but I had to literally stop myself from throat punching her on four different occasions.

She finished ripping my face off and moved on to my hair. "Where's Nicki?" I asked, realizing I hadn't seen her since I got back. Sarah slowly let go of my head and remained quiet. I turned around to read her expression and could tell something was up. "What?" I asked.

"Um, she bonded out."

"Oh?" I said, trying to process my emotions.

"She said to tell you bye, and that you probably wouldn't care. Um, she said she was only staying here for you, but I guess you guys got into a fight or something, so she called her drug dealer. Also, you should know, she was, um, with Tonya in here," she said, averting her eyes.

"What do you mean, 'with Tonya'?"

She grimaced, and I could tell she felt awkward about telling me.

"They did it," she blurted.

"Did what?"

"Ugh, okay. They did it, ya know, had sex. In here. Right where I'm sitting, actually. They had a blanket blocking them, but you could hear it. It was gross, Tonya is such a slu—"

"Okay," I said holding up my hand. I didn't want to hear anymore. Why was I feeling so jealous?

Sarah parted my hair and began braiding one side. She had been telling me about how her boyfriend came to visit but all

I could think about was Nicki. I was about to start questioning Sarah about what exactly happened, but she suddenly stopped midsentence. She took my braid and lifted it, then dropped it abruptly.

"OH, MY FUCKING GOD!" she yelled.

She screamed it so loud that a bunch of nosey girls started peeking into the cell.

"What? What the hell, what?" I asked beginning to panic.

"Dude, your head is fucking infested with lice."

Chapter Seventeen

"Lice?" I whispered, trying to keep this quiet, because the last thing I needed was for the other girls to hear.

Too late.

"Ewww, hell naw. You heard what dat girl just said? Bitch has lice, bruh," Kiesha said standing up from the table near my cell and walking away.

"Not uh, who?" another girl said, scratching her head.

"Dat girl right there," Kiesha said, pointing to me.

The next thing I know – all hell was breaking loose.

Everyone began scurrying away, trying to protect their heads from any stray lice. Apparently, lice is a big problem in jail. Once one girl has it, it's usually followed by numerous other girls contracting it. I remembered the way the last girl who had it was treated by the inmates, and I was dreading receiving that same backlash.

They all retreated to their cells to check each other's hair. Some girls were dramatically scratching their heads saying they felt itchy and there were plenty of curse words and threats being tossed my way.

To say I felt embarrassed would be an understatement. I wanted to crawl into a hole and disappear, but I was trapped. "Hey, don't worry about it, Tiff," Sarah said trying to lift my spirits, "I'm gonna let the guards know and we will get it taken care of. Okay?"

She was a good friend. She could have run away like everyone else – but she stayed.

Just then the pod doors swung open and Miss Riggins came flying in. "Which one of you nasty bitches got bugs in your hair?" Apparently, someone already alerted them.

"Cell five got em. The tall girl wit da glasses. Get her outta here, Miss Riggins, ain't nobody want no lice."

All the girls were looking at me with disgusted expressions, including Miss Riggins. "Let's go. Don't come near me, just head to the door," she said, pointing to the exit. Everyone was watching me, everyone knew what was happening, and they were all being so damn mean about it.

The lack of compassion was shocking; they were treating me like a dog with rabies.

As Sarah followed me to the exit, Miss Riggins yelled behind her. "I don't know where the hell you think you going, Carnwell, but this ain't no buddy system, you need to get yo ass back in your cell."

What Sarah said next made me stop dead in my tracks.

"I have lice too, Miss Riggins. I need to be treated as well."

My heart exploded with gratitude. This girl just outed herself, in front of everyone, so she could come support me. I was speechless.

"Oh hell naw. Go. Hurry up and go on out, Deputy Silva will take ya'll to medical" Riggins said giving a disgusted shiver and scratching her head. "Ya'll nasty bitches makin me wanna get checked."

Sarah and I entered medical and were met with looks of disdain from several deputies. "Don't bring them over here, toss em right into holding cell two," someone said, referring to us. I could hear them murmuring about how we both were infested with lice, how gross we were, and how if we didn't walk the streets and sleep on the sides of roads, that we wouldn't be having this problem.

I wanted to tell them to shut the fuck up. That I had been here for two months, and someone else must have brought it in with them. But speaking to them in a disrespectful tone would get me sent to lock, and I'd rather eat the lice than go to lock.

When the door shut behind us, I gave Sarah a grin so big that it hurt my cheeks. "I can't believe you did that. You don't have lice, do you?" I asked.

"No. But I couldn't let you come down here alone. Besides, it's Valentine's Day. I thought this would be a nice romantic getaway for the two of us," she said.

I burst out with laughter and it was immediately cut short by someone banging on the window. "Shut up in there! There's nothing funny about lice."

I rolled my eyes and turned back toward Sarah. "Holy crap, it's Valentine's Day? I forgot all about that. I just realized I've spent Thanksgiving, Christmas, New Year's and now Valentine's Day behind bars. That fucking sucks, dude."

The door swung open and a guard threw two boxes of Rid inside our cell, and promptly slammed it shut. I guess they were afraid my lice would jump out and attack him if he kept it open any longer.

"Well, Tiff, the good news is, this is the last holiday you will spend here, and I have planned a beautiful day for us. We will begin by lovingly picking nits from one another's scalps. Then, we will lather ourselves up with this highly-toxic lice killer, followed by a romantic hose down by a random deputy; it's gonna be incredible," Sarah said, picking the boxes up from the floor.

It had been a real long time since I'd had a true friend. One who didn't use me, and expected nothing but friendship in return. Sarah was a good friend, and in that moment I felt incredibly grateful to have met her.

After getting stripped and hosed down, Sarah and I were brought back to general population. When we entered the pod, everyone was staring and moving away as we walked past. I wanted to run around and start hugging people and shaking my hair all over them, but decided against it.

"The lice has been treated, you guys can go back to playing cards and snorting headache medicine now, nothing to see here," Sarah said as we walked into my cell.

"Hey, thank you so much for doing that for me. You didn't have to. It really means a lot," I said. "Aww, you're welcome. I'd chose picking lice out of your hair, over hanging out with these whores any day," she said smiling.

"Who is Big T?" Jayda, an inmate who had been released and re-arrested three times since I'd been here yelled from the day room. My ears perked up. My friend Keke who used to be in our pod but got moved to high security next door used to call me that.

"Anybody in here go by Big T?" Jayda said again. I walked to the entrance of my cell and stuck my head out. I saw her showing something to another girl and heard her say, "I don't know, someone named Keke slipped it under the door from high security." The girls began laughing at whatever it was.

"Me! I think it's for me," I said, walking toward her. "Did you say it's from Keke?"

"Yeah, are you Big T? Here," she said, handing me the piece of paper. I took it out of her hand and glanced down at it. It was a note, in the shape of a penis and balls, and I immediately knew who'd sent it. It read:

Hey boo, I miss you and your jokes soooo much, I'm trying to get back over to that pod soon. It sucks over here. Write me back and slip it under the door.

I love you!

Keke

A bunch of girls came over to look and everyone thought it was hilarious that it was a penis. We were like six-year-olds who had never seen a male body part before. I didn't even know you could slip notes through the door. "Girl, you better flush that shit down the toilet asap before you get caught," Tonya said. Tonya was the last person I wanted to take advice from. Homewrecker.

"She's right, Tiff, you should get rid of it," Sarah said quietly.

"Okay, SARAH, I will," I said staring straight at Tonya, I didn't want her to think I was doing it because SHE told me to. "I didn't do anything wrong though, I can't get in trouble for receiving a note. I didn't ask her to write it," I said, taking it to my cell and flushing it down the toilet.

I watched it swirl in circles as it went down the toilet and I jumped as the pod doors flew open.

"EVERYBODY ON THE GROUND, NOW!"

A team of guards I didn't recognize came busting through the door and ordered everyone down. I dropped to the floor by the toilet and turned my head to see what the hell was going on.

I watched as they marched over to Jayda and pulled her arms behind her back. They handcuffed her and dragged her out of the pod. Then they began walking to my cell.

I watched their boots as they got closer and closer then stopped about an inch from my head. The next thing I knew it felt as if my arms were being dislocated from my shoulders.

"What did you flush!?" the guard yelled.

"What? I—"

"WHAT THE FUCK DID YOU FLUSH, DAMNIT?! Was it drugs?" they said, pulling me to my feet by my wrists and patting me down.

"We saw that something was retrieved from the other pod under the door. We witnessed you bring it in here then flush something. What was it?"

"A note! A penis shaped note! It was nothing!"

"Let's go," she said, pulling me backwards out of the pod.

"Search these cells!" she yelled over her shoulder to the remaining deputies.

All this over a note? What the hell? Where were they taking me?

We took a flight of stairs to an area I had never been before, and I noticed a wall of red cell doors. The deputy holding me radioed in for someone to open cell #1. Once open, she pushed me through the door and shut it behind me.

"Put your hands through the slot, now," she said. I turned around to back my hands up to the slot and took a survey of the cell while she was uncuffing me. It was no larger than a closet. There was a toilet, a sink, and a cement slab with no mattress. There were no windows and I could stick my arms straight out to my sides and touch both walls.

Once the cuffs were off I turned around to face the deputy. "Where am I and why am I here?" I asked pleadingly.

"Receiving and possessing contraband is in direct violation of the rules. You are currently in Solitary Confinement. You will not be permitted to make phone calls, have visitation or receive mail unless it is from an attorney. You will be taken down to shower on Mondays, Wednesdays and Fridays and you will receive one roll of toilet paper per week – so use it sparingly."

"What? For what? The note? How long do I have to stay here?"

"Sixty days. You will be spending the remainder of your sentence in here. I will bring you toilet paper soon, try not to go before I get back," she said, slamming the slot shut and walking away.

Chapter Eighteen

Two hundred forty-six. I had counted at least a thousand times. There were two hundred forty-six concrete bricks used to make the walls of this dungeon in which I was forced to exist. I won't say live in, because I wasn't living, I was existing. My body was physically here, my mind however was gone.

I couldn't tell you how many days I had been in here. There were no clocks and no windows, just the flickering, buzzing fluorescent lights. The days and nights blended together into a continuous span of torturous boredom.

We weren't allowed any personal items in isolation, therefore I couldn't read, write or draw. I couldn't play cards or laugh with friends or take a damn shower. It was just me, my mind, and the occasional clanging of doors in the distance.

Periodically, animalistic wails would echo through the hallways. At first, I thought whoever was making these noises must be crazy. They sounded inhuman. Over time however, I started to understand those noises and could relate to what that person was feeling. Every moment that passed, I found myself slipping further and further away from reality.

I know it had to be at least nine days, because I had been keeping track of the meals I was offered, most of which I flushed down the toilet. I had lost a lot of weight, I could tell because the clothes were loose now. The food was so different in isolation. For breakfast they served a hideous bread pudding loaf, which had bits of what I can only assume was fruit and flecks of something green and translucent.

I had no appetite and this environment was not conducive to someone with a history of depression. I had replayed every moment of my life like a movie in my head. I had rehashed every terrible thing I had ever done because there was nothing available to distract me from the reality of what my life had become.

I had enough. I began thinking about how long I'd been in here and how many days were left. I thought about sitting here in silence with only my thoughts for another month in a half and it became incredibly overwhelming to imagine.

Very suddenly I began sweating, profusely. I curled up into a ball on the floor and my feet began tapping rapidly on the ground. I could hear my blood as it gushed through my veins each time my heart beat. It was becoming harder and harder to inhale the oxygen around me, the air felt hot and sticky.

A noise I didn't recognize escaped my throat and I jumped to my feet with unexpected determination. I pushed my face to the glass on my door and began roaring, like a lion trapped in a cage.

I couldn't control myself. I had officially lost my shit.

I pounded on the doors until my hands were sore and even then, I continued slamming them into the metal. "SOME-BODY GET ME THE FUCK OUT OF HERRRE!"

No one came. There wasn't a soul in sight. I started to break down crying, but it was as if someone was controlling my emotions with a lever. The crying stopped just as suddenly as it began and was once again replaced with violent rage.

I began hurling my body into the door repeatedly. I figured maybe if I injured myself they would have no choice but to let me out of here. I would have stopped at nothing to step out of that room, even if just for a moment.

My mind was gone, all logic had disappeared. My sole focus was to free myself from this prison within a prison. Without hesitation, I began slamming my forearm onto the edge of the sink. I needed to break my arm. If I broke my arm they would have no choice but to take me to a hospital, I would be free.

I would choose immense pain over another minute in here in an instant. I was swinging my arm as if I was chopping wood, hammering it down onto the metal surface. I kept listening each time for the bone to snap, but it wasn't happening. I began growing increasingly frustrated and started visually searching the room for another way.

The door to my cell suddenly swung up and a guard was in my face before I could turn my head to look.

"What the hell are you doing?" he asked, gripping my bad arm with immense pressure.

"Please, please. I need to get out of here. I can't take it." He was staring at me in shock and confusion, after what he just witnessed through the window.

"If you are trying to kill yourself in here, we have to take you to the observation tank," he said, pulling me toward the door. The "Observation Tank," I'd been there before. That was just as bad as this place except you are in a fishbowl and everyone can see you, naked, in your Velcro suit.

"NO! No, I'm not trying to kill myself, please. I don't want to die. I mean, this place makes me kinda wanna die but I don't, I really don't want to. No one has come by my cell in days other than the trustees delivering food. I haven't brushed my teeth in like two weeks, they keep saying they are gonna get me a toothbrush and never do. Sir, I've showered once, they are supposed to take me three times a week. I still don't have a blanket, they never gave me one. Listen, they hate me and I can't fucking handle this. I'm losing it, man," I whimpered.

His eyebrows relaxed as he took a step back and loosened his grip. Just then another officer rushed in behind him and he turned to face her. "Hey, um, can you tell Rodriguez I'm coming down to talk to him in a sec, we are fine in here." The woman nodded and exited the room as he swung his head back toward me and cocked it sideways.

"Is everything you just said to me true?" He glanced past me to my bed and noted that there was only a sheet. He turned to face the sink and saw there wasn't a toothbrush or toothpaste in sight.

He finally let go of my arm and placed his hands on his hips. "You gotta be fucking kidding me. Give me a minute, I'll be right back," he said, shaking his head and exiting the room.

I sat on the edge of my bed and my breathing began slowing. Finally, someone had listened to me. I prayed this guy was coming back with a toothbrush and toothpaste, because even though I'd barely eaten, the plaque on my teeth felt like rocks. My hair was matted and oily and I had smelled like a jock strap for about a week now.

Once my heart rate returned to normal and the adrenaline had left my body, all my aches and pains suddenly became very evident. I looked down at my arm and the entire length of my forearm was swollen and beginning to bruise. I reached up to rub my shoulder when the door of my cell suddenly swung open.

The officer was back, but he was empty handed. My heart sunk.

He stared at me for a moment and took a few steps toward me. "Look, obviously you got yourself into this here mess and all but, I'm sorry about the um, the way things have gone since you've been up here. It's not supposed to be like that. I talked to my superior about what's been going on, and when he realized what you were in lock for, we both agreed that you have more than paid the consequences of your actions."

I jumped up from the bed and he took a step back, placing his hand out to stop me from coming any further.

"I'm sorry. I am just excited... I think? What exactly are you saying?" I asked, my heart beating with anticipation.

"I'm saying, we are gonna get you back to population".

I began sobbing. I was overcome with relief and gratitude and if I didn't think I'd get tased, I would have jumped on him and kissed him on the lips. There were no words to describe how I felt. He rolled his eyes in response and headed toward the door. "You can sit here and cry, or you can come with me, your choice."

I skipped out the door behind him. "No, no skipping," he said holding up his hand.

"No, I know, you're right... Sorry."

Once I was handcuffed, he began leading me toward population. He pushed the button on his radio and said, "One incoming, medical." I was confused, was he talking about me? He could tell I was looking at him because he turned to me. "We gotta take you by medical first, your arm is pretty bad. They will probably wanna give you a physical too before sending you to pop, just to make sure you don't hurt anyone or yourself again."

"Oh." It made sense. I wasn't even mad. I was grateful to be out of that dungeon. We arrived at the door of medical and while we waited for them to open it, he turned to me with a look of regret on his face. "I really am sorry about how things went up there, I'm planning on talking to a few people to see what happened. Probably a miscommunication." Yeah, that was it.

The door popped open and he led me to medical cell 7. "Take care of yourself," he said, opening the door.

"Thank you, I will," I said smiling as he shut it behind me. I turned around to check out my new cell and was surprised to see another inmate. It had been so long, I was relieved to finally have someone to talk to.

She was asleep in the corner and I didn't want to wake her, so I tip-toed to the bed across from her and laid down. I turned to face her to see what she looked like and when I caught a glimpse of her face my hand shot up over my mouth to keep from screaming.

Fucking Daniels...

Chapter Nineteen

I couldn't help but laugh to myself, honestly. Like, of all the places in the entire jail I could be placed, I was locked in a closet with my arch nemesis.

I stared at her sleeping face for a moment, noticing how sweet and peaceful she appeared while dreaming. I knew that the moment her eyes flipped open however, it was going to be a different story.

What the hell am I supposed to do here? She's gonna wake up and turn into the Tasmanian Devil. There will be hair and fists flying all over the place. I could beat her ass while I had the advantage. I could pummel her while she slept, and by the time she realized what was happening, it would be too late. The guards would run in and separate us.

Wait, they would move me back to isolation, I'd rather her just wake up and murder me. I could fashion a flower out of toilet paper, and when she wakes up, smile and hand it to her and be like, "friends?" Perhaps I'll just hide under my covers and play dead. I mean that's really the only reasonable option here.

I pulled the wool blanket up over my face and immediately realized what a terrible idea this was. Not only was it impossible to breathe, but I was inhaling lint and pubic hairs.

Fuck it. I'm not gonna hide, I didn't do a damn thing to this girl. She sucker-punched me, all I did was retaliate with a damn pillow. No, I'm done playing nice. I refuse to spend another second stressing over this little Chihuahua.

I stood up from my bunk, and walked over to hers. I quickly tapped her on the shoulder before I had a chance to change my mind. She started to stir, but pulled the blanket up over her head and began snoring again.

Shit. My heart was pounding out of my chest.

I tapped again. This time she cussed from beneath her fort. "Go the fuck away, man." I was so nervous, that my hands were shaking, but I couldn't sit back down and obsess about what was gonna happen. I needed to make something happen. If we were going to fight, I just wanted it to be over with.

"Hey, Daniels. Wake up. It's Johnson," I said, taking a step back, in case she decided to come out swinging.

"You gotta be fucking kidding me," she said.

"Yeah, I know, that's what I said."

She began laughing. Literally, laughing. I wasn't sure if she genuinely thought this predicament was hilarious, or if it was the laugh a serial killer does before ripping someone's face off and making a hat.

"So, anyway," I began, "I figured we could just, um, get this out of the way now, since we are both obviously stuck in here.

I don't wanna get sucker punched when I'm sleepin', ya know?" I said.

She sat up, like straight up. She kept her head under the blanket and just, sat the hell up. It was as if I'd just awoken a vampire from its slumber.

She ripped the blanket down and squinted at me, her eyes swollen from sleep.

"Aright, what's up then?" she said, remaining seated – which was a good sign.

"What's up, with you...Then?" I said. I am the fucking worst at come-backs.

She tilted her head to the side and looked up at me. Her expression wasn't threatening, she looked... Tired.

"Aright, you want it? Here it is. Im'a be real witchu, okay? You are the reason my two-year-old ain't never gonna see his daddy. You went and fucking snitched on my baby daddy, and now, he's off to – God knows where, but he's gone. Cuz the fucking poh-leece is lookin' for him, because of you."

She looked down at her feet and shook her head, then looked back up at me with tears welling in her eyes. She was trying to keep her chin from quivering, and looked away to hide the tears falling from her eyes.

Well, damn.

My muscles relaxed a bit, and my heart felt heavy. Although, technically, I didn't force this dude to buy these guns, I was partly responsible for the fact that this poor toddler wasn't going to know his father, because when the police finally did catch up with him, he was going to be put away for a very long time.

I thought about that little boy, and felt a knot begin to form in my throat.

"You know what the worst part is?" she said, staring past me, at the wall.

Ugh, it gets worse?

She turned to face me and was hiccupping back sobs. "I'm five months pregnant, and he ain't gonna be around for his daughter. He won't be there for the birth, he won't be there to buy diapers, or help me out. I gotta do this shit by myself. Because of you. So yeah, I don't like you, in fact, I fucking hate your ass, but I ain't gonna fight you. I've got bigger things to worry about. Now, if you don't mind, I'm gonna get some fucking sleep."

I stared in stunned silence as she laid back down and rolled over to face the wall.

My very first thought was – thank God I only hit her with a pillow.

My second thought was... Well now I feel like a big a\*\*hole.

The things I did while using didn't only affect me, or my victims, or my family; they affected a family I wasn't even aware existed. The consequences of my actions rippled outward like a rock thrown into a pond.

I stared at the outline of Daniels' body for a moment. The guilt was overwhelming. I don't blame her for being angry, I would be too. She is a single mother with an addiction, I can't imagine having to leave a child behind while I did time. Even harder to imagine was how difficult it would be to go through this hell – jail – with a baby inside me.

"What the hell am I doing?" I said under my breath as I walked over and sat down at the foot of her bunk.

"Hey, Daniels," I called as I tapped her leg, "hey real quick, before you go to sleep."

"I already was asleep, hoe, why the hell you on my bed?" she said looking at me like I was crazy.

I took a deep breath and began speaking, I couldn't hold back my emotions as the words started spilling from my lips like an overflowing sink...

"I need you to know, that I'm sorry, okay," She rolled her eyes.

Then I said, "I am, I really am sorry. I don't have kids, so I can't imagine how hard it must be to raise them. But I do know it has got to be 10 times harder without a dad in the picture."

She sat up and inched backward away from me, until her back pressed against the wall.

"I didn't know Lazarus had kids, I was over there all the time and he never said a word. Honestly though, it wouldn't have mattered to me. I would have done the same thing anyway. He asked if I could get guns, he said he would hook me up with pills. I am an addict, okay, I wasn't thinking about the repercussions of what I was doing. I was thinking about getting high." She rolled her eyes again, and I was certain that she wasn't processing a thing I was saying, but I didn't care. I had to say it.

"For the record, he texted me about the guns. Okay? There was record of him asking. I didn't have to snitch, he snitched on himself. I am sorry about your son, I am sorry about your unborn daughter, I am. You need to know I'm sorry, I never meant for any of this to happen, I was sick. I am sick. I need help."

She stared down at the bed in silence, she didn't say a word. She began anxiously shaking her foot, and I could tell something was happening inside her head. I just didn't know what.

"Look, I appreciate you being real with me. Apologies are hard to come by in this place," she said quietly. I felt so grateful that she was receptive to my apology, the goosebumps prickled up on my skin because it felt like we had a break-through. I opened my mouth to respond but she interrupted suddenly.

"He wants you dead," she blurted.

"I'm sorry?" I said, confused by her sudden outburst.

"Lazarus, he wants you dead, or at least hurt bad. He prolly ain't tryna kill you but, he's a man of his word, and he doesn't play. I talked to my cousin and she said that Lazarus told Greg to check online for when you get released. He's gonna find you, he will. He's a crazy motherfucker, man. You done got yourself into some deep shit. You kept it real wit me, so I wanted to return the favor. Just watch your back out there."

I stared at her for a moment, I had so many questions, but couldn't find the words. My mind began racing through thou-sands of scenarios, and images of my murder were playing like a movie in my head.

"Can you please get off my bed now?"

"Yup," I said, standing abruptly.

"Hey, um. There's something else," she said, as she laid back down.

"God, what?"

"Your friend, Trisha I think her name is? I guess she told Lazarus where your sister live at. You might want to call her... Just saying."

Chapter Twenty

Once the nurses determined that I was no longer a danger to myself or anyone else, they sent me back to population.

Although Daniels and I were stuck in the same cell for around sixteen hours together, her warning was the last words she spoke to me. She slept the rest of the time and honestly, I was fine with that.

Her being asleep gave me the chance to not fuck up the good rapport we had established by saying something stupid – for which I'm notorious.

When they opened the doors to the female pod, all eyes were fixed on me. I ignored them. I was on a mission and didn't have time to entertain the curiosities of the other women.

I needed to give my sister the heads up. My brother, whom had spent around 16 years in prison himself, had put some money on my books when he'd heard about my incarceration. I hadn't spoken to him in over ten years, but having been in a similar situation himself, he hooked it up.

However, I had used all that money up on toiletries, boxers and socks, and had been broke for a few weeks now. My father and sister had refused to give me any money, and initially, I was pretty bitter about it.

Over time, and the more my senses started coming back to me, I came to understand. I assume they wanted to make this experience as uncomfortable as possible for me. And I'll tell you what, watching every other woman carry giant sacks of snacks back to their cells on commissary day, was certainly a cruel punishment.

I needed someone to give me a call. It cost $2.50 per phone call, and girls in here weren't exactly the most giving of people, so I knew this wasn't going to be easy.

I began by begging, running from girl to girl, flashing my best impression of a sad puppy, and being met with rejection left and right.

I tried bargaining. "Someone can have my breakfast tray for the next three days – unless it's pancakes – if you give me a call!" I yelled from the top of the stairs. Crickets. Apparently, everyone in here had suddenly gone deaf.

My mind was racing, I had to figure out a way to call my sister. Visions of her cheerfully answering her front door and being met with a gunshot haunted me.

Tears began welling into my eyes and my throat knotted up. I didn't want to cry, because I was afraid that if I started, I wouldn't stop. I felt so...helpless.

Then it dawned on me. I had something, one thing that every girl in here wanted.

I ran to my room and ripped my shirt off (calm down, this isn't going where you're thinking).

I pulled my sports bra off and put my shirt back on. Sports bras were like crack in here. They were $20 on commissary, and when faced with the choice of phone calls to baby daddies or letting their boobs hang loose, these girls chose the phone calls every time.

I marched to the center of the dayroom and proudly thrust my bra into the air. "Alright ladies, deal of the century. This gorgeous white sports bra could be yours for the taking, all I need, is one phone call!" I yelled triumphantly.

"Man, sit cho ass down, ain't nobody wants your dusty ass sports bra, get the hell outta here," Shonda said, her face twisted in disgust.

I dropped my hand to my side and let out a sigh.

"Come on, man, I really need to call my sister. And for the record it isn't dusty. I just got it back from laundry today and have only worn it for like five seconds. Anyway, pleeease. someone. I'm begging. It's basically life or death."

"I'll take it."

I gasped and whipped my head in the direction of the angelic voice who had come to the rescue.

It was a girl I didn't recognize. She must have arrived while I was in medical. I ran over to the gate of her cell and pressed my face up to the bars. "Oh my God, thank you so much. I really need to make this call. I'm Tiffany by the way."

"I'm Alicia."

Alicia, my new best friend, punched her code into the phone and dialed my sister's number.

"It's ringing," she said, handing me the phone.

My heart was pounding. "Please pick up, please pick up."

"Hello?"

My heart leapt from my chest. Thank God. I smiled at Alicia and gave her a thumbs-up, she raised her eyebrows pretending to be excited.

"You have a collect call from The Marco County Jail. Inmate: Alicia Dober, is on the line. To accept this call, press one."

I waited for her to punch the button, but instead I heard 'click,' followed by a dial tone.

I gasped. "Hello?" I said into the receiver. "Helllllllo?"

She had hung up.

My heart began pounding even faster and anxiety had twisted up my insides like a pretzel.

I looked over at Alicia as I slowly hung up the phone.

"If ya'll are done you need to move. We only have ten minutes left to use the phone and I am next in line," a girl said behind me.

My head twisted around like the exorcist. "Hold the fuck on." She backed up and crossed her arms, but didn't say a word. I'm sure she could tell from my expression that now was not the time to try me.

"Can you please call her back, Alicia? One more time? It didn't charge your account because she didn't accept the call. It said your name when she picked up, so she was probably confused," I pleaded.

"Yeah, aright. I'll try again. But we gotta make this quick because I need a call too."

She dialed the number and handed me the phone. It rang twice, and I was sent to voicemail.

I took a deep breath trying to calm myself. I don't know why the hell my sister just did that. It's obvious it was me calling even though it wasn't my name. Who the hell else would be calling her from jail.

I started to feel angry.

Now, not only were my boobs flopping around like a National Geographic documentary, but I still didn't get to warn my sister and my arm was killing me. It was black and blue in a bunch of different places and felt like it was on fire. Drugs sounded really fucking good right about now.

I lay in my bed, staring at the ceiling, and suddenly my mind was consumed with thoughts of getting high. The physical pain combined with the emotional pain was too much to handle while sober. This was all still new to me, I didn't know how to cope. The nurse in medical said that if I start to become overwhelmed with my current situation, instead of panicking and letting anxiety cause me to make rash decisions, I needed to try praying.

I laughed in her face.

There was no such thing as a God. I know this for a fact. When my mom died people tried to pull that bullshit with me: "God has a plan." "There's a reason for everything." "God needed your mother with Him in Heaven."

It's complete and utter bullshit. I needed her here, with me. FUCK God. I'm not gonna "pray," I'm gonna get high. Drugs have always been there for me, God never has.

A gnawing, aching, overwhelming need to feel the drugs coursing through my veins became my main focus.

My hands began shaking as desperation crept in. I needed to find drugs, and I knew someone in this hell hole had them.

I stood up with a burst of adrenaline and marched out of my cell. I knew these bitches in here had drugs, girls were always getting high. I just had to figure out who had them.

I remembered a rumor about a girl named Sheila in cell 1. Evidently, she had smuggled fifty Xanax bars in here in her, "back door." I had never given the story a second thought, until today.

I bounded toward her cell near the entrance of the pod, determined to do whatever it took to get one of her pills. As I passed the entrance, the door to the pod swung open. I stopped dead in my tracks as two young girls, who didn't look a day over seventeen, came walking in wearing regular clothes and holding clipboards.

I made eye contact with the girl closest to me as the door shut behind them. I was frozen, confused about why the jail would let these innocent-looking teenagers loose in here with an army of felonious addicts.

The girl smiled and took a step closer to me.

"Hello," she said.

"Hi," I replied cautiously.

"How are you?"

"Shitty."

"I'm sorry to hear that. Why do you look so confused?"

"I'm just. Um. Trying to figure out why there are teenagers with clipboards in here. Is this for a project or something?"

She turned to the other girl and laughed, then smiled back at me. "I'm not a teenager, I'm twenty-three, but thanks for the compliment."

"Okayyy, sooo, what's going on?" I said, looking back and forth at her and the other girl.

She stuck out her hand for me to shake, and I hesitated, but stuck mine out as well.

"My name is Ryanne, and I'm here to talk to some of the girls. What are your plans when you get out of here?"

"I have to go to rehab for six months. Why?" I said, crossing my arms.

She smiled. "It's fate!"

"What is?"

"You, being the first person I saw when I came in."

"Oh? Why is that?"

"Because I am here to find girls who are interested in attending our Faith Based Rehabilitation program."

"Faith based as in..."

"Faith based as in – God," she said with a smile.

I looked up to the ceiling and began laughing, hysterically. I'll tell you what, if there is a God – He certainly has a fucked-up sense of humor.

## Chapter Twenty-One

I poked around at the carrots on my dinner tray, reflecting on the conversation Ryanne and I had earlier.

I spoke with her for a while, and listened as she explained the road she had taken that led her to where she was today. Looking at her, I couldn't have imagined the dark past she'd experienced. She looked young, and sweet. I imagined her working at an ice cream shop or Petland. Not recruiting girls from jail to join her rehab program.

At first, I was hesitant to speak with her, I had been on a mission to find drugs. My foot had been tapping wildly under the table and my mind was elsewhere through most of our conversation. Her mouth was moving, words were coming out, but I wasn't processing a thing. Until she said something that caught me by surprise. "You hate God, don't you?"

My foot stopped tapping and my eyes focused on hers. "What did you say?"

"You resent Him, and don't believe He is real. I can see it in your eyes, and that's okay. If I may ask, did you lose someone close to you?" she said, leaning forward and placing her hand on my forearm.

Images of my mother began flipping through my mind like a photo album. Memories played in my head like a movie I wasn't prepared to watch. Her laughing, her smiling, her dancing around with me in the kitchen, lip-synching to ZZ Top. Her getting sick, withering away, breathing her last breath...

I tried to push the memories away, because each heart-breaking scene made my stomach turn. My mom's bright blue eyes flashed in my mind for a moment and I felt a rogue tear fall from my eye. My hand flew up to wipe it, hoping she didn't notice. I could feel my chin quivering as I tried to keep the flood gates from bursting. I hadn't yet grieved for my mom, and I sure as hell wasn't going to start today.

I looked down at the floor, trying to avoid eye contact. "It's okay to be sad, you know. You don't need to tell me what's going on, but you need to know that it's okay to feel, it's a good thing."

I didn't respond.

"I want to share something with you, and then I have to go," she said, glancing at her watch. "I lost my mom. I was very angry at God for taking her, but I have learned so much about God, and the miracles He performs daily. I now realize that He didn't 'take' her. She is in a place more beautiful than you and I could begin to imagine and I know in my heart we will see each other again, and it will be beautiful.

"I know that when I leave here, your feelings for God will be the same as when I came," she continued, "but I think it would be really great if you came and lived with us, and gave yourself the chance to learn about Him and see first-hand how amazing He truly is. I don't think it was a coincidence that you were basically waiting at the door for me. And I don't think it's a coincidence that today was the day we were approved to come here. God arranged this meeting, and I hope you will consider giving Him a chance."

I replayed our encounter over and over again in my head. For some reason, for the first time in my life, the urge to get high just – went away. It went away on its own. Anytime I wanted to get high in the past, the moment the thought entered my head, I did whatever it took to get my drugs. And I mean...Whatever it took. I'll spare you the gory details, but let's just say that stealing razors from the dollar store and shaving in the car to "prepare" on my way to my drug dealer's house – was not uncommon.

"Earth to Tiffany," Sarah said, waving her hand in front of my face. "You were somewhere far away just now, I've been trying to get your attention."

"I'm sorry, I was. I just have a lot on my mind. I have to find a way to get ahold of my attorney, I think I want to go to Leap of Faith rehab. Anyway, what were you saying?" I asked, realizing I had been completely oblivious to the fact she was even next to me, let alone talking.

"I saaaid, are you gonna eat your bread pudding, dinner is almost over, and you haven't eaten anything. You know they will make you throw it away and I don't want it to go to waste," she said, pulling it off my plate before I could even respond.

"Do you believe in God?" I asked as she took a bite.

"What?" she said, her mouth full.

"Do you believe in God, like, do you think there is such a thing?"

"Oh definitely. I mean, there's some stuff that doesn't make sense like, okay for example: A guy lived in a whale's stomach for a few days? C'mon. Or, or some guy was just chillin' by a bush and all of a sudden it caught on fire and started talking to him?"

"Right." I nodded, agreeing that it sounded preposterous.

"So, what I have chosen to do, is take the things that do make sense, and focus on them. If I get too wrapped up in the things that sound crazy, my faith will go out the window completely and–."

Suddenly, I felt sick. Nauseous. I felt my body begin to sway slightly as I raised my eyebrows trying to focus on Sarah as she spoke. She must have noticed something was off, because she stopped mid-sentence. She asked if I was okay, but her words came out slow and slurred.

I reach out to grab something, anything, and all I could grasp was air. I felt my eyes roll back into my head and then everything suddenly went – black.

When my eyes fluttered open, I was shocked by searing pain all over every inch of my body. My muscles felt like they had just been through a marathon, and my neck was aching like it had whenever I had slept on it wrong. What the hell?

I slowly reached up to my face and my arm felt like it weighed a thousand pounds. I wiped away the drool surrounding my mouth and squinted my eyes as they adjusted to the light. I was moving. Down a hallway. I glanced down and realized I was in a wheelchair.

"She's awake!" someone behind me said, and as I turned to face them I realized she had a look of serious concern. "You okay, Johnson?" Deputy Cash asked as she walked briskly beside my wheelchair. I opened my mouth to speak, but didn't have the energy. "It's okay, just relax."

I was exhausted, and I had no clue what the hell was happening. "Did I... Faint?" I managed to muster. I had fainted plenty of times in the past, but it had never felt like this. "What's going on?"

The wheelchair stopped abruptly, and Deputy Cash crouched down in front of me to look in my eyes. I could feel them rolling back into my head and I tried desperately to focus on her face. Something was wrong. "Johnson, look at me for a second, can you look at me?" It hurt to breathe. I wanted to lay down and sleep, I needed to rest. I stared blankly at where I felt her eyes should be, but it was as if my muscles weren't listening to my brain.

I felt my eyes roll back and the last thing I heard was "Aw, fuck. Here we go agai–."

I came to on the cold concrete floor. I could see the wheelchair I had just been sitting in off to the side. I was surrounded by deputies and medical personnel, and instantly began crying. Fuck my body hurt so bad. It felt as if I had been punched in the head twenty times. I reached my hand to the back of my skull and the nurse taking my pulse yelled, "No, don't do tha–" Too late. I pulled my hand down in front of my face and realized it was covered in blood.

Panic rose up within me and I rolled over to my side to see the floor where I'd been lying, it was covered in blood and hair. "What the fu–" I stopped midsentence because my tongue was on fire. I was sobbing by this point and the sobbing itself was excruciating. The nurse could tell I was having a nervous breakdown, because she pulled me close and gently hugged me.

"Shhh. Shhh, it's alright, relax. You have to stay still. Okay, you are injured. You had a couple of seizures, honey, okay."

"Wha–" I tried to scream. Electric pain inside my mouth vibrated through every cell of my body. I screamed in response, another shot of unbearable pain radiating from my mouth. Seizures? I'd never had a fucking seizure a day in my life, that's impossible.

"Sweetie, please don't speak. Okay? You have a very large gash in the back of your head, you are probably going to need stitches. And...You must have bitten your tongue, because it's only hanging on by a thread..."

Chapter Twenty-Two

I was taken to the hospital via ambulance, and had been handcuffed to the stretcher like a dog chained to a pole. I'd had plenty of hospital visits in the past, but I'd never arrived via police escorts, covered in blood and handcuffed.

Each person we passed in the hallways of the hospital, looked at me like I was Hannibal Lecter. Women clutched their purses tightly to their sides and pulled their children close to them, while the hospital employees whispered to one another and giggled at the "freakshow" being wheeled by.

I stared straight up at the ceiling, counting the fluorescent lights as we passed underneath them. Although this was probably the only opportunity to be a part of the outside world and see colors, hear elevator music and smell various fragrances I'd had in a long time, I chose to stare straight up at the ceiling.

The embarrassment and shame were almost more painful than my physical injuries. My tongue was throbbing, my body felt like it had been hit by a truck and I was completely exhausted. They didn't want me to go to sleep until they gave me a brain scan and determined I didn't have a concussion.

"Here ya go," the paramedic said as he snapped the brakes on the stretcher into place once I was in the room. I nodded, because speaking was too painful. It hurt to swallow, but it also hurt to allow the saliva to pool on my tongue. I needed pain pills and was secretly praying that the doctors would determine that my injuries were so severe that I needed sedation.

As the paramedic exited the room, the deputy escorting me, one I'd never seen before, followed behind without saying a word. I felt so insignificant, unworthy of a "good luck" or "I hope you feel better;" he just left.

Forty-seven minutes had passed before anyone came in again, and unfortunately, it was the hospital Registrar. The teenager smiled nervously in my direction, but immediately averted his eyes when I forced a smile in response.

His voice was shaking as he asked me the questions, I'm assuming he was concerned that I may try to eat his face off. I wanted to run with it, really play it up. Start growling and writhing around in bed like I was possessed. But luckily for him, I was way too tired.

"Your name?"

"Titthany Honthin"

"Address?"

"No."

He glanced up at me briefly, down at my handcuffs, and back at the computer.

"Marital status?"

"Thingle."

"Insurance?"

"No."

"Emergency contact?"

I paused. My heart sunk to the floor. I didn't know who to say. My emergency contact person hated my guts, my father was sick in the hospital and my sister would probably allow me to bleed to death if it came down to it. I was all alone in this world. I had done this to myself.

I began crying, and it was excruciatingly painful. I tried to control the tears, but I couldn't. I wanted my Mom. I wanted someone. I was hurt and alone and felt lower than I ever had once I realized that there wasn't a damn person on this planet who gave a shit about me.

The kid quickly wrapped it up once he saw that I was beginning to get agitated, and he must have told someone once he left because shortly after the doctor came in.

"Hello, Mrs. Johnson, I'm Dr. Fuller. You feeling okay?" he asked staring down at the papers on his clipboard.

I think he meant Dr. McSteamy, because holy shit.

I shook my head and muttered, "Mmm mmm." He placed the clipboard on the counter and put a pair of gloves on to examine the damage. "I would ask you to tell me what happened," he said, gently feeling around my skull as if he was examining a melon for ripeness, "but I'm assuming that speaking is the last thing you wanna do."

I closed my eyes as he rubbed around on my head and for a moment the pain disappeared. I hadn't been touched in so long, let alone by a man. It didn't even feel sexual, it just felt...Nice to have human contact. You don't realize how important it is until you no longer have it.

He pulled his gloves off, tossed them into the trash and leaned up against the counter.

"Okay, the good news is, you don't need stitches. The bad news is, your tongue looks like hamburger meat. Since you are currently, um, incarcerated, we obviously can't do any pain management with narcotics."

Suddenly I hated him.

"The tongue is one of the fastest healing parts of the body though so don't worry. It will be better within 1 – 2 weeks. I am going to give you a salt rinse and some Advil for the pain. Our options are limited here. You need to rinse with the salt three times a day, and Hydrogen Peroxide once per day."

I rolled my eyes as he continued listing off the bullshit I had to do to heal my mangled tongue, none of which consisted of drugs. I wanted to punch him in the kneecap. Maybe that's why they keep us handcuffed in here.

"As for your muscles, when a person has a seizure, just about every muscle in your body tenses up as tight as it possibly can. When you shake the tense muscles, it stretches them beyond their capacity. So, it feels like you were hit by a truck, but it's basically the same as if you had just had a good workout. The Advil should help," he said heading toward the door.

"Ha ha."

The Advil should help. I'm a fucking junkie. I shoot 100 mgs of Dilaudid into my veins at a time without blinking. This guy is a fucking idiot.

"I'm gonna send you down for a Cat Scan to make sure there's no damage there, they said you hit your head pretty hard. We will just wait for those results and if they are clear, we will go ahead and send you home—I mean, send you back. Okay?"

I didn't nod. I didn't smile. I wanted to scream and demand pills, but I couldn't. I turned to face the wall as tears began streaming down my cheeks. I had gotten my hopes up for drugs, I had been anticipating feeling better, and instead I'm getting salt water and baby Aspirin.

I was devastated.

The scans checked out fine and I was sent back to jail. I had to stay in medical for three days, so they could monitor me and make sure my tongue was healing. They were also concerned about my seizure. I'd never had one before, and since I wasn't withdrawing off anything, it was unusual for me to have one. The nurse assumed it was stress related.

I was also given an anti-seizure medication that made me really sleepy, which was good, because every minute in medical was torture, so the more time I could spend unconscious the better.

This is certainly not how I wanted to spend my last month in jail. My emotions had been on more roller coaster rides than I could handle. One minute things were good, the next they were terrible, then they were great, then I blink and my tongue is broken and my head is cracked open.

The worst part of all of it was, I couldn't blame anyone but myself. I stole from people, I lied, I broke the law, I chased the high, did the drugs and ruined my life. It was my fault that all the bridges were burned and I had no one to turn to. When you have no one to blame but yourself, you have no choice but to internalize that anger, and having no clue how to release it in a productive way – I knew I was a ticking time bomb.

I only had twenty-eight days left in jail. I was in the home stretch. All I had to do was keep it together for a little while longer and I'd be out of here. I made a vow right then and there that for the next few weeks I would mind my own business, keep to myself, and focus on my future. The past is the past and I was almost finished with this chapter, and into the beginning of a new one.

My new mantra had certainly improved my mood, and I had begun to feel optimistic. That lasted for about three hours – until I was served a subpoena to testify in court against the drug dealer who wanted to kill me...

Chapter Twenty-Three

"Was it scary?" Sarah asked, taking a bite of her honey bun.

"Ha!" I replied, still shaking from adrenaline. I had been back from court for about two hours, and my heart was still pounding like a drum. "Scary isn't even the word. It was one of the worst experiences of my life."

Her eyes grew wide with surprise. "What happened?!"

I had been dreading going to court and testifying against Lazarus. I knew that I would forever be labeled a snitch, and if he didn't want to kill me before, he certainly would now.

"I...I can't tell you."

Her face twisted into an expression of confusion and annoyance. "The fuck you mean you can't tell me?"

"My lawyer said I can't talk to anyone about the details of the trial because it's ongoing, I guess."

"Hell no, first of all, I don't count as 'anyone' and second of all, I've been waiting all day to hear the details and you're telling me I can't? I literally feel like I'm gonna cry. Come onnn. There's zero excitement in here, give me sommme-thing."

I remained silent for a moment, contemplating whether or not it truthfully mattered if I told her. According to my attorney I could be prosecuted for divulging confidential information regarding an ongoing trial, but I highly doubted Sarah would run and tell anyone.

Besides, I needed to vent.

"Okay, I'm not going to tell you details of the case specifically, but I will tell you that the defense attorney is a fucking asshole and made me look like an idiot," I said crossing my legs and getting comfortable. I could tell she was excited by the gossip, because her eyes grew wide and she inched her chair closer.

"The guy basically said that I was a piece of shit felon and no one could take me seriously because I'm a known liar and thief."

"What!? No he diiidn't!"

"Swear. And thennn, this asshole has the audacity to turn to the sheriffs in the courtroom asking if they could believe a word I said, given the fact that I stole from one of their 'brothers in blue' and lied to the entire Sheriff's Department for three years straight."

"Nooo."

"Yes, and then—"

"Tiff, it's for you!" someone yelled from the dayroom, interrupting my story right before the good part. I leaned back on my bed and looked through the space between the bars of my cell to see who was calling out to me.

Shelly was standing at the public defender phone clutching the receiver to her chest as another anxious inmate tried to grab for it. "Stop, hoe!" Shelly yelled. "He ain't call for you."

I was already running to the phone, anxious to see what my public defender wanted.

"Hello?!" I breathed heavily into the mouthpiece.

"Yeah, hey, listen. I wanted to let you know I just got an email from Bridges in St. Pete. They accepted your application and are going to be here to pick you up on your release date next week."

I had filled out the application for Bridges rehab when I first arrived in jail. I was desperate to attend a rehab rather than go away to prison, so I filled out a bunch and mailed them out to different places.

This was before I knew my father had cancer. I would be so far away from him. This was before I met Ryanne from Leap of Faith rehab. This was before everything, I didn't want to go.

"Oh... Okay, um, I was kind of hoping to go to Leap of Faith. It's much closer to my dad and —"

"No."

"Oh. Wait, what?" I asked, taken aback.

"No. Absolutely not."

"Absolutely not, what?"

"Let me get this straight, you don't want to go to Bridges, a structured, reputable rehabilitation center. You want to go to Leap of Faith, where girls can come and go as they please, meet up with their dealer in the parking lot and get high right in the facility?"

"I ...Um...I don't even know what you're t–"

"Let me ask you, why would you want to go there?"

"Well, because I would like to work on building a relationship with God and–"

"Bullshit."

"Uh, excuse me?!"

"You want to get high, and you heard that you can do it there. I wasn't born yesterday. I've met tons of girls like you who want to take the easy way out at Leap of Faith and I'm sick of it. The place is a joke, you are going to Bridges and they will be there next week to get you. Goodbye." 'Click.'

I slowly hung up the receiver, baffled by what had just occurred.

He spoke so fast, so matter-of-factly. I had to sit down for a moment and process this. Why did he say I wanted to get high? Was there something he knew about the rehab that I didn't?

I guess it doesn't matter now. I'm going to Bridges, and there's evidently nothing I can do about it.

It was toiletry day, and everyone had lined up for their items by the time I'd gotten off the phone. I headed to the end of the line and my friend Charlotte was standing in front of me.

"Do you know anything about Bridges?" I asked her. She turned around to answer but before she could, the girl in front of her whipped her head around to face me.

"You said Bridges?" she asked.

"Yeah, my public defender said that's where I'm going when I get released."

Her eyebrows arched and she turned back to face the front of the line without saying a word.

"Have you heard of it?" I asked, stepping up as the line slowly moved forward.

"Girl, I been there. You might as well stay here. It's run by the Department of Corrections. It's basically jail."

My heart dropped. I had been so happy that my release day was approaching, and this girl said that basically I had another six months of this shit. I wanted to cry.

"What do you mean it's like jail?" I asked feeling more and more panicked.

"Um, let's see. You can only bring six personal items with you, you wear a uniform, you are told when to eat, sleep and shit and you are bunked up with six other girls. The rules are the same there as they are here. The only difference is you go to stupid ass NA and AA classes," she said, crossing her arms. "I couldn't take it, I ran. That's why I'm here."

I was still processing what the girl had said when the corrections officer screamed at me. "I SAID, what. Do. You. Need." I snapped back into reality and was met with a pair of glaring eyes.

"Oh, sorry. Um, toothpaste, and toilet paper. Please," I said quickly.

"No razor?"

"No thank you, not tonight."

"Nasty ass," the deputy said under her breath, thrusting a roll of toilet paper into my outstretched hands.

I rolled my eyes and headed to the cell. They gave us one hour with the razors, and in that hour, all the women are clamoring to get into a shower stall and speed shave before the razors had to be returned. I wasn't in the mood.

Besides if I got my hands on a razor, I'd probably cut my fucking wrists right now.

The following week was a haze. I spent most of time sleeping because of my seizure medication, and when I was awake, I was crying and dreading my release. I didn't want to go to Bridges. I wanted to be close to my family. I wanted to learn about God and I wanted to wear regular clothes and hear music.

I had felt such a connection to Ryanne the day she came in and I was heartbroken at the prospect of being shipped to another city when I thought for sure God had a plan, and had sent her to bring me to a place I belonged.

"Two more days ya lucky bitch. You excited?" my Bunkie Candice asked while munching on a Chick-O-Stick.

"Not really. You know what's funny?" I began. "The whole time I've been here, every single time the voice came over the loudspeaker and told someone to roll it up to go home, I've been insanely jealous. I have longed to hear the words 'roll it up' since I've been here and now, I'm dreading it."

I stared out the window of my cell. The sky was dark gray, and beads of rain began peppering the window. I missed the rain. The way it pelted my skin as I ran to seek shelter from it. I would lay flat on the grass and let it drench me if I had the chance. Grass, I missed grass.

"Are you Tiffany?" a voice said from behind me. I spun around and saw a blonde woman in high heels and a bright pink shirt, smiling at me from the entrance of my cell.

"Um, I am. Who are you?" I asked, looking her up and down.

"My name is Felicity, and I'm the owner of Leap of Faith. I heard you spoke with Ryanne."

Holy shit. You're a day late and a dollar short, lady, I thought.

"Yeah, I did. I really wanted to come to your program but, apparently that's not going to happen," I said, feeling defeated.

I couldn't help but wonder what kind of sick joke God was playing on me. Two days before my release this lady shows up, now that it's too late.

"Well," she said, smiling. "I wouldn't be too sure if I were you."

"What?"

"Let's just say, I have a way of getting what I want. Ryanne spoke very highly of you, so I did some research. There's a loophole in your sentencing guidelines. I may be able to work something out. Would you be interested?" She seemed so confident in herself.

"Um, I mean my attorney said it wasn't going to happen, but of course I'd rather go with you than to Bridges."

"That's all I needed to know," she said as she gave me a wink. She turned around and walked away, her heels clicking loudly throughout the dayroom until she disappeared out the door.

What the hell is this lady planning? And how is she planning on doing it in one day?

I slowly raised my head to the sky and smiled. "Okay, God, let's see what you got."

Chapter Twenty-Four

Yesterday was my release date. Yet here I was, laying beneath the scratchy wool of my blanket in my cell. It had been pouring rain all day yesterday, I'd hoped maybe that was the reason Bridges didn't send a bus to get me. They didn't want to drive that far in a thunderstorm, and I understood.

I mean, a call would have been nice, but I wasn't exactly in position to demand that sort of courtesy.

"What the hell, man. My bin has been packed up since the day before yesterday, I already gave my shampoo and conditioner away, and I traded the last of my friggin' snacks to Shelley for a phone call. Where the fuck are these people to pick me up?" I said as I pulled my uniform top off.

"Maybe they forgot about you," Sarah said, smirking.

"Helpful, Sarah, really." I rolled my eyes.

"No, dude, Bridges is notorious for not picking girls up on time," Charlotte said as she flopped down off the top bunk. "They never come when they say they will and the worst part is, every minute you sit here past your release date, doesn't count for shit. You are basically stuck doing more time than the judge ordered for nothing."

"Awesome, thank you guys so much for the reassurance. I feel a million times better."

We grabbed our dirty uniforms and headed toward the laundry line. We got new uniforms three times per week, and I thought for sure this was the last polyester piece of shit I'd ever have to wear. But nope, I'm about to get a new jumpsuit and who the fuck knows how many more I'll have to wear after that.

"God, there is seriously nothing more frustrating than not knowing. Like, I feel like the past four months have been nothing but waiting and wondering, and having no say over what the hell happens," I said, inching forward in the line.

"Welcome to jail," Charlotte said as she grabbed a jumpsuit from the deputy and headed to the cell.

Before changing into the new uniform, I decided to take a shower. I didn't want to put a new uniform onto my dirty body, so I borrowed some shampoo from Sarah and headed to wait in line.

I glanced nervously at the clock as each girl went in to take a shower. Six stalls for hundreds of women meant a lot of sitting around with soap in hand, waiting for one to open. Finally, with ten minutes and no hot water left, it was my turn. I shut the door to the shower and glanced around the small area.

Pubic hairs and lint had collected at the drain and the walls were covered in soap scum and hair. Jesus, I couldn't wait to shower in a clean bathroom. Thank God for shower shoes, Lord knows how many diseases my feet would have collected by now otherwise.

I twisted the faucet and was hit with a stream of freezing cold water. It warmed up immediately, but never reached a temperature above lukewarm. I was shaking as I hurriedly squirted the shampoo into my hair and began rubbing it into a lather.

As I leaned my head back into the water to rinse the soap from my hair, suddenly someone was banging on the shower door. I fumbled for my glasses and shut the water off to see what the fuss was all about.

"What the hell?" I asked, wiping condensation from the lens, trying to see who was interrupting my long-awaited shower.

I wrapped my towel around my body and cracked open the door to peer out. As soon as the room came into focus I noticed that everyone, literally everyone... Was staring at me.

"1, 2, 3! Johnson! ROLL IT UP!"

Goosebumps covered every inch of my body as I realized what just happened. Everyone began clapping and cheering as my jaw hung to the floor.

## Chapter Twenty-Five

"Are you serious?" I asked, afraid to get my hopes up.

"Yes, Bitch! They just called your name in your cell! Now hurry the hell up before they change their minds," Tanya said laughing.

I didn't even rinse the rest of the shampoo out of my hair, I sprinted across the dayroom in a towel (which was super illegal but, what were they gonna do? Arrest me?)

As I started throwing my new uniform on, tears of gratitude began filling my eyes. I excitedly looked over at Sarah and realized her hand was covering her mouth and she was quietly sobbing.

"Oh my God, Sarah," I said, walking toward her with my arms outstretched. She wrapped her arms tightly around my waist and cried into my chest. "How the hell am I supposed to make it in here without you? You are the realest friend I've ever had," she sniffled.

"Aw, Babes. You are gonna be just fine! And I'll be done with Bridges in six months and we can hang out. Maybe get dinner or go to the beach."

"Johnson," a voice interrupted over the intercom. "You got two minutes and the bus is leaving."

"Go, go. I'm sorry. I am so happy for you, Tiff, and so proud. You are going to do amazing I just know it."

"Thank you, Sarah, and thank you for showing me what a true friend is supposed to be."

Despite how grateful I was to be getting out, I suddenly found myself quite heartbroken about having to leave.

This had been my home for a long time, and I'd spent 24 hours a day with the people in it. It felt like summer camp had come to an end, and it was time to say goodbye to all the wonderful friends I'd made.

Girls began flooding my cell. Some to see if I had any leftover commissary, but most to say goodbye and wish me luck.

I gave a few quick hugs and excitedly pushed my way past them with my mattress and belongings in hand. As I headed toward the main door, I heard some of the girls begin singing and before I knew it, everyone joined in. "Nah nah nah nah, nah nah nah nah, hey hey hey, gooodbye." I choked back the tears and exited the doors of Female Pod West accompanied by my own soundtrack, for the very last time.

I was brought down to the lobby where a deputy asked me to turn around. I will never forget the 'click' of the handcuffs I'd been wearing springing free. That was it. I was in a room full of deputies and not wearing handcuffs. I was no longer an inmate.

"Here," a big male deputy said as he thrust a paper bag into my stomach. "You can change in there," he said pointing to a holding cell.

I shut the door behind me and ripped open the bag. The scent of my old perfume filled the room and nostalgia washed over me. It had been so long since I'd smelled anything other than mold, shit and grits.

I pulled the clothes out of the bag and up to my face and took in a deep breath. My eyes closed as memories of my old life came rushing into my mind, playing like a silent movie. For a brief moment, I was home.

A knock at the door pulled me back to reality. "You okay in there? You got people waiting on you."

"I'm coming!" I yelled as I yanked my prison clothes off for the last time and dressed into the clothes I was arrested in. I smiled at the sight of my flip flops. I had never been so grateful to slide my feet into them. No more shower shoes for this b***! I'm outta here.

"Where should I put these?" I asked holding out my crumpled uniform. "In there," the guard said pointing to an empty room nearby. When I returned to where he was standing, I glanced around unsure of what to do next.

"Here ya go," he said handing me a sheet of paper. "I'll walk you out."

Out. He will walk me out. Out of this jail. I couldn't believe I was leaving.

He pointed to a closed door and told me they were waiting for me in there. I headed toward the door and when I pulled it open, my eyes grew wide and my jaw hit the floor.

"Let's get the hell out of here," Ryanne said with a big smile holding the door open.

"Wait, what? What are you doing here? I thought Bridges was coming?" A combination of confusion and worry danced around in my mind. I was thrilled to see her, but felt like this was wrong.

"It's fine, everything is fine. Felicity found a loophole in your sentencing. It said, 'she is to be released to 'A' 6-month residential treatment program,' – it doesn't specify which one. So, basically, it's whoever gets here first and- SUPRISE!" she said throwing her arms into the air. "Now let's go, Raquel is waiting in the car."

A smile crossed my face so wide that my cheeks burned.

And I ran. I ran past Ryanne, ran through the hallway, and pushed the exit doors open so hard they slammed against the wall. The chilly air and sunshine hit my face all at once and I dropped to my knees. I felt the grass under my skin as the breeze blew through my hair.

Tears began falling from my eyes as I took my first breath of fresh air in one hundred and twenty days. I listened to the birds singing in the background, the cars zooming past in the distance and the hum of the air conditioner on the side of the building. It was the most beautiful moment I'd ever experienced in my entire life.

"I don't want to ruin this moment for you, but uh, we have Dr. Danner at the house waiting for you," Ryanne whispered.

Nothing could have ruined that moment for me. I was free.

"Do you smoke?" Ryanne asked as she pulled out of the parking lot. I hadn't smoked in one hundred and twenty days, and I certainly shouldn't start now.

"Yes, yes I do."

"Here," she said as she passed back a cigarette and a lighter. I couldn't believe this was happening. I closed my eyes and took a long slow drag of my cigarette. The nicotine filled my lungs and my body started tingling with relaxation as it was carried through my bloodstream.

"What is the one food you missed the most while in jail?" Ryanne asked as she reached back to retrieve her lighter.

"Okay honestly? I know it sounds stupid, but I craved Taco Bell like it was nobody's business in there. Specifically, a chicken quesadilla. I would have killed for one."

She turned up the radio and a song I didn't recognize began blaring through the speakers. The bass of the music was in sync with my heartbeat, it felt like it had been years since I'd heard the melody of a song. The moment was so surreal. Not being watched like a hawk, wearing normal clothes and smoking a cigarette and listening to music. I had taken so much of this for granted before.

I closed my eyes to listen to the words, and my eyes were still closed when she promptly turned the music down and I heard a voice say, "Thank you for choosing Taco Bell, what can I get for you?"

\*\*\*

I sat on the soft leather chair in Dr. Danner's office and watched as her fingers danced along the file folders in her cabinet. "Ah-ha," she said, stopping on one and checking the name on the label, "this is you, Miss Tiffany."

As soon as we had arrived back at the house, I was immediately sent to meet with the doctor. My throat still burned from the acid in the tacos I'd just inhaled, but it was the greatest burn I'd ever experienced.

"Okay. Welcome to Leap of Faith, I'm Dr. Danner and I'm a Certified Addiction Specialist with a Master's in Psychology.

I'd like to get some information from you before you get settled if that's alright," she said. She was beautiful, and I wondered how she could have all those fancy certificates because she seemed younger than me.

"Absolutely," I replied, fidgeting with the bottom of my shirt. Why was I nervous?

"Alright. So, you spent around four months in jail, correct?"

"Yes."

"Was that your first time?"

"It was, yes, and hopefully last," I said and laughed nervously.

"Well good, we hope so," she said, smiling. "So, what brought you to jail, Tiffany. What happened?"

"Ha. It's a long story."

"Well that's alright, I've got time."

I thought back to when it all started, and knew that there was no way in hell this lady, 'had time'."

"Yeah, it's... I don't know. Hard to explain. It's complicated and...It's kind of crazy. It would be hard to tell you what exactly happened because it's more like 1,000,000 shitty things happening to lead up to it," I said.

It had been a long day, I was tired, and this lady was sweet. If I told her what happened right off the bat, she would think I was a lunatic.

"It's okay, Tiffany, I don't have anywhere else to be. You can trust me, and I encourage you to talk to me about anything. In order to understand the type of treatment that would best suit you, I need to know what happened. Besides, there's nothing you can tell me that I haven't already heard before," she said, laughing.

This silly woman. She thought she had heard it all. She thought she was prepared for what I was about to throw at her. She had no idea what I'd been through, the things I'd done, the people I'd hurt. I'm sure she has heard her share of stories, but I know she hadn't heard anything like this. I took a deep, hesitant breath, looked into her eyes and smiled...

"Well," I started. "You asked for it."

## Chapter Twenty-Six

As I sat on Brandon's couch, stuffing Cheetos into my face and watching Animal Planet, I suddenly realized it had been exactly four months since I left rehab.

Which means it was exactly four months and two weeks since my mom died.

I knew that my mom's friend set up a trust fund for us with an insane amount of money. I also knew that if I was given access to that money – I would buy all the drugs in the world and do them in one shot.

I confessed to her friend that I'd been popping pills and felt sick without them, so he spent $30,000 on rehab. The money, ended up going to drugs anyway-in a roundabout way. I would have detoxed in my fucking car if I'd known he was spending my trust fund money on that bogus-ass place.

I thought back to the last time I saw my mom and cringed. I was holding her hand when she passed. Having to rub her head and tell her that it was "okay to let go" was the hardest fucking sentence I'd ever uttered in my life. I didn't want her to "let go." I wanted her to stay. I wanted her to get up out of the hospice bed and dance around the living room to Tom Petty like she used to.

I wanted her to sit in the front row of my wedding, beaming with pride. I wanted her to rock my future children to sleep in her arms as she hummed, "You are my sunshine" like she used to with me. I didn't want her to let go. She did anyway.

Anytime my sister and I had left the house as teenagers, my mom would walk us out and stand at the end of the driveway giving us the "princess wave." So, when they carried her out and drove her away for the last time, my sister and I did the same. We stood at the end of the driveway, and waved goodbye.

FUCK man, why was I thinking about this right now?

"Pass that shit, will you?" I said to Brandon reaching for the blunt. He ignored me, staring at the zebras on TV in amazement. "PASS THAT SHIT, MAN!" I said louder, bringing him back to reality.

"Oh, here," he said and handed it to me without taking his eyes off the screen. Brandon was my roommate. I moved in with when I left rehab, mainly because he was one of the only true friends I'd had, and he didn't do pills. So, I was safe here.

I held the blunt between my fingers and inhaled a long, slow drag deep into my lungs. I held it there for a moment and closed my eyes. Thank God for weed. I wouldn't have made it through all this shit if I didn't have it. The people at the rehab tried to tell me I couldn't smoke weed and I stood straight up out of my chair and called them on their bullshit. Weed was a plant, and weed wasn't my problem, pills were, and they were crazy if they thought I wasn't gonna smoke when I got out of there.

Things are good right now, and I wouldn't do anything to fuck that up. I haven't done pills in like four months and I have a steady job. Weed doesn't make me sick if I don't have it, it just makes me feel awesome when I do.

"You want a beer?" Brandon said, standing up and heading to the fridge.

"Ummm, screw it I have the day off tomorrow why not?" I replied.

Oh, and I drink.

But I don't get drunk like I used to, I drink at home. I know my tolerance level and I never get drunk. Just a beer after work to take the edge off. Besides I'm afraid to get too drunk around Brandon, because even though he had a girlfriend, he's always giving me "the look," you know? The "I would bang you in a second if I had a chance" look.

My phone buzzed from the coffee table and I was immediately overwhelmed with dread. I hated talking to people when I was high, especially my boyfriend. He knew I smoked, but he didn't approve of it, and he hated talking to me when I was high.

"Uh oh. You better answer," he said, looking down at the caller ID and seeing who it was the same time I did. It was him.

"Nope. I can't. Let me drink a few more of these and I'll just drunk dial him and blame it on the beer," I said, taking a big swig of my bottle. I loved the way the ice-cold bubbles lathered in my throat. How the hell is anyone supposed to go their entire life without drinking? Dumbest shit I ever heard.

One hour and multiple bong rips later, Brandon stood up abruptly and grabbed his keys.

"Whoa, dude, don't move so fucking fast, you scared the shit out of me. I thought the fucking cops were here or something," I said placing my hand on my heart.

"You wish," he chuckled, shoving his Marlboro's into the pocket of his jeans.

"Oh yeah, I would love for the cops to show up to my pot-growing roommate's house when I can barely open my fucking eyes, idiot."

"I'm going to Stacey's, don't wait up," he said giving me a wink. Honestly it creeped me out. Stacy was his cousin and I'm pretty sure they were banging, but that's a whole other story.

"Aright. Hey, well if you are gonna be gone all night can you leave me some green?" I said giving him the puppy dog eyes. They worked every time.

"Just grab it when you want, it's in my top drawer. Leave me some though, Cheech, I know how you get when I'm not here to regulate your smoking," he said laughing.

"Shut the hell up," I said chucking a pillow at him as he left. It bounced off the door as he shut it behind him.

I decided to call my boyfriend before I melted into the couch in a hazy fog. I took a deep breath and dialed his number. It rang, and rang and rang. I was relieved when the voicemail picked up and quickly hung up. Not wanting to leave evidence of my current state on a recording.

Alrighty then, I tried, I thought as I stood up from the couch.

I shut all the lights off, locked the front door, and headed to grab some buds out of Brandon's secret stash. I flipped his bedroom lights on and glanced around his filthy room. Cigarette ashes and empty fast food wrappers littered the floor. I stepped over a pair of dirty boxers and pulled the top drawer of his oak dresser open. Knives and random objects began thumping around in the drawer as I rifled through to locate the bag.

Where the hell was this thing?

Suddenly my fingers hit something hard and plastic, and the familiarity of the object sent shivers up my spine. I began to sweat as my knuckles turned white from grasping the tube so hard. I gave it a shake and my suspicions were confirmed.

Pills rattled inside the bottle as I pulled it out from under the socks to observe it. I should have let go and ran out of the room, but curiosity had gotten the best of me. I looked at the label and didn't recognize the name of the person they were prescribed to, but I recognized the drug immediately. They were Oxy 80's.

One of the most powerful pills one could get. One pill costs like 40 bucks. What the fuck was he doing with these?

My palms were clammy around the bottle, but I couldn't let go. My heart was rapping the insides of my ribcage and I began salivating. It felt like I was possessed.

"Put them back, you fucking idiot. You are clean. You got clean for your mother. She is watching you right now. Don't do this," I said to myself. There was an inner battle going on in my mind between my addiction, and myself, turmoil and angst swarmed around inside me like bees.

Suddenly, and before I had time to think, I threw the bottle into the drawer and left the room, I didn't even bother closing the drawer, I had to get out of there. I wasn't going to let my addiction win this time. I had come so far and was not about to give up now.

I made it two steps out of the bedroom door when suddenly my mind was hijacked. A dark force took over the helm and I was merely a helpless bystander. I watched from somewhere far away as my body turned around and my legs began moving toward the dresser before my brain could process what was happening.

"Stop" I yelled out loud to myself. "Nooo!" The tears began streaming down my face. I couldn't stop what was happening. I was powerless.

The familiar "pop" of the lid being opened was the most rewarding and heartbreaking sound I'd ever heard. I knew what came next.

I shook a few pills into the palm of my hand and returned the bottle to its resting place.

A few moments later I was staring down at the white line in front of me. It looked like powdered snow. I had licked the coating off the Oxy and smashed it to smithereens without a single thought. It was mechanical, I'd done it so many times that it was programmed into my mind.

Without hesitation, I placed the straw in my nose, leaned down and snorted deeply. The powder coated the back of my throat as the familiar burn in my nose greeted me like an old friend.

I shoved the straw into my bra just as my brain turned to Jello, and the warm sensation of liquid relaxation began flowing through my veins. Goddamnit I missed this feeling. Fuck, why would anyone voluntarily stop taking these things?

It felt as if I was being wrapped in a warm hug. A hug I couldn't receive from anyone else.

All at once the world around me began to slow down and my arms felt as if they were 20 pounds each. I rolled onto my side to light a cigarette and realized I could hardly move a muscle. I closed my eyes, and when I opened them again, I was in the same position, but light was beaming through my blinds and onto the wall. I checked the time on my phone and realized I'd missed three calls and two texts from my boyfriend. Panic rose within me and I racked my brain trying to remember when I fell asleep. More importantly, why the hell I was sleeping with my shoes on?

The memories of the night before suddenly came rushing in like a tidal wave.

Oh my God. I relapsed.

I reached down to my bra and felt the plastic straw and froze. It happened. It wasn't a dream. My head started pounding and I felt nauseous. I leaned over the side of my bed and vomited all over the clean clothes I'd been neglecting to fold.

My head rested on my arm as a million thoughts zoomed through my mind. This was too much. The disappointment, guilt and shame was overwhelming. How could I do this? I wept as I realized how badly I fucked up and immediately decided I didn't want to feel this way anymore. I needed to numb it, make this hurt go away long enough for me to sort my thoughts. I needed a line.

I began crushing the second half of last night's pill, when a knock at the door made me jump ten feet into the air.

I quickly shoved the paraphernalia into my top drawer and pulled the blinds down to peek outside and see who the hell was here. My heart dropped when my eyes focused on the visitor.

A cop car was sitting in the driveway.

You gotta be kidding me. I glanced quickly at myself in the mirror and attempted to fix my hair as I sprinted toward the front door. I took a deep breath, swung it open and smiled...

"Well helllo, officer. Visiting me while on duty? How romantic!" I exclaimed, leaning forward to give my boyfriend a kiss.

## Chapter Twenty-Seven

"Okay, um, hold on," Dr. Danner said holding up her hand. She was staring at me with her mouth hanging open and her eyebrows raised to her hairline. I was used to this look by now.

"I'm sorry, it's just – what?" she said, obviously perplexed by something I'd said.

"What? Did you not read my file? I'm confused." I hadn't even gotten to any of the crazy parts, what the hell was up with this lady's face? She's a doctor, or psychiatrist or something I mean, is she not used to talking to whackjobs?

"Um, well," she uttered looking uneasy, "apparently I missed some things while reviewing your folder. I read your charges from the jail, but, I didn't realize that he..."

"Was my boyfriend?" I interrupted.

"Right." She looked nervous, or uncomfortable. I wasn't sure.

"Yeah, I know. Sounds like something out of a movie, right?" I laughed. I didn't find my situation funny it's just, suddenly I felt really awkward. I mean what are you supposed to say at this point? Like, "OMG I know, I'm a total piece of shit, right? High-five."

She stared at me over the brim of her glasses for a moment and it reminded me of the look my mother used to give me right before she grounded the shit out of me. I think I'm in trouble.

"Should we, I'm sorry, should we stop? Do you want me to stop? Because if you need to like review my file some more or somet–"

"No. No, we will keep going. I apologize. I'm just surprised is all. You can keep going we will just, um, see how far we get. Okay?" she said nervously, glancing at her watch.

"Okay, so, where should I... Um... Start from, then?"

"Well, why don't you tell me what happened that morning when he showed up at your house, after you relapsed?"

"Sure," I said, leaning back in my seat to get comfortable. I wondered for a moment if I should sugarcoat it. Maybe she wasn't prepared for this kind of thing and I certainly didn't want to overwhelm her. Fuck it, I thought, might as well get it all out in the open so she actually has a shot at fixing whatever's broken inside my fucked-up head.

The morning he showed up at my house – uninvited might I add – nothing remarkable happened. He didn't come in, thankfully, because our home smelled like they were filming "Half-Baked 2" in a back room somewhere.

He had just stopped by to bring me a coffee and we chatted for a bit and parted ways. As I watched his tail lights fade from view I felt a pang of guilt. He looked so happy today. How the hell was I supposed to tell him I relapsed and break his heart? This was going to be harder than I thought.

He was the kindest man I'd ever met, and I suddenly felt terrible that he fell for a piece of shit like me. He deserved so much better.

I called off work because I knew there was no fucking way I could be nice to strangers when my world was crumbling around me. It was not an ideal day to call off either, as I just received a promotion and was now basically a manager. I was supposed to train to do the end of shift deposits, but that shit was not happening.

Instead I spent most of the day lying in bed, smoking weed, and contemplating how I was going to word this break-up.

"Hey, babe, remember how I told you I used to be addicted to drugs? Well, surprise!" Shit – no, that wasn't good.

"Hi, honey, quick question, on a scale of 1 – 10, guess who relapsed last night?" Son of a bitch.

"Sweetie, hey, remember how you told me how amazing I was and how you thought you were falling in love with me? Well, I snorted a bunch of drugs last night while you were out protecting the community because I'm a fucking loser and I'm sorry, but we can't be together." Sounds about right.

I grabbed my phone and decided to call my best friend. She's the one who drove me to rehab. Well, technically I drove, and she was in the passenger seat crushing pills and lining them up for me, so I didn't have to take my hands off the steering wheel.

We got addicted to pills together and hadn't really hung out much since I'd gotten out of rehab, she was still using and it was hard for me to be around it. So, I'd kept my distance up until this point.

"Hello?" she answered.

"Hey."

"Hey?"

"What's up?"

"Um, nothing, what's wrong?" We had a close bond, she could tell from my voice something was wrong.

"I fucked up."

"Shut up."

"Swear."

"Tiffany."

"I know."

"I'm on my way."

Now, you would think, she was coming over to give me a shoulder to cry on, maybe give me some words of encouragement, but when I hung up that phone, we both knew why she was coming.

We spent the next two hours snorting lines and smoking cigarettes.

I told her what had happened, and she laughed and shook her head at my predicament. I mean, I was in a fucking relationship with a Deputy for Christ's sake, one whom was about to be dumped by his junkie girlfriend tonight. What the hell is wrong with me?

"I'm doing him a favor, really," I said as I licked the remaining powder off the card I'd used to crush my pill. "I mean, it's better that he knows now rather than later. Honestly like, I think part of the reason I relapsed also was like, the pressure you know? Of dating a cop?"

Kayla nodded in slow motion, through squinted eyes. I knew she wasn't comprehending a word I'd said but it felt good to process my thoughts. I'd decided to get good and high before meeting up with Chuck. It was going to be an incredibly difficult conversation and I needed to take the edge off.

"I'm done after tonight anyway," I said scratching an invisible itch on my arm. "I can't get addicted again, but I'm still gonna end it with him because I feel like I'm only gonna hurt him mo—"

Before I could finish my sentence a thick stream of vomit spewed from my face like a water hose, landing all over my pants and Brandon's suede couch.

"What...the fuck?" Kayla said, suddenly wide awake. "Are you okay?"

I couldn't stop. Wave after wave of nausea rose up from my belly and I lurched forward attempting to miss the couch. I choked and gagged on my vomit and mid-hurl, I heard the front door slam shut.

"Jesus Christ."

Brandon, my roommate, was home.

"What the hell, Kayla?"

"It's not me! I didn't do anything! She just, she's not feeling good."

"Bullshit. You gotta go, now," Brandon said with authority.

"Oh my God, whatever," I felt her weight leave the couch as she stood up to leave. "Call me later, Tiff, I hope you feel better. You're an Asshole, Brandon, I had nothing to do with this," she said, slamming the door behind her.

"Tiff," He said, placing his hand on my back, "I told you that you didn't need to be hanging out with her anymore, now look at you."

I leaned back into the couch and took a deep breath, wiping the puke from my mouth. I turned my head to face him and tears started falling. "I know, I didn't want to do it, I've been doing so good. But she just pulled the pills out in front of me. When she asked if I wanted some, I couldn't say no." I forced out a couple of sobs and I knew when he shook his head in disappointment, he was buying it.

"Damnit, man. What are you gonna do about Chuck?"

"He gets off in a few hours, I'm going to shower and then head over there to break the news. I can't believe this happened. I should have known when she asked to stop by that it was a bad idea, I just missed her, you know?"

"I know, Tiff, this isn't your fault, she should have known better. I'm sorry this happened," he said, patting my back sympathetically.

As I took one last look at myself in the mirror before heading to Chuck's, I couldn't help but feel disgusted about the person I'd become.

I used to be a happy kid.

I used to be captain of the cheerleading squad.

I was voted class clown and Valentine Queen at my high school dance – and now – I'm a 23-year old junkie piece of shit with nothing to show for my life. My mom is gone, my sister won't talk to me and my dad – who the hell knows what's going on with my dad.

I had pulled my car over on the way to Chuck's to do a line. I felt like if I didn't have something to calm my nerves I wouldn't have the guts to go. I was going to tell him I was high anyway, so it didn't matter if he noticed.

The walk up to his front door was the most terrifying 30 seconds of my life. I almost turned around twice, and my heart felt like it may die from pumping too hard and too fast.

My eyes were swollen from the tears, and the disappointment I was bearing made my whole body feel 20 pounds heavier.

I took a deep, deliberate breath and quickly hit the doorbell before I could change my mind. I heard footsteps and things clamoring behind the door as my heart pounded even faster. Here we go, moment of truth.

I heard the metal click as the door unlocked from the inside and as the door swung open I was hit in the face with something, silly string? It all happened in slow motion.

His dad and mom off to the side smiling, his brother laughing and his brother's wife clapping excitedly. There were ten other people standing behind Chuck, but I couldn't process who they were. Music suddenly started blaring and simultaneously everyone screamed:

"SUPRISE!!!"

I stared in stunned silence and realized the house was adorned with balloons and streamers. Chuck reached out for my hand, but I was frozen. He laughed as he pulled me close and placed his lips next to my ear and my jaw dropped in horror when he whispered, "Congratulations on your promotion, this accomplishment is worthy of a celebration, sweetheart. We are so proud of you."

Chapter Twenty-Eight

As I clung to the cold, ceramic sink, I had trouble pulling air into my lungs. It was as if I were trapped inside a bad dream – one in which my deputy boyfriend and his entire family were about to realize that they wasted perfectly good balloons, on a drug-addicted loser.

The excited voices of Chuck's family and friends echoed within the walls of the bathroom. I could hear bits and pieces of the conversations; all of which revolved around me. "She's such a wonderful girl." "It's about time Chuck got himself a good girl." "She deserves to be celebrated."

Jesus Christ. These people had no idea. I was none of those things. I was broken, lost and scarred so deeply that if any of these people truly knew the real me, they would furiously rip those streamers down while 'shooing' me out the door.

I stared desperately at my reflection in the mirror, looking for answers. What the fuck was I supposed to do here? I realized I'd already been in the bathroom for ten minutes, I needed to come up with a plan – and fast.

It seemed as if my brain was trembling in response to the influx of ideas that began circling my head. Amid the chaos going on inside my mind, two things became incredibly clear: I was high as fuck. And no one could know.

As I pulled the handle to the bathroom door open, I still didn't have a plan, but time had run out and I found myself with no choice but to face it.

The country music grew louder as I swung the door open and I was instantly met with my boyfriend's smiling face. "Jesus," I said grasping my heart, "were you standing outside the door waiting for me, creeper?" I joked, careful not to make eye contact.

I didn't wait for a response. Chuck's parents were drinkers, so I knew damn well that there was bound to be various liquor bottles waiting to be consumed around here somewhere. If I began drinking immediately, any erratic behavior could easily be explained away by my inability to control my liquor. Story of my life.

I wasn't going to drink the alcohol, but I had to make it appear as if I were.

"Whoa ho-ho, someone's in the celebrating mood tonight," Chuck said over my shoulder as I made myself a Jack and Coke.

"I know, right? I've had a rough day today, just been thinking about my mom a lot, ya know?" I took a swig of my drink and grimaced at the taste. "Geesh, I haven't had liquor in a long time, it feels like I'm drinking fire," I said.

"Hey! Speaking of, my mom has a fire going out back, come check it out," he said, placing his hand on the small of my back.

As we headed out toward the fire, I decided this was where I was going to spend my evening. It was dark, so he wouldn't be able to tell that my pupils were virtually non-existent. He also wouldn't be able to notice that I couldn't keep my eyes open for more than thirty seconds and most importantly – there was no one else out here.

"I'm sorry to just spring this on you, but my mom really wanted to surprise you, she really likes you." I didn't look over at him, but I could tell he was staring at me and smiling.

"Give it time," I said jokingly (but not really).

"So, this is the lucky lady," a voice from behind us called out. I turned around and could see three dark figures walking toward us. Fuck my life.

"Yup, this is her," Chuck replied throwing his arm around my shoulder.

"Tiff, I'd like you to meet Jake, Gunnar and Michelle. These guys work with me, Michelle is on the undercover unit." Perfect.

"Hi, I'm Tiffany." I stuck my hand out to shake Michelle's and she ignored it, wrapping her arms tightly around me. I wasn't prepared for this surprise hug, so my arms were awkwardly pinned to my sides. I flinched as I suddenly remembered that there was a good chance I still smelled like weed.

I held my breath as she pulled away and I could tell from her face that I was in the clear. She was obviously wasted and could hardly stand up; her heels were getting stuck in the grass as she swiveled back and forth attempting to regain her balance.

"You'll have to excuse her," Gunnar said smiling, "we usually don't take her out in public, for this very reason." Michelle laughed in response and gave him a playful slap. Gunnar was attractive, and that's putting it mildly. His perfect white teeth shined brighter than the moon and his muscles rippled underneath his Bass Pro shirt. He was much taller than I was, and his shoulders were basically taking up the whole back yard.

"Gunnar is on the K-9 Unit," Chuck said, as if he were reading my mind.

"Oh, that's cool," I said, sipping my drink and trying to seem uninterested.

"Jake's about to become a detective, ain't that right, Jakey Boy?" Chuck said giving him a pat on the back.

"God-willing," Jake replied, taking a swig of his beer.

"Chuck talks about you alll the time," Michelle randomly blurted. "It's real sweet. He needs a good girl, he's been fucked over more than anyon—"

"Ha ha, oookay, Michelle, let's not scare her off just yet, I kinda like this one," Chuck said smiling nervously.

I felt like a bigger piece of shit with each passing moment.

I observed quietly as the four of them talked about police things. I didn't understand half of it because they were speaking in code, but I couldn't help but wonder; what, in the actual fuck have I gotten myself into?

These cops were two feet away from me and I was nodding out and scratching my skin like a crackhead. I smiled and nodded along with their conversation, but I felt like a damn fish out of water.

"That had to be a strange experience for you, Tiffany," Dr. Danner said, snapping me back to reality. It was the first time she'd spoken in about forty-five minutes and to be honest, I had almost forgotten she was there.

"Yeah, strange is a good word. I'd also say terrifying, exhausting, and truth be told, a little exciting."

"Well of course, it was as if you yourself were going undercover. As a drug user, you had a behind the scenes look at what goes on in the world of Law Enforcement. This is incredibly intriguing, Tiffany." Dr. Danner glanced down at her watch and I noticed a look of disappointment crossing her face.

"As much as I hate to do this, I have to stop you there. It's getting late and we still need to get you down for bag search. What do you say we meet again next week?" As she began gathering her papers, I couldn't help but feel a bit disappointed myself.

This was the first time I'd actually talked about what happened and in a strange way, going back and processing the things that had occurred, was really therapeutic for me. It felt as if I'd been carrying a giant suitcase around with me this whole time, and while speaking with Dr. Danner, I was able to slowly begin emptying the suitcase, releasing a bit of the burden.

"Dr. Um, Danner. I...I was wondering if maybe it would be possible for me to just finish this, um, this one night. Finish telling you about this one night. I just, it, it would make me feel better if we could start fresh next week. I'm almost finished, and it would help me to just, to just get the rest out? I know it's late and honestly, I'm exhausted. But I just want to tell you about one more thing and then...we can be done. Please."

She stared at me for a moment, the way a mom stares at her child after he asks for "just one more bedtime story." She peered down at her watch, then back up at me, and took two steps back to her chair.

"Of course, Tiffany. I would love to hear the rest. I would sit here all day if we could, I just know that you have a lot of important things to do before we get you settled. Usually I'd be finished with my intake evaluation by now, but your story..." her voice trailed off. "Please, go ahead," she said, crossing her legs and adjusting her skirt.

"Thank you." I took a deep breath, and continued.

As the night progressed, I was continually introduced to more deputies and other various branches of Law Enforcement. I had to repeatedly apologize for my appearance and explain that my mother had recently passed, and I'd been crying all day. I think most of them felt sorry for me and didn't think twice about the fact that I looked like a zombie, and the rest were too drunk to notice.

I had nervously sipped through four glasses of Jack and Coke and suddenly found myself feeling very friendly. I could feel my inhibitions disappearing and the volume of my voice increasing. I was drunk.

"Whoa," Chuck said as he grabbed hold of my arm to keep me upright. "You okay, Babe?" he said laughing.

"No. Yeah! Hell yeah I'm okay. It's my party I'll get drunk if I want to," I sang, obnoxiously.

As time passed, the faces around me became a blur. It was as if the party was happening in slow motion. I could see blips of faces and hear random bursts of laughter, but the world around me was suddenly a kaleidoscope. I could feel my eyes rolling back into my head and it took every ounce of strength I had to focus my vision and when I did, Chuck's face was an inch away from my mine.

"Hey, I have a gift for you, it's in my bedroom," he said.

"Ha! Bullshit. I've fallen for that one before," I said.

He began laughing as he pulled me toward his room. "Not like that, Nerd. It's an actual gift. Here," he said as he handed me a card and a small box as he shut the door behind him.

"I hope you don't 'spect me to read words right now," I said, drunkenly tearing the paper away from the card.

"Just open the box, you can read the card tomorrow." He set the card on the nightstand and sat down next to me on the bed. I vaguely remember opening the box but I sure as hell remember what was in it.

It was a pink key.

I began crying tears of joy when I realized he'd bought me a car. My excitement was immediately extinguished when I saw the look on his face after I'd thanked him for the car.

"Honey, I didn't get you a car. It's a key to my house. I'd like you to move in with me."

My face suddenly dropped. No. No. This can't be happening. When I was driving over here to end our relationship, he was wrapping a house key for me.

Fuck. My life.

I had no choice. I couldn't let this go any further.

"Chuck," I began. "Chuck, I appreciate this, so much. It's just-"

"I know, it's soon. I just don't like the idea of you living with that stoner kid and honestly, I hate not being able to see you four days out of the week. If you lived with me, I'd be able to see you every night when I come home from work. Nothing would make me happier than waking up next to you each day. Don't make me beg...What do you say?"

I paused for a moment, taking in the look on his face. Anticipation, excitement...Hope.

I took a deep, intentional breath in and looked deep into his eyes.

"Chuck... I got high today."

Chapter Twenty-Nine

"Wait a minute," Dr. Danner said, "So...You told him?"

"Yeeeah. In hindsight, telling him I had relapsed in the middle of a party he had thrown for me probably wasn't the best idea."

"Well? How did he take it?" she asked.

Before I could respond, a knock at the door made us both jump. The door creaked open about an inch and a woman with long dark hair and leathery skin poked her head in.

"I'm so sorry to interrupt, Sylvia sent me to check and see how much longer you were going to be. Her shift is over, but Tiffany still needs to have her belongings checked, as well as a drug screen," she said.

"We are finished. Just one more moment please, Joanie." Dr. Danner smiled.

"Okay, I'll let her know," the woman said as she quietly shut the door.

"Okay, so that's going to have to be it for today, but Tiffany, wow. I have so many questions I'd like to ask, as well as get some additional information. So, if it's alright with you, I'd like to meet with you tomorrow once you get unpacked and settled in. Once we finish our meeting I will be able to set up a program that I feel works best for your recovery, sound good?" she asked, sticking out her hand to shake mine.

"Yes, that sounds great. So, um, where do I go now?" I asked, shaking her hand.

"Here, I'll walk you down to Sylvia's office. She is very nice. She handles all our intakes as well as providing transportation to the girls. She is in recovery as well and she will be able to answer any questions you have."

I followed Dr. Danner through the dimly lit hallway toward a door at the end. Apart from the light beaming from underneath the crack in the door, the rest of the place was dark, and quiet. Dr. Danner pulled the door open and gestured for me to enter.

"Okay, Tiffany," she said from behind me as I walked in, "Sylvia will take it from here, have a great night!" I waved goodbye as the door closed, and smiled nervously at the woman behind the desk.

"Sit," she said, staring down at her cell phone. I assumed she meant on the bright pink couch against the wall, because there were literally no other chairs in the room. I lowered myself down on the couch and noticed that my brown paper bag from jail was sitting in the corner of the room, it was crumpled and empty. My papers and journals were scattered across the floor as if someone had dumped the bag upside down and shaken it.

I could feel the anger growing in me as I looked at my post-cards and letters that meant so much to me, wrinkled and scattered like garbage.

"I've already gone through your items, I couldn't wait any longer," Sylvia said abruptly.

"I see," I said, staring down at the floor.

"I didn't find any contraband—however, I did find a few items of concern."

"Okay. Like?"

"Who is Nicki?"

"Um. What?"

"Nicki. Is she your girlfriend? Aside from the fact that homosexuality is a sin in God's eyes, we would prefer to be aware if any of our clients are currently in relationships," she said, staring at me through squinted eyes.

I took a deep breath, attempting to maintain my cool. I was on the verge of snapping loose and I really needed things to get off on the right foot. If I fucked it up here, I was going back to jail, and going back to jail would be a violation of my probation which meant my suspended sentence of fifteen plus years would immediately go into effect.

"She is not my girlfriend, no. She was a girl that I was... we were talking, in jail. It was nothing. I was bored and she just, helped pass the time I guess. I'm not gay."

Sylvia stared at me for a moment and then rifled through some papers on her desk.

She cleared her throat and began reading aloud: "Baby, I love you so much. I can't wait until we get out of here and can begin our life together. Are you going to get into Leap of Faith you think? If so, I live right around the corner and can come visit." She set the paper down and looked at me, as if she'd just cracked the DaVinci code. She was acting like she had caught me in a lie, and to be honest, it was getting on my nerves.

"She wrote that a while ago. A lot has happened since then and we haven't talked in forever. Listen, I'm not gay, but I am exhausted. You can keep the letters and examine them later or fingerprint them or whatever. I really just want to sleep."

She hesitated for a moment then stood up. "Okay, I'm gonna hang on to these," *I bet you are,* "and we will talk more about Nicki tomorrow."

"Sounds good," I said standing up.

"Okay, I need you to lift your shirt and grab underneath the wires of your bra, pulling them out and toward me please. I just need to make sure you don't have anything illegal on your person before I take you to your room."

223

I pulled my shirt up and exposed my breasts to her. I wasn't wearing a bra when I was arrested. And I just wanted to get this shit over with.

"Whoa. Oh. Okay. You could have just told me you weren't, um, wearing one. Jesus. Empty your pockets, please."

"I don't have pockets. These are pajamas. Obviously."

"Very well, I'll show you to your room."

I followed her through the building as she rattled off the rules of this place. To be honest, I wasn't comprehending a word she'd said. I could hardly keep my eyes open and the sheep in my mind had already begun jumping over the fence.

"Any questions?" she asked, her hand on the doorknob.

"Nope, I think I got it." I smiled, having no clue.

"Great, here you go," she said, quietly opening the door. It was dark, but the lights of several alarm clocks illuminated the room. I followed her closely as she tiptoed through the darkness and realized there were four beds on the floor. No box springs, no frame, just mattresses on the floor.

Although it seemed a bit unprofessional, I was in no position to complain. I'd been sleeping on a plastic mat with a pillow made of cardboard for half a year. This was the fucking Ritz Carlton to me.

She pointed to the bed in the corner and gave me a 'thumbs up'. I silently thanked her and watched her leave the room. I remember the other woman saying Sylvia's shift was over and wondered who the hell was watching us if she was leaving. Then I wondered who the hell "us" was.

I'm going to bed in a dark room, and waking up to a house full of strangers. I've had some pretty awkward mornings in my time, but I had a feeling that this one would take the cake.

I laid down in the same pajamas I'd been arrested in back in November. I was wearing these the last time I'd slept in a bed. This whole thing was so surreal.

My head hit the soft feathery pillow, and tears of gratitude began running down my face. The soft mattress felt as if I was laying on a cloud and I couldn't help but feel overwhelmed with joy.

"I am laying in an actual bed," I repeated over and over to myself, trying to wrap my head around the fact that I was no longer an inmate.

As my eyes adjusted to the darkness, I was able to make out the structure of the room I was in, and judging by the snoring, I ascertained there were at least two other women in the room with me. The room smelled like a mixture of paint and shampoo, I assumed that it must have recently been renovated, which would explain the smell and the mattresses on the floor.

I closed my eyes and began silently praying to God. I thanked Him for saving me from the dungeon I'd been living in and leading me to this new chapter of my life. Before I could finish my prayer, I drifted off to a peaceful sleep. The first, in a very long time.

I wasn't sure what had woken me up, perhaps a noise? My eyes shot open and I glanced over at the alarm clock a few beds down, it was 3:33 am. I closed my eyes again and heard another noise, it was coming from the corner of the bedroom. It sounded like someone was whispering.

My gut instinct was to hide under the sheets because honestly –it was creeping me the fuck out. The whispering was hurried and agitated, as if someone was yelling at someone under their breath. Was someone on a phone?

I listened intently for a moment and the whispering suddenly stopped. Had I imagined it? I closed my eyes, attempting to fall back asleep and pretend I'd never heard the voices when suddenly I had the overwhelming urge to pee. I tried to ignore it, but it was as if my bladder was at maximum capacity, and there was no way I'd be able to fall asleep without going to the bathroom.

I didn't even know where the hell the bathroom was. Fuck me. I rolled off my mattress and stood up next to my bed. I began tiptoeing through the room as the wood creaked beneath my feet.

"Looking for the bathroom?" a voice said in the darkness, stopping me dead in my tracks.

"Yes," I whispered to the stranger.

"It's the other way, that corner," the woman said sleepily, pointing to the corner in which I'd heard the whispering. Awesome, I get to go by the scary ghost voice.

I could see light coming from underneath a door around the corner and I felt my way across the wall until my hand reached the knob. My heart was pounding as I silently turned it. I pulled it open quietly, not wanting to disturb the person whose bed was directly outside the door and I silently slipped inside.

The light had been coming from a closet in the bathroom, and it illuminated the bathroom enough that I could see two stalls to my left. I breathed a sigh of relief and noted this would be the first time I took a piss behind closed doors in 121 days.

Before I could pull the door of the stall open, I heard a voice from inside.

"Did you get it?" It was a female, and she was whispering.

"No, dude, can you help me?" another voice said from the next stall over.

"Yeah gimme one sec."

Suddenly the stall flew open and I stared in horror, looking down at the redheaded girl on the toilet seat in front of me. She looked up at me and gasped when she realized I wasn't her friend. "What?" the girl said from the other stall, but the redhead didn't respond, she was staring at me in shock.

She knew there was nothing she could do or say. It was too late.

I'd already seen the belt tied tightly around her biceps, and the loaded syringe jutting out of her arm...

## Chapter Thirty

In the span of only three seconds, a lifetime of thoughts crossed my mind.

This was a rehab, correct? So why in God's name is my drug of choice being administered two feet away from me? My heart was beating against my rib cage and a tornado of jealousy was spinning in my gut.

"Who the fuck are you?" the girl asked, a hint of panic in her voice. The other stall fell silent, the other girl must have realized that they were no longer alone in the bathroom.

"Um, okay – so hi, I'm Tiffany. This is my first night here at Leap of Faith, and I was under the impression that this was a residential treatment program. Judging by the mattresses on the floor and the fact that you are shooting up in the bathroom, I'm suddenly not so sure."

The redhead pushed the door open and marched straight toward me. I thought perhaps I was about to be murdered for witnessing her crime, however she made a sharp left and knocked on the door of the other stall.

"Lexi, I need you out here. I'm not dealing with this shit alone," she said, peering over at me angrily.

"Listen, I just need to piss, okay? I don't really care about what the hell you guys are doing," I said, but it was a lie. I cared very much, actually– I was pretty pissed that I wasn't invited to this fun party. I wanted them to share. I needed them to share.

I had seen the shit loaded into the barrel of her syringe and now it was all I could think about. The other girl – who looked like she just stepped out of the Motel 8 after a night of party-ing—emerged from the stall.

"Here is how this is gonna go down," she said, trying to sound tough, "you are going to keep your mouth fucking shut, or we are going to whoop your ass in your sleep. I'm serious." The night walker glanced nervously at her redheaded friend for confirmation, and I noticed the redhead sporting her best, "we mean business" face.

The laughter escaped from my mouth before I had a chance to stop it. They were trying to intimidate me; but after spending years on the streets and months in jail, these little Spice Girls didn't faze me.

"Okay," I began, "Lexi, is it? And, what's your name?" I said, looking at the redhead.

"None of your business." She crossed her arms across her chest in defiance.

"Fair enough. Lexi, None of Your Business, I'd like to start off by saying – you don't scare me, okay? Let's get that out of the way immediately. Secondly, while I feel like perhaps this may be a trick, or a set up to test my willingness to stay clean, I'd like to state that currently I have no willingness, and I'd like to get high. Lastly, if you don't give me some of that shit immediately, I will march straight to the boss's office, you will get kicked out, and I'll carry on with my life not thinking twice about either of you. Your choice."

I casually leaned back against the sink, feeling pretty confident that the ball was suddenly in my court, and awaited their reply. I had them stuck between a rock and a hard place, and they had no choice but to share. I was moments away from feeling the glorious sensation of liquid relaxation coursing through my veins.

"We don't have any left."

"Liars."

"I swear."

"Okay, that's fine. I have no choice but to repor–,"

"Okay, stop! Fine....Jesus. I have a half a pill. I need it for tomorrow though. I can probably get my boyfriend to bring us more, but you would need to call him," Lexi said.

"Huh? I have to call him? Hell no, I just got here, I don't have a phone?"

"They let you make a phone call to your family to get your stuff. You can just call my boyfriend instead, he has the number to the office saved in his phone, so he will know what it's about. Tell him we need some. He will meet us at the Meeting tomorrow and slip it to us."

I knew I wasn't going to do it. But I needed the drugs, now. So, I agreed.

"If you fuck me over, new girl, I swea—"

"I won't damnit, just give me the shit. Once I do some it will be in my system and then you will know I'm not ratting you out. I'd fail a test too. So, pass it, damnit."

She was angry, I could see it in her eyes. I don't blame her, I'd be pissed too if I was forced to give away the last of my drugs. But I don't give a damn, I'm getting high. God put me in this bathroom at the perfect time, and I was eternally grateful.

She closed the stall behind and her and began preparing the rig for me.

"I know what it looks like when it's right, don't try and fuck me over by not putting the whole half in there," I whispered through the crack.

"Dude, shut the fuck up, I won't," she whispered angrily.

When she opened the door, I saw the syringe sitting on top of the tank on the back of the toilet. My heart was exploding inside my chest and I couldn't wait to feel high again. It had been so fucking long.

I would just do it tonight, just this once... To get the urge out of my system. Then I would start fresh with my rehab journey tomorrow. A little bit probably wouldn't do anything to me anyway and technically I hadn't started rehab yet. It was fine.

I entered the stall, shut the door behind me, and grabbed the syringe.

*** 

The next morning, Dr. Danner placed her briefcase next to her chair and sat down across from me.

"Good morning, Tiffany. I was thinking about you all night last night. Your story was so captivating. If I can be honest with you for a moment; I was anxious to get back here today and hear more."

I felt uncomfortable. Nervous. I was afraid to speak to her after what happened last night.

Before I could reply, she abruptly rose from her seat and made her way over to the couch I was sitting on. She sat down next to me and looked into my eyes; her face had fallen into an expression of sadness.

"Tiffany... I know what you did last night," she said.

My heart sank. I placed my head into my hands and began to weep. I felt so embarrassed and guilty about what I had done, and now everyone knew.

"Look at me," she said placing her hand on my back, "Tiffany, look at me."

I slowly raised my eyes to meet hers and swallowed the knot that had formed in my throat. My ribcage began convulsing as I began sobbing, I couldn't breathe.

"Shhh," she whispered, trying to comfort me. "Tiffany... What you did," she began, "takes a tremendous amount of courage. To come face to face with your drug of choice on the first night—and then have the strength to not only walk away from it; but to immediately tell the counselors so they could get those girls and their drugs out of this place—was heroic."

I shook my head.

"It wasn't fucking heroic. I'm a snitch. It's my first morning here and everybody already hates me. I feel so stupid." I sobbed.

"Listen to me, I need you to hear what I'm saying. You just saved a life, whether you realize it or not, you did. Maybe yours, maybe theirs, maybe the other girls in this house—or maybe— the girl on the street, desperate to find a safe place to get clean. The one who couldn't get into this program because it was already full. You just freed up two beds for someone who really needs them, someone willing to do whatever it takes to get clean. You don't know it today, but one day down the road it will become very clear how the choice you made last night rippled out into the universe and changed everything. I am so proud of you."

I thought about what she'd said for a moment. And she was right, I don't know it today. Today I know that I turned every light in this place on and began screaming at the top of my lungs that there were girls using in the bathroom.

Today I know that the owner of Leap of Faith came to the house at 4:30 in the morning to drug test everyone, and three girls were removed.

Today I know that the moment I looked at that needle on the back of the toilet I thought about my dad's face on the monitor in jail, and I knew that I never wanted to be forced to communicate with him through a screen again.

Today I know that I get to call him on the phone, and wrap my arms around him for the first time in a very long time, when he brings my things to me. I get to touch his skin and look him in the eyes and thank him for his unwavering love and support during the darkest times in my life.

Today I know... I am clean.

I don't know what comes next, I don't know what to expect and I don't know where the hell this life will take me. But I do know one thing for sure. There is a God, He was with me in that bathroom stall last night, and He has a beautiful plan for my life, one that is greater than I could ever imagine.

## Chapter Thirty-One

"I know I don't know you, but I would like to thank you for what you did," a woman named Claire said after introducing herself

"I knew those bitches were getting high, but I had no way to prove it. I've been clean for 99 days and I swear if it was me who walked in on them, I wouldn't have made it to 100. Especially my first day in this place, you rock," she said, sticking her hand up for a high five.

Claire was probably in her sixties and slept on the mattress directly in front of our bedroom door. She had long silver hair and her skin was weathered, apparently from many years of exposure to the sun. I glanced at the area surrounding her mattress and noticed she had very few belongings. She had lived on this earth over 60 years and had only a few outfits, an alarm clock and a stuffed Betty Boop doll to show for it.

"Yeah, thank you. I am surprised myself to be honest with you. I'm just grateful that the temptation is gone, ya know?" I said, standing up from the floor. "So, what do we do now?"

I hadn't received a schedule or orientation for this place yet since I'd gotten in so late last night. Amidst the chaos of everything they'd forgotten to show me around.

"In about 10 minutes we go to the computer shop and work for a while," she said. A look of confusion crossed my face and she noticed immediately. "Felicity–the owner of Leap of Faith, she owns a computer shop. We spend a few hours working there each day," she said.

Hold up.

"What do you mean 'working' there? What do we do? She pays us?" I had so many questions. I don't know if I'm ready for a job yet, like, I need some rehabilitation first I think.

"We fix up computers, make calls to get computer donations, sell the computers. Things like that. No, we don't get paid," she said. Okay, this woman is acting like this is normal. I didn't get sentenced to "computer salesman school," so how the hell is that supposed to help me get clean?

I tried to read her face for the slightest hint of laughter, because I knew she had to be fucking with me. "You ready?" she asked, standing up and putting her shoes on.

"Um, I mean...yeah... I guess."

I followed Claire through the front door and stopped short when she headed out to the street. I looked back over my shoulder, there was no one else around. "Claire!" I yelled in a whisper from the front porch. "Where the hell are you going?" She stopped and turned around before bursting out with laughter.

"Oh Lord, you are too funny. C'mon, it's okay. Everyone is already there," she said waving me out.

I watched as she stepped out onto the street and walked along the line of the grass down the road. What in the actual hell was this woman doing? I took a hesitant step off the porch and then one more into the grass. I was outside, unsupervised in the middle of the ghetto. This can't be right.

Claire apparently noticed I wasn't behind her and started walking back toward me. "Hurry up, we're late. The computer shop is right up here." I looked to where she was pointing and about 300 ft. in front of us was a building. I could see a young girl stepping off the back of a moving truck carrying what appeared to be a printer.

"Hey, so is it like, legal for us to be out here right now? Like, I was sentenced to a rehab and here I am walking down the damn street. It just feels wrong and I really don't want to go back to jail," I said, catching up to Claire.

"It's finnne. This shop is a branch of the rehab. It's part of it." I looked around as we walked, and while part of me was worried the SWAT team was about to bust out from behind the bushes any second now, the other part of me really loved the feeling of walking down the street like a normal human. Cars were whizzing past us and for the first time in a long time,

I didn't feel ashamed. I was just a regular person walking down a regular street.

"You must be Tiffany," said a heavyset African-American woman as we approached. I smiled and went to shake her hand, but she yanked me into a bear hug, almost knocking the wind out of me. "I'm April, and I am a house mother here. I didn't get a chance to meet you because I was on an overnight pass with my family. I just wanted to personally thank you for being so brave."

"Let's fucking go, what the hell took you guys so long?" Ryanne whined, appearing out of nowhere looking angry.

"We, um...Uh," Claire stuttered, "I'm sorry, I was filling Tiffany in on−."

"It doesn't matter," Ryanne interrupted. "We have a lot to do, let's go." I looked at April and mouthed 'sorry' and quickly followed Ryanne into the shop.

"Claire, I need you to organize the power cords in the bins. Tiffany—you come with me."

Shit.

Ryanne led me to a room in the back and shut the door behind us. I was suddenly really nervous.

"I wasn't yelling at you for the record," she began, "Claire is as slow as a fucking turtle and I'm tired of her shit." The laughter escaped my mouth before I had a chance to stop it. She just called that lady a turtle.

"Awe, she was really nice to me. She was explaining how things worked around here because like, I have no clue what's going on, basically. Like at all. I'm in a computer shop right now and I thought for sure I'd be in a meeting or reading a self-help book or something," I said.

Ryanne laughed. "Oh no! I'm sorry. With the girls getting kicked out—thanks to you, and the late night last night, things have been crazy. I'll tell you what. I'll take you back to the house and give you the rundown. Sound good?"

"Yes. That would be amazing. Thank you," I said, relieved that I didn't have to organize power cords today.

"Before we go, I have something for you. Kinda like, a thank you for what you did last night," she said.

"Oh. Wow. That is so nice, but you really didn't ha..."

"Shut up. Follow me," she interrupted.

She stood up and pulled the door open, gesturing for me to go ahead of her. I smiled and walked out...immediately stopping dead in my tracks.

I screamed at the top of my lungs and dropped to my knees, sobbing so hard I couldn't breathe.

My father and sister knelt down beside me and wrapped their arms around me.

"I am so proud of you, baby," my dad whispered into my ear before resting his head on my shoulder.

This was the first time in my entire existence that my father and I had ever hugged without a drop of drugs or alcohol in our systems. It was the most beautiful moment I'd ever experienced.

They were only allowed to stay for a half an hour, because technically visiting day wasn't until Sunday. My dad gave me a quick update on his cancer treatment and my sister filled me in on what was new with her. She had a wall up, I could tell. I didn't blame her one bit, I was just so grateful that I got to see her face...in person.

As I watched them walk back to their car to leave, the little girl inside me screamed and cried. I wanted to chase after them and go with them. I missed them so much. I kicked myself for not spending more time with them back when I had the chance, but I had been too busy getting high. The only time I called them was when I needed something and even then, I kept our encounters as brief as possible.

My thoughts drifted to the last time I'd seen my sister. When the memory found its way to the front of my mind, my stomach turned. It was no wonder she had a wall up, I had been so terrible to her.

"Hey Tiff, what are you doing today?" my sister had asked cheerfully into the phone.

"Um, not much, chillin' at the house. I don't really feel too good."

"Well that's lame. Get your ass up. I'm coming to get you. I have a surprise."

"Aw, thanks, Lane. I really appreciate it, But I'm gonna have to take a raincheck," I said, trying to sound as sick as possible.

"Bullshit. I'm already on my way. It's your fucking birthday, dude. Get your ass up I'm almost there."

I was suddenly consumed with anger. I hated hanging out with my sister. She didn't do drugs, and she knew me better than anyone, so it would take an exhausting amount of effort to maintain a somewhat normal demeanor. I wasn't in the mood to fake it all day.

"Happy Birthday," Gail the psychic said as she shuffled a deck of Tarot cards.

"Thanks," I said, pulling my sleeves down over the crease of my arm. I hated wearing long sleeves in the middle of the damn summer. But I couldn't let my sister see my arms.

"So, what can I do for you today, are you want to communicate with spirit? Or have your cards read?"

"Um, I'm not really sure. I wasn't expecting this. My sister surprised me by bringing me here, so..."

"She wants to talk to our mom," my sister chimed in. I rolled my eyes.

"Oh, okay. Please don't tell me anymore. I will see if I can channel her. Tiffany, just close your eyes and take a deep breath," she said calmly.

I slowly closed my eyes and took in a deep breath. She slapped the deck of cards down onto the table and I jerked my head up and opened my eyes. Shit...I was nodding out.

"Okay. I have a woman coming forward, a mother figure. But...okay hold on. Okay she wants to talk to you," the woman said, looking at my sister.

"Of course she does," I muttered under my breath.

"No, no, that's okay. We are here for Tiff, tell her I'll talk to her later." My sister deflected the offer. She probably knew it would have pissed me off.

"Okay, sure no problem," Gail said, looking uncomfortable. "Tiffany... do you...are you in any legal trouble?"

"What? No," I said, feeling somewhat offended. "I worked at a Law Office. My mom worked there too, maybe that's what she's talking about."

"Hmmm. Okay. I don't think that's it. Let me see." Gail got quiet for a moment and took a few deep breaths. I was getting annoyed. This was fucking stupid and I really wanted to get home and go get pills from Lazarus. I was almost out.

"Tiffany, your mom is showing me lots of pain, and anguish."

"Yeah. She died of cancer, it was pretty bad."

"No, not with her...with you."

My foot started tapping as my anxiety began taking over. I thought this was supposed to be fun. This shit is becoming a real buzzkill.

"Oh yeah?" I asked sarcastically, crossing my arms and leaning back in the chair.

"Yes. Oh Tiffany. Your mom is showing me that you have a lot going on, too much perhaps. She says you need to take it easy. She says you are her baby, and she loves you and wants you to know that she..." Her voice trailed off and she grew silent.

"She what?" I asked.

"She is stepping back now. She said that she loves you very much."

I squinted at Gail, I couldn't help but think she was keeping something from me.

"Okay, you started to say something though, I feel like there was more. Did she just back up or whatever in the middle of a sentence?" I asked.

"Yes. They do that sometimes. We only have a few minutes left, I'm going to pull some cards for you before you go. Okay?"

It was pouring by the time my depressing psychic reading was over, so my sister and I sprinted to the car. Usually I would love things like this– running in the rain with my sister. But I hated it today. My shirt was sticking to my body making the outline of the syringe I'd concealed in my bra clearly visible. We slammed the doors shut when we got in and she immediately put on the heat. I tried to place my arm across my chest to hide it. "What did you think?" she asked smiling, reaching into the back seat to grab her CD case.

"It was awesome," I lied, slipping a $20 out of her purse while she was turned around and shoving it into my pocket.

"Tiffany!" someone yelled, snapping me back to reality. "I've been calling your name for two minutes. What are you doing?" Dr. Danner smiled, noticing I was staring at the empty parking space.

"Daydreaming, sorry."

"No need to apologize. I heard your family came. That's wonderful, I'm so happy for you. Listen, I hope you don't mind, but I scheduled an impromptu session for us today. I am leaving for two weeks for Japan and wanted you to finish telling me your story if that's alright."

"Of course. Right now?"

"Yes. We will go back to the house and you can finish telling me what happened with your boyfriend, after you told him that you'd gotten high. Walk with me," she said.

As we walked back to the house, I couldn't help but feel a bit of dread. The last thing I wanted to do was take another trip down "Tiffany Is a Piece of Shit" Lane. But I knew how important this next part was. In order for the doctor to understand "me", she had to know what happened. The night of that surprise party was the beginning of an incredibly dark journey. It was time to tell the truth.

Chapter Thirty-Two

I was honest with Chuck when we first began dating, I told him that I had been an addict, but I'd recovered in treatment. Which, at the time I believed to be true. I expected him to end the relationship right then and there; instead he kissed me and said, "I don't care about your past, as long as you don't take them anymore, then it's not stopping me from being with you."

I remember being so grateful that he had such an accepting heart. I should have ran that night. Saved him the heartache. But I never expected for any of this to happen. It wasn't part of my plan.

I thought that after paying $28,000 for 28 days in rehab after my mom died, surely whatever the hell they did in there had fixed me. I thought that they worked their magic and now I was all better. After all, it had been around five months or so since I'd last used, so something must have clicked. But I was wrong. Because here I am staring into the heartbroken eyes of a man who trusted me.

I was incredibly intoxicated, but what I saw through my blurry vision is something I'll never forget. I watched all the joy immediately drain from Chuck's face, and the hope disappear from his eyes when I told him. He was crushed.

I followed him with my eyes as he stood up and walked to the foot of the bed. He closed his eyes, dropped to his knees and clasped his hands together. He was praying. This guy's first reaction was to pray. I wanted to tell him that he was wasting his time, that no one was up there, but I figured now wasn't a good time. Obviously.

The room was silent as he pleaded with God. I don't know what he was saying, but even with his eyes closed I could feel the pain behind them. He opened his eyes and looked at me as a single tear streamed down his face.

"Are you done?" he asked sternly.

"Done what? With us?" I said.

"No... are you done with the fucking pills?"

"Yes! Yes, I'm done. I didn't mean... I don't even know what happened. It was happening so fast like I couldn't control it. I didn't want to do it I swear to God."

"Then why the hell did you, Tiffany?"

How can I explain this? There's no explanation that makes any damn sense.

"I can't... I don't know how to explain it. It was like the urge was so overwhelming that I physically could not stop myself from opening the bottle."

"What bottle? Where the fuck did you get them?"

Shit, I didn't want to rat my roommate out. I could tell Chuck was getting frustrated and didn't want him to take his anger out on Brandon. It wasn't Brandon's fault that I was a junkie who couldn't be trusted.

"Kayla," I blurted.

"I fucking knew it. I told you she was bad news. You can't be around people like that, Tiff, it's too tempting to go back to your old ways," he said, his expression softening.

I could tell that his current emotion was sympathy—which was good. I really needed to take advantage of this.

"Babe, I know. I should never have invited her over. I just missed her so much. She was my best friend and, I like all the new friends I'm making—your friends, it's just that I miss the people I grew up with. I miss my mom. I feel like my old life is so far away and I guess I thought...I thought that seeing Kayla might make me feel closer to my mom. I don't know. I'm so sorry." I began to cry, I knew that the tears would seal the deal.

"Come here, Babe," he said pulling me in for a hug. "I'm so sorry about your mom, I can't imagine how hard that must be. I know that you can overcome this, you will overcome this. And I'll be right here by your side while you do. I love you."

I took a deep breath, relieved that he was being so great about this. I really did like him, maybe even loved him. I was grateful that he was able to overlook my flaws and love me despite them.

"So, what do I need to do to help you?" he asked, grabbing my hand and placing it between his.

This was a great question. What the hell could he do? The only thing that came to mind was handcuffing me and keeping me in the closet, because apparently, I wasn't able to control myself when left to my own devices.

"I think... I think I need to move in. I need to get away from town, away from the bad influences, that way I won't be so tempted, ya know?"

What am I saying? What the hell did I just do.

His eyes lit up like a Christmas tree as he reached for the box and handed it over to me. I forced out a smile and grabbed on to it, wondering if it would be inappropriate for me to throw it back at him and run full speed out the door. It was too late, I'd already said the words.

"Before I give this to you," he said keeping a firm grasp on it, "promise me that you are done with the pills." His face was serious again.

I stared into his eyes for a moment. Is this a promise I could keep? He was so amazing, and I really didn't want to end things with him. He loved me unconditionally and was the best thing that had happened to me in a really long time. I really can't fuck this up.

"I promise."

I had every intention of keeping that promise. I honestly, truthfully, wholeheartedly did. But addiction is a sneaky bitch. It doesn't care who you're dating, who you love, if you have kids, a job or goals. It doesn't care who you were... or who you plan to be. It creeps in when you least expect it, consumes your thoughts and eventually... your life.

\*\*\*

"Hello everyone, I'm Tiffany, and I'm the new shift leader. I just transferred here from Santiago store and I look forward to working with all of you," I said to my new employees.

They smiled and looked around at each other, confused by my presence. This was a last-minute decision, and none of them expected it. They all stared at me for a moment and I felt awkward, unsure of what to say next. "You're free to go," I said, and they immediately scattered like roaches, desperate to get away from the weird morning meeting.

It had been two weeks since I'd moved in with Chuck and decided to transfer stores. This one was much closer to my house and I liked the idea of starting fresh.

"Hi, I'm Kendra," a blonde, obviously pregnant girl said sticking out her hand for me to shake. "Nice to meet you, I'm Tiffany." She must have noticed I was staring at her belly, because she gently placed her hand over her belly button and rubbed it in a circular motion. "There's two of them in there," she said smiling.

"Holy shit! Congratulations! I'm pretty impressed that you are still working," I said.

"I know, it's hard. I don't have a choice though. My boyfriend left before we found out I was pregnant and has been MIA ever since," she said sadly, looking down.

"Well please let me know if there's anything I can do to make your life easier. I can only imagine how hard it must be to run around while pregnant, especially with two!" I smiled.

"Thank you so much, I will." She grabbed a tray and headed out to the dining room.

It felt really good to be in a new place. New scenery, new faces and a new start. Chuck and I hadn't spoken about my relapse since the night of the party, it was as if nothing ever happened.

My first night at the restaurant had gone fairly smoothly–apart from a few drink spills and one customer growing enraged at the sight of her tiny baked potato. Nothing I couldn't handle.

I began checking the servers out at the end of their shifts, taking their money and receipts. One by one they left for the night until it was only Kendra, David (the cook) and I. Kendra waddled in with one hand on her back and a tired look on her face. She let out a loud sigh as her and her twins plopped down in the empty seat at my desk.

"You okay?" I asked as I reached over to take her receipts.

"Yep, fine. My feet are as big as balloons, I can feel it. I can't wait to go home and soak in a warm bath," she said, stretching her legs out straight in front of her.

"Mmm I bet, that sounds really good actually." A warm bath, I might have to take one myself after I get off. Chuck is at work, so I have the house to myself.

"Well it was nice working with you, Tiffany. Happy to have a new face in here. The other manager is a real asshole. Anyway, I'm gonna take a piss then head to the bus stop. I'll see you tomorrow," she said, struggling to stand up. I jumped up and reached for her arm to help pull her up.

"What do you mean bus stop?" I asked.

"Oh, yeah I don't have a license. So, I take the bus. It's no big deal, been doin' it for years," she said as she strained to bend down for her purse on the ground.

"Hold on," I said reaching down and grabbing it for her.

"Wait!" she exclaimed as I grabbed one of the straps on her bag. As I pulled it up the weight of the contents caused the purse to turn sideways, spilling most of its contents onto the floor. Coins began clinking and her lip gloss and pens rolled in different directions.

"Oh my gosh, I am so sor–" I started to say, but stopped short when I noticed her expression. She was frozen in place with a look of horror on her face. I stared at her confused, then looked back down at the floor. I hadn't noticed it before.

I looked back at her in shock, unsure of what to say as she dropped to her knees and frantically began shoving the items back into the bag. It was too late. I'd already seen it.

"Listen..." she began. I held up my hand to stop her. "Please," she continued, "I really can't lose this job..." she pleaded. "I know this looks bad but..."

"Stop. Just stop," I said. Sitting back into my chair and thinking for a moment. So many things flashed across my mind. I had so many choices in this moment and didn't know what the hell to do. This girl was pregnant. I just started here. What the fuck.

I stood up, walked past her to make sure the restaurant was empty and shut all the lights off. "Dave, you're good to go!" I yelled over my shoulder at the cook as I stepped back into my office and shut the door.

"Please, are you gonna fire...."

"Shut the fuck up for a second!" I snapped, hurrying to type in the totals for the day. I logged off the computer and grabbed the deposit bag and my keys.

As I pulled the office door open I turned around to face her with my hand still on the knob.

"You aren't taking the bus. I'm giving you a ride home... and you're gonna give me five of those pills..." I turned off the light and headed toward the parking lot.

## Chapter Thirty-Three

"Take a left here," Kendra said unbuckling her seatbelt. I glanced over at her as I made the left turn.

"Why are you taking off your seatbelt already?" I asked, it seemed suspicious.

"What are you talking about? We are about to be at my house," she said.

"Listen, if you are planning on jumping out of this car and running inside before giving me my shit, I swear to God I will tackle you. I don't give a fuck if you are pregnant, and you certainly don't seem to care either." I pressed on the brake to slow down. "Where do I go?"

"It's this house here. I do give a shit about my twins, actually and I wasn't going to run, obviously...here." She reluctantly dropped five pills into the palm of my hand and I immediately clasped it shut. I could tell she was annoyed, but I didn't give a damn. The girl had like 500 of them in her bag. I had no intention of doing pills anymore, but it was almost as if God wanted me to find them, I mean they practically fell into my lap.

I watched her struggle to maneuver her way out of the passenger seat and smiled. Normally I would have run around to help her, but I'd lost all respect for this girl once I saw that she had no problem poisoning her twins. Once she pulled herself up, she leaned down to grab her purse. "It's not what you think, they aren't mine," she said.

"Yeah, okay. That's what they all say. If you try to tell management that I do pills, Kendra, I will have you fired faster than you can blink. There's security cameras in the office. They would probably take your babies away the minute they popped out, so don't fuck with me." I put the car into drive so that she would get the hint to shut the damn door, but she stood there for a moment and I could tell she had something more to say.

"Hello, can you shut the door, you're letting mosquitos in," I said.

She took a step back and started to shut the door, but before she did she leaned down until her eyes met mine. "You are making a big mistake. Grams isn't going to be happy about this."

"What? Who the hell is Gra—", she slammed the door shut and started walking to the house. I rolled the passenger window down to call out to her. "Did you just say your Grandma isn't gonna be happy about this? Hello?" she glanced back over her shoulder one more time, then stepped into her house, shutting the door behind her.

That girl is a nutcase. What's her grandma gonna do, hit me with her Cash?

I sped the whole way home, anxious to do a pill. Most of you are probably thinking, "Why the hell would you speed? You could have gotten pulled over and arrested for possession." I feel the need to remind you that my boyfriend was an officer in this county, so there was no way in hell that I was getting more than a high-five and a "What's up," from any cop I came across.

The car was barely in park when I ripped the key out of the ignition and ran full speed inside. I felt like a kid running down the stairs on Christmas. It was strange the way my brain was able to compartmentalize certain emotions and situations. The part where I promised Chuck I would no longer do pills anymore was stuffed away in a box in the way back. The box that held my selfish wants and needs was beautifully wrapped and begging to be opened.

As I crushed the pill up on the counter, a tiny voice inside my head gently reminded me that I was making a terrible mistake, that I was supposed to be doing the right thing and staying clean. That voice was quickly muffled by the deafening roar of my addiction, screaming for me to hurry the fuck up and snort this.

It would be different this time, I told myself as I lined up the fine powder with my debit card. I would just do these few and then stop again. I had to do these, they were fucking free. What the hell was I going to do, throw them away?

"It will be different this time," I said aloud as I sniffed the entire line deep into my nose. "I promise."

Thirty seconds later, every muscle in my face began to relax. My eyelids grew heavier and I found myself moving in slow motion toward my bed. God, I missed this feeling. Why would I ever want to stop doing these? I finally felt like myself again for the first time in a long time.

I glanced over at the closet as I flopped down onto the bed and stared at Chuck's uniform hanging on the back of the door. It was as if this outfit was taunting me. "What have you done? You don't deserve Chuck. You are nothing but a junkie loser. You don't really think you'll get away with this, do you?"

"Screw you, stupid uniform." I threw a pillow at the back of the door and his uniform fell to the floor making a 'clink' sound as his name badge hit the wood floor. "Son of a bitch." I said to myself, rolling off the bed to go pick it up. When I leaned down to pick it up, the bedroom door suddenly swung open and knocked me to the floor.

I let out a scream that shook the windows and immediately placed my hands up in front of my face to protect it from the ax murderer entering my room. It was then that I heard a laugh I knew all too well.

"Geeezzz. Calm down it's just me," Chuck said.

"What the hell are you doing home? You almost gave me a freakin' heart attack!" I yelled, standing up to hug him. Not necessarily because I was in a loving mood, mainly because I was high as a fucking kite and knew he'd be able to tell the second he got a look at my face. I messed up. This was a terrible idea. What the hell am I supposed to do now?

I thought he was going to be on duty all night—so I could watch a movie and pass out and he'd never know I relapsed. I had a foolproof plan...Or so I thought.

I knew in that moment, I had no other choice but to tell him. He's already on high alert because of last time, and once he takes one look in my eyes it's going to break his heart. It's better that he hears the truth now, instead of being forced to ask. I'd already done enough damage, it was time for me to move on.

I hugged him for a moment longer, realizing this would probably be the last time I would ever be loved by someone as wonderful as him. I wanted to stay in this moment forever, because I knew the second I pulled away, life as he knew it would completely change.

I took a deep breath, and let go.

I raised my eyes to him and began to speak, but I was interrupted. "You are so beautiful, Baby," he said gazing into my eyes before pulling me in for another hug.

"Thank you, Honey, um, but we need to talk about something," I said, pulling away before he got too deep into this mood.

"Uh oh," he said, stepping back and looking down at me. "You're not pregnant, are you?" he said, laughing. I laughed too, but it was nervous laughter, so it came out as an obnoxious cackle.

"Pregnant. Ha, good one, Babe. Um, nope. Not pregnant. Thank God. Right?"

The laughter subsided, and his face returned to a look of concern. "What's up, Tiff? You okay?" I paused before speaking. I knew he already knew. "What's the matter?" he asked, a hint of panic in his voice.

"Well, I ..." I was struggling to find the words.

"Is it your job? You don't like it there do you?" he interrupted. I looked at him for a moment, trying to get a read on what he was thinking. He had a look of genuine confusion on his face, but nothing about his expression insinuated he may have thought I was high. I knew for a fact I looked high, I had just snorted an entire pill after three months of being clean. So why isn't he catching on?

"Babe, you're killing me. What is it?" he pleaded.

*He is staring in my eyes. He is looking right at me. How is he not aware of what I'm about to say?* It didn't matter, it was now or never. I had to tell the truth.

"Um, well. I met a pregnant girl at my job tonight. She's pregnant with twins and.... she was doing drugs. When I went to check her out, her purse fell on the floor and –"

His jaw dropped open and his face twisted in disgust. "You have got to be kidding me. My God, those poor babies. What the—well did you fire her?"

I stared at him for a moment, waiting for him to piece the puzzle together. Suddenly, I realized what was happening. Despite the fact that he is a professional at knowing when someone is high – he has no clue that the person a foot away from his face had faded.

Oh my God.

The script had suddenly changed. I was no longer the poor addict about to confess that once again I'd failed at making it any length of time without drugs. My new role was that of a responsible restaurant manager focused on ridding the workplace of all delinquent employees. "You bet your ass I did," I said, beaming with pride.

He smiled and pulled me in for a bear hug. "I am so proud of you, Tiffany," he whispered.

"Thank you, Babe, I told you. I am a different person now."

Chapter Thirty-Four

I looked up at Dr. Danner after realizing I had been lost in my story for a while. "I'm sorry, I got carried away."

"No, no. It's fine," she said smiling.

"Should I continue?" I asked nervously. It was incredibly odd to talk about myself for this long, she had to be growing tired of my ramblings.

She glanced quickly at her watch and folded her hands on her lap. "Please do, we have plenty of time. Perhaps we can finish your story before I have to leave, that way I don't have to wait a week to hear the rest." She laughed, slipping her heels off and crossing her legs underneath her on the couch.

"Okay." I smiled as I leaned back and got comfy, too. Dr. Danner was in for a doozy with this next part...

Once I had realized that I could get away with being high– that Chuck didn't notice, things escalated quickly. One month later– to the day– I made a choice that would alter the course of my life indefinitely.

"I can't come in today, I'm really sick, Don."

Before calling up to work, I laid backwards on the bed with my head hanging off the edge. I heard that this position tightens your throat and makes you sound sick. I was sick, sicker than I've ever been. But it wasn't a cold or the flu, it was much worse.

"Tiffany, you've been missing a lot of work lately, are you sure everything is okay?" Don asked sounding slightly agitated.

"Yes, I don't know what's going on, I need to go to the hospital I think, I'll go today probably." I lied. I didn't need a fucking doctor, I needed a Roxy.

"Make sure you bring a note with you tomorrow. You are coming tomorrow, right?"

"Yes. I should definitely be better by then. Thank you."

I hung up the phone before he had a chance to reply, I honestly didn't care if he fired me at this point. I didn't care about anything except finding money so that I could make this pain stop.

I rolled back up onto the bed and let out a growl as a wave of nausea made its way up from my belly into my throat. I ran to the bathroom, but it was too late. Vomit shot out of my mouth before I could open the lid of the toilet, covering my shirt and the bathroom mat.

I crawled through the vomit and lifted the lid, but couldn't muster the strength to stand up. I laid my head onto the cold ceramic seat and closed my eyes waiting for the nausea to pass.

It felt as if my bones were in a vice grip, at any moment I was certain they would snap. It was as if my body was on fire and I was trapped inside. I wanted to shed my skin, this weak human flesh that was revolting without its fix. I needed a pill, I needed something.

With a sudden burst of energy, I remembered that Chuck had a half a bottle of vodka in the pantry. I ran like I was trying out for the Olympics and threw the pantry door open with enough force that it knocked a few magnets of the fridge.

I lunged for the bottle and chugged until it was empty. The bitter alcohol burned the walls of my esophagus as it made its way down, but I didn't care. I needed the pain to stop.

I reached for my phone in my back pocket and mashed the numbers to Lazarus's cell.

Each ring felt like an eternity. "Yo, you know what to do." BEEP.

I cursed out loud and frantically dialed again. Ring, ring, ring. "Yo, you know what to do." BEEP.

Tears of desperation streamed down my face as I opened my text messages. I needed pills and I need him to answer. I began typing:

"Hey Laz. Remember that thing we talked about last week? When I said I couldn't because I have a boyfriend? I changed my mind, please call me back ASAP."

What the hell am I doing?

Lazarus had tried to offer me pills in exchange for sex a million times, I always said no. I would never sleep with him for thousands of reasons but the main one being–I love my boyfriend very much.

Therein lies the problem. I'm broke and I have no money for pills. I love Chuck so much that I need to do whatever the hell I can to ensure he doesn't know I'm detoxing. Four hours from now when he gets home, the pain of this withdrawal will have doubled by then. He would know I was using and it would kill him. I can't do that to him, it would ruin him. Two minutes of meaningless sex was much better than destroying this wonderful man's future.

I had to make this pain stop so that I can make it through the night. One more night, then I'll try and get clean tomorrow.

I picked up the phone to call Kayla. We hadn't spoken much since Chuck and I had gotten back together because he thinks she's a bad influence. Which is precisely why I needed to get ahold of her right this second.

"Hello?" she answered, sounding surprised. I don't know what it was about the sound of her voice, I instantly broke down into sobs.

"Holy shit, Tiff, what's wrong?" she asked.

"Dude, I am so fucking sick. I've been getting high this whole time and I am detoxing so bad. Lazarus isn't answering, and I have no money and honestly, Kay... I want to die." I could barely get the words out.

"Oh my God. I can't believe you didn't call me sooner, idiot. I don't have Roxies, but I have D's," she said.

"What the hell is a "D"?" I asked. Why did she know about something that I didn't know about? We started using at the same time.

"You haven't heard of them? It's a pill. It fucks you up. The only thing is–"

"I don't care, please. Please bring me one. I'll do anything," I pleaded.

"Okay, I'll be there in like twenty. I'm so happy you called, I've missed you so much," she said.

"Please! Just come. We can talk when you get here," I said. I didn't want to reminisce. I needed her to shut the hell up and get here with drugs.

I laid on the floor of the kitchen twisting in agony for what seemed like a lifetime. The vodka didn't do a damn thing to help with the pain, it was almost as if I was immune to it during withdrawal. Each second felt like three hours. I imagine that this is what people in a gas chamber must feel like moments before taking their last breath. I was suffocating from the pain.

A burst of adrenaline and joy shot through my veins as I heard acrylic nails tapping on my front door. "Oh my God come in!"

I didn't move from the floor, I was going to snort whatever the hell this pill was right off the tile below me. "Where are you?" Kayla asked, apparently unable to see my lifeless body by the dishwasher.

"In here," I mumbled.

"Oh my God, Tiff. You are such a dork," Kayla said, rounding the corner.

"Fuck you, where is it?"

Before she could respond, Kayla's friend Javier appeared from behind her and smiled down at me. "Hey down there. You okay?" he asked with a look of sympathy on his face.

"Not really. I'd offer you a drink, but I can't move. Why the hell are you here?"

"Tiffany!" Kayla scolded, obviously embarrassed.

"Sorry! I just wasn't expecting company, and was wondering...what he was doing here. So, what are you doing here?"

"It's his stuff, asshole, so be nice." Kayla laughed, setting her purse on the counter. "Are you just gonna stay down there?"

"Yup."

"Ha ha. Okay, give me a sec to get it ready," she said, pulling the stuff from her purse.

I closed my eyes and took deep breaths, anxiously anticipating the feeling of the powder filling my nose and dripping down my throat. It took her a few minutes to get ready, but it seemed like it had been a week.

"Ready?" Javier asked.

"Hell yeah." I replied, with my eyes still closed. "Just set it on the floor next to me, I'm not joking, I can't move."

The room was silent. I opened my eyes and gasped. "What the fuck are you doing?" I asked him when I realized he was about to strangle me with a belt. "Are you trying to murder me?" I screamed, jumping to my feet.

"Tiffany, calm down. I tried to tell you on the phone, but you cut me off," Kayla said calmly. "The belt isn't for your neck, it's for your arm."

I looked at the belt, then looked back at Kayla. I hadn't noticed before because I was laying down. Her arms... they were bruised, and covered in track marks. The world was suddenly spinning around me as I came to terms with what was going on.

I looked at Javier, and looked down at his hand. He was holding a syringe, loaded with drugs.

"Sooo," Kayla began, "what do you want to do?"

I looked at her, looked back at Javier then down at the needle. I had never shot up before, junkies shot up, and I wasn't a junkie. I had three choices here. Continue detoxing and destroy my relationship. Shoot myself in the head with a gun and make it easier on everyone, or have some strange dude I don't know shoot me up in the kitchen of my cop boyfriend's house...

"Fuck it, let's do it." I said, rolling up my sleeve.

## Chapter Thirty-Five

"I need you to stay really still, okay?" Javier said looking in my eyes.

"You will feel a pinch and you can't flinch when you do. After I untie the belt, you need to stay seated or you'll fall. I'm serious, your knees are gonna give out. You ready?"

My heart was pounding out of control. I had heard so many stories about people shooting up. They always end up living under bridges and contracting diseases. Javier wasn't a doctor, he was a dishwasher at Barron's Roadhouse for Christ's sake. What the hell am I doing?

"Are you sure that this will take away the withdrawal? I won't feel sick anymore?" I asked nervously.

"Tiff, I promise. You know I wouldn't let him do this if I didn't think it would help. I promise you will feel better. It's up to you though, if you don't want to do it then don't. I don't want you to think we are forcing you," Kayla said.

"No, I know. I'm just scared. I would honestly rather die than feel another second of this shit. I want to do it—I have to, I just. I'm scared." My legs had been restless for the past two hours. I was tapping my foot uncontrollably hoping the muscles would get so tired that they would stop aching.

"I can't... I can't take it anymore. Just do it. Hurry up." I squeezed my eyes shut and took a deep breath.

"You have to stop shaking your leg," he said, grabbing ahold of my arm.

"Fuck, I can't, man," I whimpered in frustration.

"Ready?" he asked.

I nodded furiously while keeping my eyes clenched shut. He tapped the vein in my arm twice then pushed the needle in. My eyes rolled behind my closed eyelids from the pain and I tried not to move. Two seconds later I felt him untie the belt and I opened my eyes to see that the needle was already out.

Before I could open my mouth to say anything, a wave of liquid relaxation began at the tip of my head, and slowly made its way down my body. It was as if I'd been trapped in a snowstorm all day, and someone finally placing a heated blanket on top of me. Every place this blanket touched instantly transformed to jelly. Suddenly—every ounce of pain I'd been experiencing for hours was just—gone. It had disappeared, all of it. I felt normal. I felt... amazing.

I began laughing but the sounds were coming out in slow motion. I could see Kayla and Javier looking at each other and smiling. "I think it worked," he said, glancing back at me.

"Duh, told you she'd love it," Kayla said, smiling with satisfaction. She was my best friend, she knew me better than anyone.

"Hoooly shit, you guys. Thank you so much. I thought I was going to die for a minute there. I feel so much better. I work tomorrow, I'll pay you back I promise." I went to stand up and Javier jumped toward me gently placing a hand on my shoulder to keep me in the seat.

"Easy. You may want to give it a minute," he said.

"I'm fine, I'm fine," I assured him as I stood up. I wanted to hug Kayla and thank her for being such a wonderful friend. But when I tried to take a step toward her the world suddenly went black.

I could feel my knees hit the tile and heard a bang as my head fall back into the cabinet. My vision returned, and I could see them drop down next to me to check on me.

"Duuude. I just got so light headed!" I laughed. "I should have listened to you, probably."

"Are you okay?" Kayla asked while checking me for injuries.

"I'm fine. I just wasn't expecting that. Why does that happen?" I asked.

"It's way different than snorting a pill, this goes straight into your bloodstream, it's a lot stronger."

He said, "Yo, Kayla, we gotta go, man, I don't want to be here when her man gets home ya know what I'm sayin'?"

"Are you gonna be okay if we go, Tiff?" she asked standing up and reaching to pull me up.

"I am, yeah, I'm probably just gonna get some sleep, now that I can. I don't want to start shooting this shit all the time, it was just a one-time thing—an emergency. I'm actually gonna try to get some Suboxone tomorrow, I'm sick of doing this shit," I said.

"I hear you, I'm gonna quit soon too. Maybe we can do it together?" she said as she hugged me goodbye.

"That sounds good, friend. I'll call you tomorrow, thanks again. Bye, Javier!" I called behind them.

As soon as the front door shut, I glanced around the kitchen to make sure there wasn't any evidence and headed to the room. It felt like I had run a marathon, the twisting in agony, restless legs and stomach cramps from throwing up had really taken a toll on my body.

I laid down in bed and checked my phone, there was a message from Lazarus.

"Wassup girl, I'm straight, you comin' through?"

"Hell no," I said to myself as I reread the text. I was desperate to stop the pain when I'd sent him that text, I'm fine now. There's no way I'm going over there to hook up with him.

His text got me thinking though, if this stuff goes straight into my bloodstream, it would probably fade off a lot faster. I would be sick again before the sun came up tomorrow. I should probably make a plan to get more now that I'm feeling normal again. My mind began flipping through its rolodex of people I could ask for money. Not my sister, I just borrowed money from her two days ago. I can't ask my dad, he probably has no money.... think, think, think...

Oh, I could ask my friend Meagan. I hadn't talked to her in a while, but she had no clue I did drugs, so the call would seem random, but believable.

"Hey, Tiff! I haven't heard from you in forever!" Meagan said excitedly upon answering.

"I knooow. I've been so freakin' busy with work it's been insane. How are you?" I asked, not really giving a shit how she was.

"I'm great, just working a lot. My mom is sick, so she's been staying with me. She hurt her back."

"Damn, that sucks. I'm so sorry to hear that. Hey, so I have a super random question. No pressure at all, I'm just in a bind. I work tomorrow at 3:00, but I completely freakin' forgot that my power is about to get shut off. They sent a bunch of late notices and I've been so busy it just slipped my mind. They said I have until midnight to pay or we will lose power...Is there ANY way I can borrow like $50 until I get off work tomorrow?"

I felt bad lying to her, but I would feel a lot worse come the morning if I didn't do this. Besides, I could pay her back when I got off tomorrow.

"Aw, friend, of course. You remember where I live, right?" she asked. Thank God.

"Yes I do, oh my God you are a lifesaver, thank you so much...I'm on my way," I said sprinting to the car.

"What's up?" Lazarus said answering his phone.

"Hey! Are you still straight?" I asked.

"Ya."

"Cool, can I come through?"

"For sure, lil' mama." He hung up before I could respond.

As soon as I hung up, my boyfriend's picture popped up on my screen, it was like he was watching me or something. "Hey Babe!" I said cheerfully into the phone.

"Hey, where are you?" he asked. I glanced down at the clock and wondered what he meant. He wasn't supposed to be home for an hour and a half.

"I'm at Walmart. Where are you?" I lied.

"Well I came home an hour early to surprise you with a Redbox movie, but you aren't here."

"No way! Aw, Babe. That's so exciting! I'm leaving now and should be home in like thirty, I'm at the Walmart by the house." God, I was a terrible person. He was doing something nice for me while I was buying drugs. I am such a piece of shit.

"Okay, I'm gonna shower and stuff, I'll see you when you get here."

"Okay, see you soon. Bye."

"Bye."

The guilt was an emotion I'd grown accustomed to. Just about every decision I made in my life was followed with a cloud of guilt. The only way I knew to get rid of the cloud, was to bury it with more drugs. They made it go away, they made everything go away.

As I sped to Laz's, I gripped the money tightly in my hand. I was so grateful that I wouldn't have to worry about getting some tomorrow, these pills I was about to get would hold me over until I got off work tomorrow night.

I gently knocked on the door and as soon as Laz swung it open, I was immediately hit with a cloud of smoke. "Jesus." I said, wafting it away from my face, "are you guys hot-boxing this place or what?" I asked stepping inside behind him.

"Nah, it's just me here. I just hit the bong, you want some?" he asked holding up a ridiculously oversized glass bong. It was the length of his entire body, and I would be in a damn coma if I hit that thing.

"Hell no, thanks." Ever since I'd moved in with Chuck I hardly smoked. It made me too paranoid.

I followed Laz into his room and glanced around as he shut the door behind us. I'd never been in here before, it was surprisingly neat and tidy, not what I expected of a drug dealer.

"So, what you tryin' to do, Mama?" he said, giving me a flirty smile.

"Just two of them please?" I said, staring at the Goodfellas poster above his bed. I didn't know people still hung posters up.

"Aright, aright. Sooo.... What you gonna do for it?"

"What do you mea—" I looked over at him just as he pulled his shirt over his head. Suddenly, I realized what was happening.

"Oh, oh no. No, I have money. I don't need... We don't need to do anything. I can pay. Sorry, I meant to tell you that," I said awkwardly.

His face fell, and he plopped down on to the edge of his bed. "How much you got?"

"Fifty."

"Aight, I'll give you four blues."

"But, fifty only gets me two. I was gonna use the leftover $10 for gas because I'm almost out." I said, feeling confused.

He didn't say anything, he was staring at the floor. Was he gonna hook me up with extra? Because that would be amazing. He did that sometimes on days he was feeling generous. Today must have been one of those days.

"Give me the $50, I'll give you four, and you can give me a 'blow job'," he said matter-of-factly.

"Ah. No, that's okay. Thank you, but I'll just take the t–"

He was lunging toward me before I could finish my sentence. He wrapped his hands around my arms and squeezed so tightly it felt like my bones were breaking.

"Hey!" I screamed trying to wriggle away. "Stop, man. What the hell are you doing?"

His voice softened, and he loosened his grip a bit, but didn't let go. "You said you wanted to hook up, I been thinkin' that's what was finna happen dis whole time, I mean look," he said, grabbing his junk, "you got me all excited."

"Listen, Laz, I'm sorry about this, it's my bad. I should have told you. Maybe we can do this another time. Okay? I just...I have to be somewhere soon, so I don't have time. Let's just do it tomorrow, cool?" I said trying to diffuse the situation.

He let go of my arm and bounded over to his dresser. For a split second I thought for sure he was about to whip out a pistol and force me to have sex with him, instead he opened a baggie and scooped out some pills.

"Here, man. Sorry about grabbing you. I just been wantin' you for a long time you know? It's driving me crazy." He dropped a few pills into my hand and I handed him the fifty.

"I'll call you tomorrow, okay?" I said heading to the door, wanting to run full speed but trying to remain as calm as possible.

"Aight, Momma," he said, looking me up and down as he shut the door behind me.

I sprinted to the car and locked the doors as soon as I got in. I was in shock about what had just occurred. I'd been going to Laz for years and he never tried me like that.

I wanted to tell my boyfriend about it, but obviously, couldn't. I couldn't tell Kayla either because she was best friends with Laz, and she would probably say something that would piss him off. I couldn't tell anyone. I would just have to bury it, like I do every other fucked up thing that has ever happened to me.

As I went to put the pills into the secret compartment of my purse, I realized that Laz had given me seven of them. I was so shaken up in his room I didn't even realize it. I'm not going to lie, it made me feel a little better about the situation.

I pulled out of his driveway and headed down the road, I decided to do a pill before the long drive home, I needed to calm my nerves. I pulled over on a dark side street and crushed quickly crushed one up. I was in a dangerous part of town, but I didn't want to wait until I got into the main part of town to do one, I needed to get fucked up as soon as possible after what just happened.

I quickly snorted the pill and licked the remaining powder off the car manual I'd crushed it up on. As I turned the headlights on and hit the gas, the car didn't move. I pushed the gas again and...nothing.

Panic rose within me as I checked all the lights and switches to see what was happening when suddenly it dawned on me. I never got the $10 from Laz. Oh my God. Chuck was sitting home waiting for me to get back from the store five minutes from our house and I just ran out of gas at midnight in the middle of the ghetto on the opposite side of town... How the hell was I supposed to explain this?

## Chapter Thirty-Six

I paused for a moment trying to get a read on Dr. Danner. I knew she had a flight to Japan this evening, and I didn't want my ramblings to hold her up. It felt as though I had been talking for hours, but in reality, it had been only minutes.

Dr. Danner was looking at me as if she were in the car with me when it wouldn't start. Her face looked terrified, like she was just as screwed as I was in that moment. I didn't even ask if she wanted me to stop this time, I figured she would let me know when she had to go.

I furiously slammed my foot against the gas pedal as Kayla's voicemail picked up for the tenth time in a row. I threw the phone into the passenger seat then pounded the steering wheel out of frustration. What the fuck am I supposed to do? I don't want to call Lazarus, he would probably invite me to stay there—and we all know how that would turn out.

I can't call Chuck, because I'm supposed to be at Walmart five minutes from the house...

Think, Tiffany, think.

I began flipping through my internal Rolodex once again. It's amazing how quickly one's mind can race when it's in "scheme and manipulation" mode. Each person that popped into my head was immediately shot down for various reasons, and each moment that passed made it harder for me to avoid being caught in this predicament.

Suddenly it hit me... Jacob.

Jacob and I used to be best friends, well, the kind of best friends that slept together often. Anyway, I would spend every waking moment with him and if I'm being honest, one of the main reasons was because he was a drug dealer, and he was ridiculously rich.

Jake was born into money and always had everything he ever wanted. Once he became the biggest dealer in my town... The guy had so much money he didn't know what to do with it. He would buy motorcycles for his friends, just so he had people to ride with. We would go to a movie and he would buy every ticket for the row in front of us just so he didn't have to look over people's heads. He was fun to be around, but he was crazy.

I hadn't spoken to him since... Crap. Since I robbed him and ran out of his house with ten pills... Damnit, Tiffany, why can't you just be a normal person, I thought as I dialed his number anyway out of desperation. Maybe he forgot.

My heart pounded as I waited for him to answer.

"Well, well, well. I thought you had my number blocked. I'm amazed you were able to find it after all these years."

"Heeey, Jake, what's up, man," I said sheepishly.

"Oh, not much. Just um, ya know, wondering where the hell my pills are that you stole from me three years ago. I would have asked you a while ago, but... You blocked my number, and you blocked me on Facebook and then...Ya know, moved to another town. So, other than that... not much is up," he said, clearly making his point.

"Listen, Jake, I know. I am so sorry, I never should have done that to you and I feel like a real asshole about it. I have the money, I can pay you back." Liar. I am a liar why the hell did I just tell him that. I don't have $250.00 fucking dollars. What the hell is wrong with me?

He was silent for a while and I could tell he was thinking.

"Tiff, it's not about the money. You hurt me. You were like a sister to me and then you just disappeared."

I tried my best not to be offended after he referred to me as a sister, seeing as how we had done things that normal siblings don't do.

I had to win him over again and I hoped that he would miss me so much that he would be willing to overlook this small blunder on my part.

"No, I know, Jake. Like, when people ask me if I have a brother I'm always like 'yeahhh but...we don't talk anymore it's so sad, ya know? Cuz you're like, totally my bro, bro."

I glanced nervously at the clock and began to panic. I should have been home by now.

"Listen....Jacob, I know you hate me. I don't blame you. But I have no one else to turn to and I'm in a bind. If you can help me out tonight, I will owe you my life. I will pay you back with interest. I'm begging."

I did my best impression of a damsel in distress as I explained my predicament. I told him everything—minus the fact that my boyfriend was a cop—and pleaded with him to bring me a can of gas.

I could hear his engine before I could see his car, but I knew it was him. No one else in this part of town had a car that purred like that. His Lamborghini pulled up beside me and he rolled down his window and smiled.

"Hey, pretty lady, you need a lift?" he joked, in a terrible country accent.

"Shut the hell up and put the gas in before someone steals your car, idiot, you do realize where we are, right? I can't believe you brought that car." He owned so many cars, he could have picked a more inconspicuous choice.

After he finished putting the gas in, he climbed into the passenger seat of my car and shut the door. He had a briefcase on his lap and was smiling at me awkwardly without saying a word. He was probably on shrooms.

"What's... up?" I asked, nervously glancing at the clock. Now was not the time for small talk, I had to fucking go.

"I miss you," he said giving me a puppy dog pout. Jesus Christ. What is this?

"I miss you too, man. Thanks so much for saving me, it really means the wo–"

"Yeah, so on the way over I did some thinkin'" he interrupted. "And, I thought of a way that you could repay me for... well for the money you owe me and for tonight."

Oh God. Here we go. Two guys trying to get me to do sexual favors in one night... This was getting out of hand.

"Look, Jake, I can't do anything with you anymore, okay? I'm in a relationship with a great guy. I told you I could get you the mon–"

"Shhh," he said placing his finger over my lips. "I'm not trying to bang you, don't worry about that. Speaking of, have you been putting on weight? I hear when you get into a relationship you let yourself go but Jesu–"

"Fuck you, Dick. What the hell do you want? Do you want pills? I just got like ten of them, you can have a couple, I just need like four for tomorrow." I was growing more and more impatient by the minute and just wanted him out. And now I felt fat on top of everything else.

"Here's what you are gonna do," he said, sitting up straight. "I'm giving this briefcase to you. You are in charge of it. You need to get rid of everything that's inside it and once you do, you will not only have made enough money to pay me back, you will also have a couple hundred left over for yourself. Sound good?"

"Um, well no. Not really. It doesn't sound good at all, actually. What the hell is in there?" I asked.

"Just take it, open it when you get home. I'll text you the code to unlock it once you get to your house," he said opening the passenger door.

"No, dude, this is weird, and sounds complicated and... I'll just give you the money, okay? I'll pay you interest for the um... years that have passed since I took your stuff."

"Nope. I'd like you to take the suitcase. It would be helping me a great deal, and it would also make me feel better because it would show that you genuinely do care about our friendship. I'm leaving it here," he said, standing up out of the car.

"No thanks."

"Yes."

"No."

"Yes."

"What the hell is this 'Deal or No Deal?' I don't want the fucking briefcase. Listen, I have a feeling I know what's inside and honestly, I can't mess with stuff like that. I didn't tell you before but... My boyfriend, he's actually in Law Enforcement, so I gotta be really careful what I do," I said, knowing damn well the minute he heard that he would run for the hills.

He laughed.

"You think I don't know your boyfriend is a cop, Tiff? It's a small town, everyone knows. All the more reason for you to take it," he said with a devilish smile.

"What the hell? That doesn't make sense. Why is the fact that my boyfriend is a cop, more of a reason for me to take your illegal briefcase of– God knows what?" I asked, desperate to go home.

"Because, I have been recording our entire encounter," he said pulling out his cell phone and waving it at me. I could see the big red record button. Just above it read 15:23 minutes, "so if you don't take this shit and get rid of it for me, I'll have no choice but to let him listen to it. He will probably be surprised don't you think? I mean you're a pretty good liar, just look at how you lied and pretended you missed me just so I'd help you. You are a user, a thief, and a liar. It sucks it has to be like this, but I've been hurt for a lot of years, Tiff, now it's your turn." He slammed my door shut... and walked away.

I stared out my windshield in shock and listened as his Lambo started up and peeled away. It wasn't until my phone rang that I snapped back to reality and realized I had somewhere to be.

"Shit. Hey Babe, I'm so sorry. I'm on my way now. The lines were so long and then my card wouldn't work and for some reason my car wasn't starting but I got some chick to jump it and ... whew. I'm on my way. I need a hug when I get home, okay?" I said. The last part was true. I needed someone to hold me and tell me everything was going to be okay because right now it felt like everything was falling apart.

As I reached for the handle of the front door of my home, it swung open and Chuck was standing there with a sympathetic look on his face. "Come here, Baby. I am so sorry you had a bad night." His hug momentarily made everything disappear. I took a deep breath inside of his embrace and desperately wished that I were someone else, anyone else. I wished I could be normal, he deserved normal. I hated myself and wanted desperately to crawl into a hole and never come out.

"What's in the briefcase?"

His question sent a shiver down my spine and I gripped the handle tightly in the palm of my hand. "Oh...it's, my boss, Kathy, the female manager bought it for me. She said I could use it for the deposits and stuff at work." I lied.

"Well look at you, Miss Business Woman Pants. I made some popcorn and have the movie ready whenever you are," he said following me inside.

"Awesome. Just give me one second. I want to pee and change into something comfy."

I texted Jacob as I entered the bedroom and shut the door behind me. I was pulling my pajama shirt over my head I heard my text message alert go off. My heart started racing, he had sent me the code.

I opened the text and read:

"Thanks again for all your help, great catching up. Hope to hear from you soon. 669."

I threw the phone down on the bed and picked up the briefcase. I didn't know what was inside, but I knew I had no choice but to look. I was still in shock about the whole interaction, mainly because I thought I was the one doing the manipulating. In actuality, he had one up on me the entire time.

I shut the bathroom door behind me and sat on top of the toilet seat. "What the hell have I gotten myself into?" I said, pulling the leather briefcase up onto my lap. My hands shook as I fumbled to line the numbers up on the combination lock. 6... 6... Deep breath... 9. "*Click.*"

Chapter Thirty-Seven

The briefcase squeaked as I pulled it open, I already knew what was inside before I looked. But the moment my eyes fell onto its contents and my suspicions were confirmed, I couldn't help but gasp.

I slammed the lid shut immediately and took a deep breath. My heart was pounding, and the room began to spin, this can't be real.

I opened the lid slightly and peered inside. Hundreds of little plastic baggies were thrown in haphazardly, a kaleidoscope of illegal substances. There were countless bags of Roxicodone – my drug of choice–and each bag contained about 10 pills. There were also baggies filled with a white substance which I can only assume was cocaine, as well as weed and other pills I didn't recognize.

I was sitting in a cop's house, with a briefcase full of thousands of dollars' worth of pills on my lap. Even if I wanted to sell all this, I wouldn't know where to begin—and it would take me years to get rid of all of it. Did Jacob seriously think I was going to ride around town slinging drugs out of my damn trunk? Jesus, what if I got caught with this thing? I could see it now; "Cop's girlfriend arrested with 6 billion pounds of narcotics."

This was bad. This was really bad. A few hours ago, I was withdrawing on my kitchen floor and wanting to die, then I was injected with drugs for the first time, almost molested by my drug dealer, ran out of gas in the ghetto and rescued by an old friend who forced me to take a suitcase filled with a pharmacy's worth of drugs. What the hell kind of Twilight Zone episode had my life become?

I tucked the briefcase into the closet under a pile of clothes and headed out to the living room where Chuck was waiting patiently; a bowl of popcorn in his lap and the movie paused. He picked a movie titled "Sinister", how fitting.

Two weeks had passed since I'd acquired the briefcase and I must say–I was doing surprisingly well unloading the merchandise. I had researched "How to Be A Good Drug Dealer" and learned some pretty neat tips, the most helpful being that people would buy more, if you offered them a discounted rate for buying in bulk. I had gone straight to Lazarus and made him an offer he couldn't refuse. I'm not gonna lie, it felt pretty awesome slingin' drugs out of my leather suitcase– I considered asking people to start calling me Pablina Escobar, but didn't want to get ahead of myself.

Also, I'm pretty sure Pablo Escobar never injected himself with his own supply. I knew it was going to happen the minute I saw all those bags in the case. I'm an addict for God's sake.

It's like giving a kid an ice cream cone, and telling him not to eat it.

I wasn't planning on shooting up again, but Kayla said she tried shooting up a Roxie and it was way better than snorting it. So, naturally, believing one must try everything once before completely ruling it out—I gave it a shot (no pun intended.) I didn't enjoy it as much as I enjoyed my first time with the Dilaudid, but I found that when I injected the drugs, I didn't need to do as much. It was a smart financial move on my part to give up snorting the drugs.

I was already in debt before receiving the briefcase and now the debt had tripled. I needed to come up with a plan—and quick—before I was forced to leave the country and hide from Jacob for the rest of my life.

"If we were to get a puppy, what kind would you want to get?" Chuck asked, scrolling through pictures of dogs on the phone.

"A small, cute, fluffy one. Preferably one that doesn't poop." I replied. I had been begging Chuck for a puppy for a long time since I'd never had a pet of my own. He always refused, but I finally got him to cave. We were leaving the house in an hour and returning with a new member of the family. I couldn't wait.

My phone buzzed on the table and as I went to reach for it Chuck stopped me. "That better not be work trying to get you to come in, this is our only day off together. Plus, we are puppy shopping," he said giving me an annoyed face.

"Stoppp. It's not work, and even if it is, I'll tell them I can't. I've been wanting a dog forever, you think I'd leave to go get yelled at by customers?" I said opening the text.

From: Kendra.

"Hey girl, I know we haven't talked since I left for maternity leave. But Jett told me you had gotten some green for him, and I was wondering if you could get me some Blues. I need 50. I'll give you $35 apiece. Let me know."

"Babe… I gotta go," I said jumping up from the couch. Chuck's face fell, and he looked both confused and frustrated. "I'm sorry, honey, it's an emergency. One of the managers got sick and had to go home. They don't have anyone else. I'll be gone two hours tops. I promise, then we can go to the pet store. I'm so sorry," I said kissing his forehead and running into the bedroom before he could respond.

I grabbed five baggies and shoved them into my bra while quickly throwing on my work clothes. I know it was wrong for me to lie to him. But honestly, I couldn't pass up this offer. Blues go for $20 apiece and this idiot was desperate enough to pay double. If I had any chance of paying Jake back the money—I had to go, and I had to go now.

Thirty minutes later I was in her driveway. I remembered where it was from the night I dropped her off after blackmailing her into giving me five of her pills. I didn't even feel bad about it, she was poisoning the twins in her belly and didn't give a shit. She knew she was wrong, and that's probably why she had no problem reaching out to me for these.

The front door swung open and I saw Kendra smiling and holding one of her babies. I couldn't believe how thin she'd gotten. Clearly, she hadn't cut back on the drugs.

"Hey, Kendra," I said as I approached, "who's this little guy?"

"This is Liam, his sister is sleeping so... shhh." She tiptoed into the house and I followed closely behind. If I'm being honest, I was almost certain that Child Protective Services would have taken her babies away the minute she popped them out, considering that she had 500 pills on her at any given time. Liam looked... surprisingly healthy for a baby born addicted to drugs.

"Where's your grandma?" I asked looking around as she shut the door behind me.

"My grandma? What are you talking about?" she asked looking puzzled.

"Yeah, your Grandma, Grams or whatever. The lady who was gonna beat me up. That night I dropped you off here you said she wasn't going to be happy with me."

She started rocking Liam suddenly and 'shushing' him, which was weird because he wasn't even crying. "He's getting fussy, I'm gonna go lay him down," she said turning and heading down the hallway. Maybe she had super Mom powers and could tell when her baby was about to get fussy, because he looked fine to me. Weird.

Once she was out of sight, I began surveying the living room. There were dirty diapers and cigarette butts littering the floor, and I suddenly felt so sad for these babies. Not only was their mother an addict, but they had to live in this fil–...

"Hey bitch," The man's voice interrupted my thought process and I spun on my heels to face him.

Kendra was nowhere in sight, neither were the babies. It was a large African-American man, maybe 6ft 3 wearing a wife beater and jeans.

"Oh. Hello," I said, confused as to who the hell he was and why he was calling me a 'bitch'. He stepped closer, and that was when I noticed the gun tucked into his waistband.

"Sit down," he ordered, pointing to the couch.

Not wanting to argue with an armed man, I reluctantly headed to couch and sat down slowly. I glanced around nervously for Kendra thinking this was some sort of a mistake, but she was nowhere to be found.

"So, you the Trick that stole from me? Huh?" he said menacingly, stepping closer. Trick, doesn't that mean, prostitute? What the hell...

"Wait, what? Okay, clearly this is some sort of a mistake. I don't even know you. And I'm certainly not a prostitute." I was relieved once I realized he had the wrong person. "Where's Kendra?" I asked glancing past him.

"Don't worry about Kendra, BITCH. She ain't your friend."

He slid one of the kitchen chairs across the room and slammed it down in front of me. He plopped down into it, releasing his gun from his waistband and setting it flat on his lap. My heart was pounding out of my chest and I was struggling to breathe. I was pretty sure I was about to die.

"Listen...Sir. I feel like there is a misunderstanding. Kendra called and asked me to bring her some–"

"Shut the fuck up. This is how it's gonna go down. You came here with 50 pills, right? Guess what? They're mine now. Hand 'em over," he said leaning forward and sticking his hand out. I suddenly realized what was going on. I was getting robbed.

I wanted to speak, but something inside me told me it would only make it worse.

"Hand them the fuck over, NOW!" he screamed. It looked like his eyes were about to pop out of his head, he looked scary as shit. I jumped in response to his yell and began fumbling around in my bra for the bag of pills. Pablo Escobar would have shot this guy by now... I handed over the bag and he snatched it from my hand.

"See you thought you were all 'big and bad' because you were the 'manager' of a fucking restaurant? You thought that gave you power? You don't know the first thing about fucking power. What the hell is wrong with you, stealing from a damn pregnant woman."

His voice was so deep and so loud it vibrated my chest as he spoke.

"Yeah. I know all about what happened between you and her," he said, leaning forward in the chair and lowering his voice. "See, Kendra was married to my brother and he up and left her, pregnant and alone. I felt bad and told her she could live with me—on one condition. She helps me out. Kendra doesn't even do pills you stupid cunt. You think she would risk her babies lives? My niece and nephew? She loves them more than anything."

I sank into the couch as the realization of what was happening set in. I felt like I was going to pass out.

"Those pills weren't hers," he continued, "she was just the messenger. She gets the pills from her dad, and brings them to me. The pills you forced her to give you? They were MINE."

I opened my mouth to speak and he held his hand up to stop me.

"You lucky I don't kill you where you sit, girl. If it wasn't for Kendra telling me to take it easy on you—you'd be dead and buried in the back yard, I don't fuck around bout mine. Get yo ass up, and get the hell out of my damn house. Now."

I jumped up from the couch and ran toward the door. Out of the corner of my eye I saw Kendra emerge from one of the bedrooms and into the hallway rocking her baby. I couldn't help but feel foolish. I had chastised her for being a terrible mother and the pills weren't even hers, she didn't do drugs.

When I pulled the front door open, my eyes were locked on my car, preparing to run full speed the second I stepped outside. Before I left, I heard the man's cell phone ring and when he answered, everything suddenly made sense.

"Yo, this is Grams... what's up."

My adrenaline was exploding like fireworks inside my body and I needed to get high to calm the hell down. I was set up, and I almost died.

I pulled into a McDonalds and parked under a tree. My windows were tinted enough that I could do a shot right here and no one would ever know. My hands trembled as I pulled the syringe and spoon from my purse. I smashed a pill into powder on one of my cd cases and dropped the powder into the spoon. Before I could mix it up, my phone rang.

Shit, it was Chuck.

"Hey Babe," I said, trying my best not to sound like I'd just escaped certain death.

"Hey," he said abruptly.

"What's up?"

There was silence on the other end.

"Hello?" I said, mixing up the solution and uncapping the syringe.

"Where you at?" he asked.

"I'm still at work, I should be done soon. What's up?" I tied the belt around my arm and began growing impatient. He needed to hurry up and spit it out, so I could do this before I lost my damn mind.

"Just wondering. It's weird though, because... I came here to get something to eat and figured we could just leave for the pet store straight from here. But, guess what?"

Chills suddenly crept up my spine. I dropped the syringe into the passenger seat and covered my mouth with my hand.

"Your manager said you're not here, he actually said they never texted you to come in. So... I'll ask you again. Where are you?"

Chapter Thirty-Eight

I was so grateful that Chuck was confronting me over the phone, because my face immediately flushed with embarrassment. He had caught me red-handed, smack dab in the middle of a big fat lie. Part of me wanted to hang up immediately and pretend I'd lost service, but I knew that would be too obvious.

The thing about my addiction is, it has enabled me to be the record holder for "The most believable lies ever told" as well as "Quickest thinker during times of distress." It was as if there were no limits to my lies, because my moral compass had broken a long time ago. Therefore, I was able to say the wildest shit without feeling bad about it. I had to do whatever was necessary to keep this dark side of me hidden – and this time was no different.

"I lied, I'm sorry," I said.

"Yeah, no shit," he said, "Sooo, what the hell are you doing then?"

Here we go.

"Babe, it's bad. I didn't want to tell you because I knew you'd be upset," I said.

I still had no clue where I was going with this story just yet, but I decided to just wing it.

"What's bad? Where are you? Can you just tell me?" he said sounding distraught.

My heart was pounding, and I blurted the first thing that came to mind.

"It's Kayla."

"Jesus Christ."

"I know. See, I knew you'd be upset, this is why I didn't want to tell you. Kayla texted to tell me goodbye. She said she had a gun to her head and had enough. She didn't want to live anymore. I told her to give me five minutes, that I wanted to hug her goodbye before she left. Babe, I knew if I told you, you would have called the police or something and she would have been dead before they arrived. I'm so sorry for lying, I didn't have a choice. I knew that I would be the only one able to stop her."

He was silent for a moment on the other end of the phone. I was feeling pretty damn proud of myself. This was one of those lies that he couldn't refute, because there was no way for him to prove whether or not it happened. All I had to do was text Kayla the minute I got off the phone with him and she would go along with it in a heartbeat.

"I wouldn't have called the police, Tiff. Although she probably needs to be Baker Acted, but I would have respected your wishes to let you handle it. I don't want you to feel like you can't talk to me about things. We are working on building trust, remember?"

I breathed a sigh of relief. He bought it. I should have felt bad in that moment, I'd left my faithful boyfriend on date-night to do a drug deal, that went horribly wrong – and then used the potential death of a friend to get myself out of a lie. What kind of person does that?

An addict... that's who.

"Tiffany, I hate to stop you there, but we have to wrap this up," Dr. Danner said closing her folder and sliding it into her briefcase. She stood up and silently began gathering her belongings, careful to avoid eye contact.

Usually when she decided it was time to end our session, she gave me some encouraging words or thought-provoking questions pertaining to what I'd just shared. This time, she didn't even look at me.

"Is everything okay?" I asked, wondering if perhaps she'd finally realized I was the biggest piece of shit on earth, unworthy of her time.

She stopped what she was doing, and peered at me for a moment before dropping her arms to her sides and letting out a sigh.

"Tiffany, you trust me... don't you?"

"Of course I do, why?" My heart began pounding.

"It's just. When I first ask clients 'what brought you to rehab', usually they give me a short explanation of their childhood experiences, then their drug use, followed by some sort of catastrophic event that led to them coming here." My eyes followed her as she slowly paced back and forth as she spoke.

"With you... it's almost as if you began telling a story—a fantasy if you will. I've been doing this a long time and I am familiar with avoidance habits. I get the impression that you are afraid of being transparent with me. So, you created this—incredible story, to distract yourself from the reality of what happened."

It suddenly felt as if the wind had been knocked out of me. Shock and anger began to overwhelm me...I was speechless. She must have noticed, because she began speaking once again, softer and more carefully this time.

"I am not trying to upset you, okay? I just feel like it's important that we start dealing with truth from this point on."

I stared at her—through her, unsure of how to respond. She thinks I've been making all of this up?

I stood up and peered at her. "Are you kidding me? Over the past couple of days, I've spent hours with you – HOURS— and you are telling me that you let me continue talking, all the while you were convinced that everything I was saying was a lie?! Even if it was—which, it's friggin' not— why the hell would you sit there nodding in agreement, instead of stopping me?" I was baffled and honestly, incredibly offended. I too began pacing, because the fury raging inside me was too big to remain stationary. I didn't even wait for her to answer my question.

"I thought we were connecting, I was feeling better, I thought you fucking cared. I am so stupid. I should have known that you are just like everyone else. You don't give a shit about me, I'm just another psychotic junkie living in an alternate reality." I was beside myself. This felt so unfair.

"Tiffany, please calm down. It's okay to feel angry, but you must know it isn't helping."

"What the hell do you know about helping? Huh? Do you know what you've done? You were the first person I've trusted in a long time and now – I feel like I'm a patient in a psych ward."

"Now, Tiffany, I never sai–"

"You didn't have to. I have told you things I haven't told anyone." I shook my head furiously and balled my fist as the uncontrollable anger began taking over. I wanted to scream at the top of my lungs, but I knew that would further prove her point about me being a lunatic.

"Stop. You have to understand where I'm coming from. Okay? I am sure that some of what you have shared with me is true, however I also believe some if it has been exaggerated. I have had many patients experience a form of psychosis after trauma causing them to manifest scenarios that never actually occurred."

"Oh my God." I needed to leave. I needed to get out of this room, because I was seconds away from wrapping my hands around her throat and strangling her.

"I'm done," I said marching toward the door.

"No."

"No what?"

"No. We cannot be done. I see that you are upset and don't want you storming out of here filled with resentment toward me, it will upset the other girls."

"Upset the other...you have got to be fucking kidding me." I laughed, swinging the door open so hard that it banged into the metal table. "I resent you, Dr. Danner!" I screamed over my shoulder storming out of the room.

Fuck her, fuck this place – fuck being clean. I try to do the right thing once, tell the truth once, and I still get accused of being a liar. What's the fucking point of trying?

I wasn't meant to live a normal life. I wasn't a normal person. I was a psychotic junkie loser and that's all I would ever be.

Most people are good at life, it's effortless for them. They go grocery shopping, pay their bills, go for walks. Hell, some people even bird-watch. They literally sit around and watch birds with binoculars. I can't even go ten minutes without jamming drugs into my veins and have no clue how to function without them.

I am not sure why the hell I was put on this earth, what my purpose was supposed to be, but I don't have the energy to figure it out. Living is too hard... dying would be so much easier.

I knew that by leaving this facility, I would be arrested and sent to prison for like forty years, but I didn't give a damn. At least in prison people wouldn't pretend to give a shit about me before stabbing me in the back. I stood at the front door for a moment, considering the consequences of what I was about to do. I took a deep breath... and walked out.

I inhaled the night air deep into my lungs as the gravel crunched under my sneakers. I made it to the end of the driveway and paused, realizing I'd forgotten my cigarettes on the picnic table. I stood there for a moment debating on whether to risk going back and someone stopping me. But I knew I couldn't make a proper plan without calming my nerves. I turned around and before I could take a step—bumped into someone and my heart dropped to my knees.

It was Ryanne.

"What the hell are you doing?" she asked calmly.

"Don't. Move Ryanne, please. I'm leaving."

"Why?" she asked indifferently.

"Because I don't belong here. I don't belong anywhere. Honestly, being alive hurts too much. I'm not good at life and I never asked for it. That's the worst part. I never fucking asked for this. My mom chose to have me, then she went and fucking died and left me here to fend for myself, I can't do it anymore. I give up." The last sentence came out in sobs as I collapsed to my knees in the gravel driveway.

Ryanne gently placed her hand on my back and I lost all control.

It was as if a lifetime of sadness suddenly exploded out of every pore and I was slowly emptying myself into a puddle in the driveway.

"I don't want to live anymore, Ryanne," I said into the shells on the ground.

She didn't say a word. She sat down next to me and crossed her legs, keeping her hand on my back. "That fucking doctor called me a liar. She listened to me talk for two days and finally, before hopping on a flight to Japan said she thinks 'I'm fucking psychotic and hallucinating," I said through tears.

"I hate that lady," she whispered.

I sniffled as I sat up and looked at her. "What?"

Ryanne smiled and nodded. "I do, I actually hate her guts. I've never liked her. She honestly might not even be a doctor, I'm not sure. My aunt has known her forever, that's the only reason she works here."

"Your aunt?" I asked feeling confused.

"Yeah, Felicity – the owner. She's my aunt. I've lived with her since I was a baby. After I ended up getting addicted to drugs in my teens, she decided to start a rehab center. Said it broke her heart to see young girls losing their lives. So here we are," she said gesturing toward the building.

"Do you know that I haven't even had a normal day here?" I said wiping tears away with my sleeve. "Like... Not one class, not one meeting – nothing. Other than when I went to the computer shop and met with my dad and sister, I've basically been with her or sleeping."

"Hold on," she said standing up suddenly. "She's kept you out of classes?"

I nodded.

"You haven't been to a meeting?"

I shook my head.

I could see the anger and confusion on Ryanne's face, and wondered what the hell was going on.

"If I leave you here for a second, can you promise me you won't leave?" she asked.

"No, I can't promise you that. I don't want to be here," I said standing up. I wanted to get high, and now that the thought was in my head, it was too late.

"There is so much for you to do here, you haven't even begun. That bitch should never have kept you out of classes and in a minute, I'm going to go in there and break her legs so she can't fly to Guatemala."

"Japan." I laughed.

"Whatever. Japan. Please, give me one more day. I'll tell you what. You and I can bring mattresses into the office and have a sleepover in there. We can stay up all night talking and eating popcorn and I won't judge you– I promise. I'll tell you about the time I let a homeless guy grab my boob for a hit of coke. Please don't leave," she pleaded.

I laughed, hard. I wasn't expecting it either. Usually once I get into a depressed mood it's like a landslide, there's no stopping it until everything around me is destroyed. But Ryanne's wit seemed to pull me out of my funk somehow.

She smiled and poked my cheek. "See, you are cheering up already. Stay out here as long as you need, smoke a cigarette, whatever. I'm gonna go talk to Dr. Douchebag and get our campout set up—okay?"

I took a deep breath. A sleepover sounded much better than going to jail, and it felt good to have someone on my side. I decided to give it one more day and see how things went and if I still wanted to leave in the morning, I would.

I gave her a little smile and nodded.

"Yes! Awesome. Okay, I'll see you inside," she said jogging away.

As I inhaled a drag of my cigarette, I stared up at the moon. I missed my mom, and I knew she was probably doing a happy dance in the clouds once I'd made the decision to give this another shot. I had so many emotions swirling through my head at once that it was impossible to process any of them. I wanted to die, but I wanted to live. I wanted to be clean, but I wanted to get high. I wanted to be normal, but I didn't have the energy to try. I was broken, in desperate need of repair.

As strange and unorthodox as the past couple of days at this rehab had been so far, I knew that this was the best place for me. If I had any chance of living life differently than I had, I needed to stay here long enough to hear something that made sense.

Chapter Thirty-Nine

"Okay girls, I'm leaving in five minutes, if you're not in the van- I'm leaving your asses here," I joked, heading out the door.

It had been two months since I'd almost left, and so many things had happened since that night. If Ryanne hadn't followed me out, I would probably be dead by now.

The day after I tried to leave, Ryanne put me in charge of driving the girls to the morning meeting. Everyone thought she was crazy since I was fresh out of jail and newly clean – but there was a method to her madness.

She knew something about me that even I didn't know about myself. She knew that by giving me a responsibility as great as this one, it would renew my sense of self-worth, self-reliance and self-respect. I didn't think anyone would ever trust me again after the things I'd done, so to be responsible for transporting eleven addicts in a van to and from a meeting – was huge. It made me feel good—needed—and I hadn't felt that way in a long time.

"Shotgun!" Rhonda yelled, pushing past everyone and jumping into the front seat next to me. "Haaay giiirl," she said slamming the door and reaching for the radio dial. Rhonda was a beautiful Jamaican goddess with an incredible soul, and she was one of my best friends. She flipped the radio to a rap song and peered over at me out of the corner of her eye with a rebellious smirk.

"Rhonda. Felicity said no rap music. Can you at least wait until we pull out of the driveway to start breaking the rules?" I laughed.

With driving; came responsibilities and unfortunately it often put me in a position to "mother" the other girls. Since I was the one driving, I was technically "in charge" when we left the center, which was a strange place to be for someone who was technically a client in the program.

"Boo, you're no fun." She pouted, flipping it to a Christian station.

"Everybody in?" I asked, putting the van in reverse. Most of the girls were half asleep, so I took their silence as confirmation that everyone was accounted for. We slowly pulled out of the driveway and the minute the tires hit the main road, Rhonda had Ludacris blaring from the speakers and was dancing wildly in the front seat.

"There they are!" Bill said greeting us as we sauntered into the morning meeting and found our seats. I smiled at all the familiar faces in the room and was overcome with gratitude. 7:30 a.m. every morning we stepped foot into this room. It was the same friendly faces, same lukewarm coffee and same hope being shared before the sun even rose for the day.

It was so nice to be in a routine after years of living spontaneously, compulsively and dangerously. Many of the old-timers accused me of being on a "pink cloud," a sense of euphoric bliss that a lot of "newcomers" experience upon finding recovery.

But I knew it was more than that.

I knew that for the first time, in a long time – I was making progress, and it felt damn good.

"I'm Steve, and I'm an addict," Steve said after raising his hand to share. Steve was in his seventies and always shared first. It was as if he prepared an amazing speech every morning to present to all of us and his words always had a way of putting everything into perspective for me.

"I look at these young girls over here, man," he said pointing to our row, "and I can't help but feel a bit envious. I'm 71 years old. I've got five years clean. I used for fifty years. I missed so damn much. I missed everything." His voice broke and I could tell he was getting emotional.

"I lost my wife once she finally got sick enough of my shit. My kids are adults and haven't spoken to me in over twenty years—hell—I got grandbabies I ain't even met." He stared down at the table for a moment, you could hear a pin drop in that room. When he finally looked up, he looked straight at me and stared into my eyes.

"Man, I'll tell you what.... I would give anything in this world, to go back in time, and enter these rooms when I was your fucking age. Then I might actually have something to look back on and be proud of. You girls are young enough now to get it right, to have a life and make something of yourself. Don't do what I did. Get it now so that you aren't my age looking back on your life and thinking damn...I wasted all of it."

It felt like I'd suddenly been struck by lightning. Tears began welling in my eyes as I processed what he'd just said. I imagined what it would be like to have waited until I was an old woman to get clean – if I made it that long. I imagined my children being adults and never speaking to me. The loneliness, the guilt... for what? A momentary high?

Never in my life had anyone's words saturated my skin and seeped into my soul like his just did.

I could hear other members voices mumbling as they shared their own bits of wisdom, but all I could do was replay in my head what Steve had said.

That was it. That was the moment.

Steve's words changed my life that day. The universe had carefully devised a grand plan to align our paths so we both ended up in the same room that day. Whatever higher power was out there, knew that I needed to hear what that man had just said.

As we all entered the house after the meeting I glanced at the clock and realized we had fifteen minutes before we had to leave for the computer shop. At first, I had been baffled by the idea that as rehab patients, we were required to work on computers and sell them. But as time went on and I'd seen how much money they had generated for the program – it began to make sense.

"Tiff, don't forget you have an appointment with Kelly at 11:00 a.m.," Anastacia, the house mother reminded me.

"Aw crap, I totally forgot. Thank God you reminded me."

"Yeah, I figured you did, Forgetful Frannie." She laughed.

"Hey Anastacia, you think it would be cool if I headed back a few minutes early? I really gotta go to the bathroom," I whispered.

"You gotta take a shit you mean?" she yelled at the top of her lungs over her shoulder.

"You're an Asshole," I laughed, shaking my head.

"Of course you can go, it's not like you are doing anything productive around here anyway," she joked.

I crumpled a piece of paper and threw it at her just as she closed the door.

I was lost in thought as I walked back to the house. Today was my first appointment with Kelly, the new counselor who had taken Dr. Danner's place.

Just before I made it to the driveway a police car drove past me.

It was as if time slowed down and the world was suddenly in slow motion. I followed the car with my eyes, fearing that perhaps it was Chuck. I was relieved to find a woman behind the wheel, but then my heart dropped once I realized... I knew her.

I thought back to the last time I'd seen Sharla, the officer in the car, and was immediately overcome with shame and sadness at the memory.


"How do I look?" I asked, pushing the Aviator sunglasses up on the bridge of my nose.

"Like a dork," Chuck said leaning down to kiss my forehead.

"Heyyy," I said, pretending to be hurt, "today is a big day...I have to look the part."

I could see the concern on Chuck's face. He had been putting this day off since the beginning of our relationship.

"You ready?" I asked with an eager smile.

"Babe, I hope you realize this isn't a joke. It's serious. I feel like you think it's a game," he said.

"Stoppp. I know it's not a game, okay? I'm taking this super seriously. Besides, I watch cops all the time...I know what I'm doing," I said putting my hair up into a ponytail.

"Shut the hell up and get in the car." He laughed, locking the front door behind us.

"For real though, I have a serious question," I said, sliding into the front seat of the patrol car.

"What?" he asked.

"Yes or no. If necessary, am I allowed to tase somebody?"

He tried to keep from laughing as he shook his head and pressed a button on his two-way radio.

A lady on the other end chirped back and said something I couldn't understand. He looked over at me and held his finger up to his lips to shush me before pushing his button to reply. "221, status, active." He put the car in reverse and slowly pulled out of the driveway.

"Alright, boys!" I yelled while slapping the roof, "let's catch some mothafuckin' bad guys!!"

I had been begging Chuck for years to take me on a ridealong. His answer was always a firm "no." He said it was too dangerous and that if something went wrong, and I was hurt he would never be able to forgive himself. I finally convinced him during a drunken heart to heart one night, and despite his best efforts to recant his statement, I assured him that he'd pinkie promised and those were sacred.

We had been driving around for three hours with no action. I had secretly hoped that by now we would have arrested three prostitutes and thwarted two bank robberies. Unfortunately, however, we had only responded to one call and it was an old lady who got scratched by a neighbor's cat and wanted to press charges.

She claimed the woman "sent" her cat to attack the old lady on purpose because the woman sprayed it with a hose when it was in her yard once. Chuck decided there was no way to prove this and called paramedics to check her out.

"I have to swing by the station to turn in my ride along slip, you want to wait out here or come in?" he asked pulling up to the front and parking.

"I'll come in, I've never seen the inside of a police station before, it sounds exciting," I said hopping out.

When we entered the main lobby, I immediately began scanning for a restroom. "Hey Sharla! This is my girlfriend, Tiffany," Chuck said introducing me to the pretty blonde sitting behind the counter.

"Hey Tiffany! Nice to finally meet you, Chuck has told me all about you." She stood up to shake my hand and smiled, revealing a row of perfect teeth.

Chuck was not allowed to be friends with this woman anymore I suddenly decided, she was way too pretty.

"Hi! Pleasure to meet you. Hopefully all good things." I laughed. Of course it was good things, he didn't know that I was actually a psychopathic drug addict...not yet anyway.

"Babe, I gotta pee...where's the bathroom?" I asked peering around.

"Right over there, past the 'Faces of Meth' poster," he said pointing down the hall. I excused myself and made my way down the hall pausing for a moment at the poster.

I looked at the small, square, "before and after" pictures of people, and couldn't help but feel sorry for them. They looked normal once, they were regular people. Something terrible happened in their lives between the first and second picture and they were virtually unrecognizable, droopy-eyed and covered in scars.

"Thank God I never got that bad," I said to myself as I opened the bathroom door.

I immediately made my way to the stall, having been trapped in the patrol car with Chuck for hours I'd begun to feel achy and nauseous. I locked the metal bar on the door and sat backwards on the toilet seat facing the wall. Using the sleeve of my shirt I wiped the toilet lid to make sure it was clean before pulling out my supplies.

Slowly setting the spoon down, I was careful not to make a 'clink' as it hit the ceramic toilet lid. I quickly crushed up the pill and put it into the spoon, adding a splash of water from the sink and mixing it up. As I pulled the mixture up into the barrel of the syringe, I couldn't help but laugh to myself.

*I bet I'm the first person in history to shoot up in the employee bathroom of the police station,* I thought as I tightened my belt around my biceps. Life had gotten so much easier once Javier taught Kayla and I to do this ourselves. I still wasn't sure how I was going to explain to Jacob how the majority of his supply was missing – with no money to show for it—but I would figure it out. For now, I had to hurry up and do this shot because my boyfriend was waiting.

I slid the tip into my skin and once I heard the "pop' of it entering my vein, I pulled back on the plunger a bit to confirm it was in. The blood from my vein danced up into the barrel and I immediately pushed the drugs into my bloodstream.

Once the barrel was empty I pulled it out, capped the needle and removed the belt.

I sat still for a moment as the liquid made its way through my bloodstream, massaging every cell in my body and relaxing me into bliss. This was the greatest feeling I had ever experienced in my life – and it only lasted about fifteen seconds.

The minute it was over, I craved it again. I lived for those fifteen seconds. In those seconds it felt like a wave had come through my body and when it left, it had taken all my worries and fears with it back out to sea. It was a miracle drug and I instantly felt better, normal, no longer sick, and ready to take on the world.

Before leaving the bathroom, I stared at myself in the mirror for a moment. I didn't recognize the reflection of the person staring back at me. My entire existence was a lie, every word out of my mouth – a lie. I was a con-artist.

I had been wearing a mask for years and the man on the other side of the door had no idea that he was in love with a thieving, lying, drug addict. I hated myself, who I'd become. I wish I could just quit this shit. But the thought of going through withdrawals was terrifying, I'd rather die than have to ever feel that pain.

"You ready?" Chuck asked as I entered the lobby. "I just got a call, apparently some junkie overdosed in the Walmart parking lot."

"Jesus, when the hell will these people learn?" I asked, shaking my head and waving goodbye to Sharla.

Chapter Forty

On our way to the overdose call, I couldn't help but think how ironic it was that I currently had a fresh batch of narcotics coursing through my veins.

This person did the same exact thing I had just done five minutes before, except for them– it was the last thing they would ever do. I stared out the window and wondered what the person must have been thinking. Maybe there were going to shop in Walmart but needed a fix first so the cold air hitting them as they entered the store wasn't excruciatingly painful.

Maybe they were having a bad day and just needed to forget, or maybe they had a great day and paused to do a celebratory hit.

Whatever the reason, I am certain that they did not know that they wouldn't be leaving their car ever again. That the driver's seat would be the final place they took a breath. When that person dressed themselves this morning, they had no clue that it would be the last outfit they ever wore.

Jesus, I need to stop thinking about it, it's totally killing my buzz.

As we pulled up to scene of the overdose, I noticed the vehicle was surrounded with yellow caution tape. My mom used to decorate the front of our house with it on Halloween and it was so eerie to see it in real life.

"Why don't you stay here for a minute, Babe, while I go check it out," Chuck said unbuckling his seatbelt.

"Uh, hell to the no. I've been waiting for this moment all my life. Pleassse can I go check it out? I won't look in the car or anything—I just want to see how something like this is handled in real life." I gave him my puppy dog pout in a desperate attempt to sway him. In a sick, twisted way—I figured that somehow, some way, seeing a dead body might help me stop using. Seeing the consequences of it in real life might be exactly what I need to scare me straight.

"Sorry, I need you to stay here. It's protocol that if we have a passenger on a ride-along, unless they are currently enrolled in the Police Academy they aren't allowed to be present when someone is deceased. It's a privacy thing. I'll be as quick as I can," he said shutting the door and adjusting his belt.

I watched eagerly through the windshield as Chuck made his way up to the scene. I thought about the person in the car. The person was probably a heroin user. I had heard awful things about heroin and people in my town were dying at an alarming rate. Ever since I'd started shooting up, Kayla and Javier had tried to get me to try heroin a few times, but I always declined.

I was afraid that I would like it too much, and for some reason it made me feel better about myself knowing that what I was doing was "technically" legal. Pills aren't a street drug— they're prescribed by doctors. So, I felt like it made me higher up on the "Morals" chart than those who used the hardcore stuff.

I watched as the paramedics and various Law Enforcement officers methodically worked their way around the scene. One person was taking photos, another person was opening a stretcher while others stood around with their hands rested on their belts observing. I could see Chuck pointing into the car and talking to one of his buddies about something. They all simultaneously burst out in laughter and I squinted to make sure I was seeing it right. How could they be laughing at a time like this?

Chuck made his way back to the car and leaned into the driver's side window with a smile on his face. "What is so damn funny?" I asked, unable to fathom how they could find humor at a time like this.

"Dude...it's not funny, but it's kind of funny. When I looked inside the guy's car..." he paused to laugh again, "the guy is wearing a fucking shirt that says, 'Shit Happens'."

I tried my best to force a smile, but I couldn't hide the sadness I felt. Only a twisted person could actually laugh at something like that. That was someone's son, someone's friend... He was obviously lost and alone. It was fucking tragic, and these guys were able to laugh during a time like this.

They get to go home to their families, he gets to go to the morgue. I mean granted, he clearly did this to himself, but he was a person. A person worthy of respect. I suddenly had an incredible amount of resentment toward my boyfriend bubbling just under the surface.

"The guys don't need my help, they got it covered. I'm gonna go say bye to guys and I'll be right back," he said patting the side of the car and walking away.

My phone vibrated inside my purse causing me to jump and when I saw Jacob's name on the text, my heart started to race.

"Where's my money?" he wrote. I shoved the phone back into my purse just as Chuck opened the door.

I stared out my window, because I was afraid if I looked over in his direction I would snap. "Is everything okay?" he asked me as he started the car.

I took a deep breath, trying to compose my thoughts. "No, it's not. I gotta be honest, Chuck, it kind of pisses me off that there is a dead guy inches away, and you guys are pointing and laughing like a bunch of bullies. Like, it's disgusting actually."

I glanced in his direction with a look of disdain, there was nothing he could say that would justify it.

"Babe, I totally understand how bad that probably looked. But I need you to put your anger aside for one minute and think about what I am about to say." He turned the car off and shifted in his seat to face me." Last week, I showed up to a house where the parents had left their child in the car. Completely forgot the kid was in there. I saw the boy's lifeless body, glistening with sweat. I sat next to the mother on the porch as she screamed at the top of her lungs about wanting to die. Last month, I responded to a scene where a girl blew her head off in the bathtub. I saw it all. I respond to at least two overdoses a shift, and have seen and smelled more dead bodies this past month than any normal person would in two lifetimes. I try to find something to detach myself from the situations because it makes it less real. Sometimes it manifests itself in humor— and I know it's fucked up, but if I didn't do it, I would have ended up in a looney bin by now with all the shit I see daily."

I paused for a moment processing what he'd said. It made sense. How would I react if I had to stand a foot away from pieces of brain matter and shards of bones? I'd probably be a nutcase.

"It's a tough job, Hun, it really is," he continued, "and if you don't believe me, you can come up to the door with me at our next stop," he said, turning the car back on. My phone vibrated again in my purse. I knew it was Jake. He wanted his money, and I didn't have it. I ignored the buzzing.

"Come up to the door at the next stop? What do you mean?" I asked feeling confused.

"Yeah, we gotta go notify this guy Javier's family that he just OD'd."

"Javier?" My heart started to pound as I turned to face Chuck, who suddenly turned to me with a look of realization. "Hey, he had a Barron's Roadhouse hat on, didn't your friend Kayla used to work there?" he asked looking back at the road.

## Chapter Forty-One

I realized I had been standing in the same place long after Sharla's patrol car passed by. I was physically there, but my mind was back to that awful night. The night I'd found out about Javier.

He was the first person I'd ever known to die from addiction. I had always heard stories about people overdosing, but I'd never seen it firsthand.

I remember standing in the pew at his funeral, watching his father clutch his mother as her sobs caused her knees to buckle.

Audible sniffles echoed through the church as a slideshow of his photos danced across the screen.

The pictures began when he was a young child and I remember staring at the toothless grin of this innocent boy by the Christmas tree with his mom. He had a light in his eyes that had long burned out by the time I came to know him.

He was so joyous in the pictures, so full of life and promise.

I knew that the little boy in that picture wearing a uniform with a baseball bat rested on his shoulder, had no idea that he would only have fifteen years left on this planet.

His mother had given birth to him twenty-four years ago. And now... he was gone. All that remained was a body in a coffin sitting on stage in front of a hundred broken hearts.

"Are you coming?" a voice said, snapping me back to reality.

"Yeah...I, sorry, yes," I said, trotting over to Kelly's office door.

Kelly was the new therapist, the one who had taken Dr. Danner's place when she was fired. She was the polar-opposite of Dr. Danner in every single way and I had grown really close to her over the past few months.

Dr. Danner didn't get fired because of me. I had nothing to do with it, surprisingly. Apparently, she had been writing prescriptions for Claire in return for half of Claire's disability checks. Claire obviously tested positive for narcotics and was kicked out of Leap of Faith. The last I heard she was staying in a motel with some old guy.

"So, what was going on out there?" Kelly asked shutting the door behind me.

"Nothing. I... just saw someone I knew, and I guess I got lost in a memory for a second."

"Anything you wanna talk about?"

"Nah, I'm okay." I smiled.

"Okay. How has your week been going?" she asked, kicking her Converse shoes up on her desk.

"Good, really good. I've been doing bag checks for the new intakes. Felicity says I'm better than a bloodhound. I've found more hidden drugs this week than they have since the place has been opened," I said, proudly.

"Wow. Well it makes sense, you probably know all the good hiding places," she said laughing.

"Exactly."

"You gotta be careful with that, you know," she warned.

"I know."

"I know you know, Tiff. But addiction is a sneaky bitch, so just make sure you aren't putting yourself in dangerous situations."

"Thank you. I won't, I promise. There's usually always someone there with me anyway. It helps," I said.

"Well good. I'll stop lecturing you then. Alright, let's see," she said pulling out my file and flipping it open. "Last week you and I had just started talking about Jacob, the gun and how it made you feel, before the session ended. Do you want to pick up where we left off?"

"I do. Yeah. Because, it was the closest I'd come to being caught in the whole two years that Chuck and I had been together. It was actually a pivotal moment for me."

"Okay. Good. So, if I remember correctly, there was a knock at your front door, correct?" she asked.

"Yes."

"And you and Chuck had been playing video games at that point?"

"Yup."

"Okay, why don't you pick up from there. I'm interested to hear how you were able to maintain your 'dual personality' – so to speak– in the presence of both Jacob and Chuck."

I glanced up at the clock and realized we only had 34 minutes left in our session. It never seemed like enough time to me.

Chuck and I had been playing video games for about an hour that night when there was suddenly a knock at the door.

He paused the game and pulled his headset down off his ear to get a better listen. "Did the doorbell just ring?" he asked, looking surprised.

Before I could answer, he was off the couch and jogging toward our bedroom—the opposite direction of the front door. I knew what he was doing. He was grabbing his off-duty weapon.

"Be careful, Babe," I whispered nervously, cowering in the corner of the room. I watched as he peeked out the peephole, the gun resting by his right side.

"Who is it?" he barked, attempting to make his voice lower to sound more masculine.

"Hi, it's Jacob, Tiffany's friend—is she home?"

My blood ran cold as Chuck whipped his head around, giving me a puzzled look. My eyes grew wide and I furiously shook my head back and forth.

"Who?" Chuck asked again.

"It's Jacob, I'm an old friend of Tiffany's and I've been trying to reach her for a while now, is she home?"

"Bro, it's midnight. Is there some kind of emergency or something?" Chuck asked before mouthing "What the fuck" to me.

"Well," Jake began, sounding calm and collected, "I guess you could say so, yeah. It's somewhat of an emergency. She has something of mine and I'd like to have it back."

My heart raced as I shook with fear. It was over, despite my innate ability to get out of any situation, this one would be impossible. And to be honest I wasn't sure who I was more frightened of, the psycho drug dealer on the other side of the door—or my gun-toting boyfriend.

Before Chuck could reply to Jake, I ran toward the door. I held my hand up to calm Chuck and gently began speaking through the door.

"Jake, my phone has been off. I have your old yearbook, and I will meet with you tomorrow."

"Yearbook?" Jake asked, sounding confused.

FUCK.

"Ohhh, I get it. I see what you're doing. You are pretending to have something less valuable and less illegal of mine so as, to not tip off your Deputy boyfriend. Ahh, good idea. Okay, cool. Well you just give me a call tomorrow then, Tiffany, and you can bring my 'yearbook' to me. If for some reason I don't hear from you, I'll just come back, okay?" he said.

It was a threat. I knew that, but I was desperate for him to leave.

"Okay! Sounds good, bye!" I said quickly, walking past Chuck and heading toward the bedroom.

I collapsed onto the bed and closed my eyes. When I was a kid, I used to think that when I squeezed my eyes shut, no one could see me. I wished now, more than anything that that were true. I tried it anyway, just in case.

"Um. You wanna tell me what the hell is going on?" Chuck's voice boomed from the doorway.

Shit, it didn't work.

"Honey, it's complicated," I said, trying to buy time.

"Oh, is it? Okay well never mind then. If it was easy to explain I'd tell you to go ahead and explain, but since it's complicated—don't even worry about it. I probably couldn't keep up anyway," he said.

I breathed a sigh of relief.

"Thank you. Yeah, it's a lot and I'd rather not get int—"

"You have five fucking seconds to tell me everything or you can get your shit and get the hell out," he snapped.

"Oh, so you were being sarcastic."

"One...Two...-"

"Okay, Jacob is a drug dealer," I said quickly—like an idiot.

Before he could reply, I continued, "Jacob is a drug dealer and... The last time I relapsed, I ... I took a bunch of money, and drugs from him."

I watched his face fall and his arms go limp at his sides. He was still holding the gun, and a small part of me secretly wished he would just point it at me and pull the trigger.

"I owe him a lot of money. I don't know how he knows where I live, and honestly, I forgot all about it. I'm so sorry, Babe," I said, as tears started flowing from my eyes. Mostly because I knew that crying was like kryptonite to him, but also because the sadness in his eyes made me want to die. He hadn't asked for any of this, and it was clear he was beside himself with shock.

"So, you've got a drug dealer knocking on MY DOOR at midnight, because you robbed him?"

"Okay, no. See, technically I didn't rob him. He gave me like, over $7,000 worth of drugs and I never....um, returned them. The drugs. Never gave them back...to him. So. Technically not robbing," I said.

"Get out."

"What?"

"Get.... the FUCK out of my house."

"Your house?"

"You're God damn right my house. I bought it. I also bought all the furniture, all of the food in the fridge, all of the plates you eat off of—everything. Every God damn thing you touch in this house is mine, so I'll say it again. Get the hell out, NOW."

He dropped his gun onto the nightstand and walked into the bathroom, slamming the door behind him.

I sat there in stunned silence for a moment, staring at all the scattered pieces of my life.

I had nowhere to go.

Where the hell was I supposed to go?

It was midnight.

"Babe, please!" I cried out.

Silence.

"Chuck, I'm begging. Let me stay tonight. I'll leave tomorrow. I don't have anywhere to go, please. This all happened a long time ago. I have been doing so good...I didn't know..."

The bathroom door swung open and Chuck stepped out. He walked to the side of the bed with a look of defeat on his face, and his chin started to quiver.

"I love you so much, Tiffany. I love you more than anything in this world.... But you are making it really hard. You are making it so damn hard to love you." He sat down on the edge of the bed with his back to me and his shoulders began shaking as he sobbed into his hands.

I glanced over at the nightstand where he threw his gun.

I should grab it. I should just grab it, and put it to my head. It would make everything so much easier. On him, on me, my family... I wasn't cut out for life. I wasn't any good at it. The only thing I'm good at is creating chaos and destruction.

I stared at his back in silence for what seemed like an eternity. I didn't know what to say, there was nothing to say.

"What are you going to do?" he asked, staring at the floor.

"I guess I can call my dad and see if he's awake, but he usually goes to bed early. Maybe my sis-"

"Stop. You aren't going anywhere. I'm sorry. I was angry, I am angry. But I don't know if that psycho is still out there waiting for you or something, so you just need to stay here. What are you gonna do about the money?"

I took a deep breath of gratitude and had never in my life been more thankful for my boyfriend's forgiving heart than I was tonight.

"I have my tax check, I will give that to him tomorrow. I will only owe him $2,000 after that and I think he will just be grateful that I even gave him–"

"You know what, actually. I'll tell you what. Don't say another word. I don't want to know another fucking thing, okay? I'm a fucking deputy–in case you've forgotten. So, whatever deals you have with your old dealers–I don't want to know about them. I'm going to sleep on the couch. Goodnight."

I jumped as the door slammed behind him.

I sat there for a moment, replaying everything that had just occurred, in my head. I couldn't have Jacob coming back here tomorrow, I had to fix it. I needed a plan.

I got up from the bed and walked into the bathroom. I felt like shit, physically–and emotionally. I locked the door behind me and pulled the remaining bag of pills from the briefcase out of my tampon box. I had been holding on to these in hopes of salvaging some money to give back to him. But he was probably going to kill me tomorrow, anyway. So, it didn't matter.

My mind raced as I filled the syringe. How the hell could I get $2,000 by tomorrow? It would be impossible. I wouldn't be able to get the money and Jacob would either beat me to death, or show up here and tell Chuck the whole truth...and then kill me.

I thought about Chuck laying on the couch, probably staring at the ceiling wondering what the hell he had gotten himself into. I needed to leave him. It was for his own good. His soul is beautiful, and pure while mine is tarnished, and evil and... Empty. I probably didn't even have a soul. Someone with a soul wouldn't do the things I did.

As I pushed the drugs into my vein I closed my eyes and took a deep breath. Suddenly, a lightbulb went off in my brain.

Oh my God. I got it. I don't know how I didn't think of this before. I smiled to myself just as the drugs hit my heart and rocketed through my body.

It wasn't going to be easy – but I knew exactly how I was going to get Jake the money before tomorrow night.

Chapter Forty-Two

"Hi. Um, how much can I get for this?"

My hands trembled as I held out the sterling silver neck-lace my grandmother had given me, for the clerk to inspect.

The man behind the counter, a tall angry looking Spanish guy looked me up and down, then grabbed the necklace from my hand. He held it closely to his face and squinted.

"I can give you $20," he said firmly.

The necklace had been a gift from my grandmother for my tenth birthday. I managed to hang on to it all these years simply because I refused to wear it. I was terrified of losing it, as it was the only memento I possessed from when she was still here.

My heart sank when I heard his offer. "$20? It's real silver. And I'm certain the diamond in the cross is real as well," I said, challenging him.

"I can give you $20 for it. No more."

I stared at him desperately for a moment. Sweat had begun to collect on my brow and the withdrawals were in full effect. I'd used the last of Jake's stash the night before and really needed something to make me feel better while I carried out my plan of action.

"Listen, man, I'm begging. I've never done this before but I'm desperate. I know the necklace is worth more than that, I googled it. Please," I pleaded.

"Ma'am, I have other customers. Do you want the money or not?"

As shitty as I currently felt, there was no way I could get rid of this keepsake for a measly 20 bucks. "No thanks," I snapped, snatching my necklace from his fist. Kayla had recently informed me that she was having trouble paying the bills since Javier's passing and she'd begun pawning her possessions, and purchasing them back once she received her paychecks.

I had no idea how pawn shops worked and had been excited at the prospect of selling belongings for cash –up until today that is. I punched the steering wheel once inside the vehicle. What the fuck was I supposed to do now?

My mind had raced the entire drive home. I'd conjured up a thousand plans to obtain the money, all of which I tossed aside once I realized how impossible they would be. Things like; robbing a house, selling our TV, I even considered selling my car to pay Jake back. I figured I'd have enough money left over to buy more pills, and once I had those I could think clearly enough to come up with a good excuse as to where the hell my car was.

As I entered my house, the cold air inside stabbed my skin like a million microscopic razorblades. Every hair on my body stood on end as I ran to seek refuge beneath my covers.

My bones ached while I watched the ceiling fan spin in circles above my head in the bedroom. I wanted to get up and turn it off because the humming sound it made was making me nauseous, but I didn't have the energy.

"Fuck!" I screamed out in frustration. How the hell am I supposed to get money when it hurts to even move my fucking eyes.

In general, if I go longer than four hours without a hit, my mental withdrawals begin – the obsession. When I go more than five hours without a hit, the physical symptoms surface. It had been fourteen hours since my last hit and the thought of suicide began taunting me for the thousandth time.

The voices of my subconscious were tempting and relentless. "How can you live like this?" they said. "This pain is excruciating. You can't take much more of it."

"Chuck will be home in three hours and you've already had the flu three times this month, you can't fool him again. Just end it. End it now."

I glanced over at the nightstand where Chuck kept his off-duty weapon. It would only take one pull of the drawer handle, and one pull of the trigger for all the agony and mental torture to end. My legs were restless, and it felt as if thousands of fire ants were gnawing on the muscles of my calves. No matter how much I moved my legs or how hard I squeezed them, the pain refused to let up. "You could end it in a second. I could make it go away."

I whimpered and curled up into the fetal position, rocking back and forth attempting to alleviate the pain. I couldn't escape it – it was everywhere. It was inside of me, a part of me. And it always would be, the pills were the only thing keeping it at bay. The moment I stopped feeding it, it tore my body apart.

Without hesitation I pulled myself over to his nightstand and opened the drawer. I couldn't take another second of this torture. I should have let the guy take my stupid necklace, the $20 could have at least gotten me a pill and I would be fine right now. Instead, I'm going to die.

As I pulled the gun up out of the drawer, the jingle of my text message startled me, causing me to drop the gun into the empty drawer. I could see who it was from, from where I was sprawled on the bed.

Lazarus.

I lunged for the phone and frantically opened the text.

"I'm straight," it said.

"Of course you are you son of a bitch. You ALWAYS have pills when I don't have any God damn money, you fuck!" I shrieked at the screen. On days when I had hundreds of dollars, Laz would be out of pills. Every single time I was broke– without fail–I received a text from him, waving my drug of choice in front of my face when I couldn't have it.

Knowing that an entire bag of pills was five miles away from me, made my stomach turn. All I needed was one. One pill and I would be fine. One pill and every single horrific symptom I was experiencing would disappear in an instant, an INSTANT. I just needed one.

"I don't have money right now. I will tonight. Can I get one and I'll pay you back later, please," I begged.

My foot tapped anxiously as I awaited his reply. It seemed like a century had passed before he responded.

"Nah."

Desperate sobs escaped my throat and tears blurred my eyes until I could no longer see his heartbreaking reply. I threw the phone across the room and screamed until my throat was raw. It felt like I was drowning, and someone had walked up with an oxygen mask– only to pull it away as soon as I reached for it.

Suddenly it was if I were possessed. All the crying ceased immediately, all the stress disappeared. Something came over me, I was no longer in control. I picked the phone up off the floor and texted him back.

"I will do whatever you want."

I hit send and began to put my sneakers on. I was no longer myself, the real me seemed to have completely detached from my physical body and something else had taken over. I was on auto-pilot.

"Come over," he replied.

"I'm on my way."

The apartment was completely dark inside when I pulled up, all I could see were periodic flashes of light from the TV.

I knocked on the door and the butterflies began swirling around in my gut. Not the good kind of butterflies, the kind you get when you are about to do something bad.

"Hey gorgeous," Lazarus said swinging the door open.

I felt lightheaded. I wanted to turn and run but my feet wouldn't allow it. I was inches away from relieving this pain, I couldn't turn around now.

"Come in." He smiled, ushering me inside.

My heart was exploding inside my chest as I stepped in. I didn't want to be here. I wanted to be anywhere but here.

"What made you change your mind?" he asked from behind me. I wanted to blurt out 'desperation,' but figured that wouldn't go over well.

"Well, you told me the offer always stands. I figured today would be a good day to take you up on it," I said, forcing a smile.

It took whatever miniscule amount of strength I had left in my body to keep from crying. As I watched him unbuckle his pants my heart shattered into a thousand pieces.

I was sad for Chuck, the wonderful man who stood by me, supported me and loved me unconditionally. But the true sadness, the sadness that emanated from my soul was the grief of having to say goodbye to the person I used to be.

The little girl who rode her pink bike around the neighborhood with her sister and giggled wildly without a care in the world.

The girl whose mother used to hold back her hair as she blew out the birthday candles on her cake.

The girl who danced around the living room in her princess pajamas singing "The Little Mermaid" while her parents clapped and sang along.

The girl who had dreams, hopes, and ambitions.

She was gone. That girl died a long time ago and tonight, tonight was the night she was lowered into the ground, never to be seen again. I was someone else, something else... I was a waste of flesh and breath.

Lazarus took a step toward me and put his arm around my shoulder. It felt like a slimy reptile, unwanted and intrusive on my skin. I thought he was going to hug me, instead he pushed me down to my knees on the tile floor.

The world around me slowed down, my eyes glazed over, and my brain shut down. I was no longer a living thing. I was a body, that this repulsive stranger was using for his own pleasure. I didn't want to have any part of it, so I left. Not physically, but mentally I was gone. I could feel what was happening, but with my eyes squeezed shut I took myself someplace else.

To the future. To ten minutes from now when the pills were making their way through my veins and everything that had ever happened to me, today and before, would disappear. I would once again be in my comfortable haze of existing without a worry in the world.

It would be worth it. This would be worth it and my reward for allowing him to use my body would be my ticket to forget. I would forget this happened the moment I left. I would tuck it so far away that it would be lost in the sea of shameful things I'd done deep in the back of my mind.

That night, on my knees in that filthy apartment, I mourned the loss of the person I was supposed to be, and accepted the fact that I was nothing more than a junkie whore.

The tears formed a puddle on the floor beneath me in Kelly's office. Reliving that memory that I'd worked so hard to forget made a tidal wave of painful emotions wash over my body. I couldn't bring myself to look at her, the shame was paralyzing. I had never told this truth to another soul and honestly couldn't believe I had spoken it out loud, making it real. Making it true.

As I struggled to catch my breath I could feel the warmth of her body as she softly sat down next to me and wrapped her arms around my shoulders in a tight embrace. "That must have taken a lot of courage to admit, Tiffany, I am so proud of you," she whispered.

I looked up at her, my face twisted in confusion. "How can you be proud of me? Did you hear what I said? I did a sexual favor to get high. That makes me whore. Not just a whore, a cheating whore. Why the hell would you say you are proud of me?" I was almost offended. It was as if she were babying me, coddling me. I didn't know what the hell her angle was, but I didn't like it.

She shook her head and raised her eyebrows. "You aren't any of those things Tiffany, you have to know that. Withdrawal is one of the most mentally and physically painful experiences anyone can have," she began, letting go of me and leaning back onto the couch. "You know, it brings me back to something a woman told me a few years back and it has always stuck with me. If you were on fire, would you stand still and burn? Or would you seek water to put it out?"

I nodded, understanding where she was going with this. "When most addicts experience withdrawal symptoms," she continued, "they will do whatever it takes to relieve the pain, to make it stop. The real you would never had done what you did that night. You... were on fire."

I sat still for a moment and processed her analogy. It made sense, I would have done anything to make the pain stop – I had been moments away from shooting myself when Lazarus texted. What I ended up doing was a better alternative at the time, but it didn't make it right.

"I appreciate that you're trying to make me feel better, I really do. But to be honest, I'm not sure anything anyone says will give me peace about what I did. It was something I said I'd never do. Sure, it would be easy to blame on the drugs, but the fact remains it happened. And it haunts me," I said.

"We all do things we regret, Tiffany. It's part of life, much more so for an addict. I don't expect you to be free of guilt after ten minutes. We will work through those struggles and you will go even more in depth into your past and the things that haunt you, once you get a sponsor and start working the steps."

"Okay, cool," I said, wiping away the evidence of my emotions from my cheeks.

"That was the first time I've seen you get emotional since we have started our sessions. That shows me you're making progress. I'm really proud of you."

I rolled my eyes in response and a half smile spread across my lips. It felt good to hear someone say that to me, it had been a long time.

"So, you said that you owed Jake the money the next day— after the night with Lazarus, and I know what happened two days after that. I'd like to briefly go over that while you are here if that's okay," Kelly said, grabbing a cigarette and waving me outside with her.

"But, Dating and Marriage 101 starts in fifteen minutes, I'm supposed to be there," I said.

"I know – I already texted the teacher. This is important, come on," she said, nodding for me to continue.

Chapter Forty-Three

"Hey, guys, table sixteen says they didn't want any pink in their steak, I need you to throw this on the grill please, quickly," I said, shoving the plate through the window of the cook line.

"Hey, Tiff, sorry to bug you. Um, the guy at table 47 wants to see a manager?" Gina said nervously.

"About?" I asked.

"Uh, I'm not really sure. I brought him the water he asked for, and then he immediately asked for a manager, so. I don't really know, he doesn't seem upset or anything. He actually seems... happy," she said.

I let out a sigh as I brushed past her. I really didn't have time for this, I still had to count the inventory in the cooler and we closed in an hour. I walked through the dining room giving a fake smile to each guest as I passed, when I rounded the corner near table 47 my heart fell to my knees.

"Hello." I said. "What can I do for you?" I glanced around nervously as I awaited his reply.

"Well, hello," he said smiling. "I was looking over the menu and I was having trouble finding something, I was hoping you could help me."

I crossed my arms and took a deep breath. "What is it?"

"Yes, it's $7,000. Can you show me where it is?" He smiled, holding up his menu like a smart-ass.

"Jake, you can't just fucking show up to my job like this. Are you serious right now?" I whispered frantically.

"I've given you more than enough time, too much time, actually. I thought for sure the idea of your boyfriend finding out who you really are, would be enough motivation for you to return my money, but evidently I was mistaken."

"Listen, it's not that," I said, "Of course I don't want him to know, it would destroy him. It's just. It's not easy to get that kind of money, especially when...." My voice trailed off.

"Especially when, what? You're a junkie and have to feed your addiction first? I get it. Which is why I figured I'd give you some incentive."

My heart began to pound as I wondered where he was going with this.

I quickly glanced around the restaurant and noticed a few servers were standing by the computer waiting impatiently for me to come put my manager code in for them. "I have to go, Jake. Give me one more week. I'm trying, I really am."

"Do you remember Cinco De Mayo?" he asked calmly, unfolding his napkin and placing it on his lap.

"What the fuck? Cinco De Mayo? Like six years ago? Yeah. We went to the party downtown then crashed at your house.

What does that have to do with anything?" I asked, feeling confused and growing impatient.

The fact that he was moving so slow and talking like he was some kind of gangster in a movie was really getting on my nerves.

"Do you remember what happened when we got back to my place?" he asked.

Jesus Christ, dude, I don't have time for this. Just tell me what the hell–." I stopped midsentence as the memory of that night resurfaced. He smiled in response to my sudden realization.

"You are a liar," I snarled, feeling enraged that he would threaten me like this.

"Am I?" he said with a look of confusion. My eyes fell to his pocket as he reached in it to pull something out.

"I actually thought you might say that." He held his phone up, so the screen faced me, my blood ran cold once I registered the image.

"You have five days to get me my money or everyone on the internet gets to see your performance," he said standing up. I stared at him in disbelief as he threw a $20 bill on the table and smiled at me. "Keep the change."

He made it two steps, before turning around and snatching it back up from the table. "Actually, I'll go ahead and keep this.

Just give me $6,980 by Friday." He winked, and headed toward the door.

Three days had passed since Jake showed up at my workplace to threaten me. I had already pawned everything valuable of mine, as well as lots of things that belonged to Chuck. Things he wouldn't notice missing from around the house. I had nothing left to pawn and two days to get Jake the money or... Something terrible was going to happen.

As the hours passed and my desperation grew, my moral compass started to shift. It was as if my conscience, that had always told me right from wrong had faded, as my need to obtain money had grown.

I had begun dipping into my tax check to support my habit, because there was no way I would be able to continue to work– and continue to think of ways to make this money– all while keeping it hidden from Chuck and trying to remain as normal-seeming as possible. It was like trying to shovel during a blizzard, as soon as I made money—I had to spend it to not get sick. I couldn't get ahead of it.

I couldn't have Chuck find out that I was a junkie– not like this.

I cranked the music up in my car and banged the pill I'd just gotten from my friend Danny. I had been avoiding Lazarus since the other night and a pang of guilt kicked me in the gut every time the memory crossed my mind.

I listened to the rhythm of the music as the wave of bliss hit me. I closed my eyes to enjoy this moment, this split second as the drug entered my bloodstream. Because it was in this second—that nothing mattered. In this moment, I was thoughtless, weightless, I was free.

The feeling faded, and slowly the hideous world around me became louder, more apparent. All the lies, negative thoughts and twisted situations I'd gotten myself into rushed back in like a dam had been flung open.

If I could have that fifteen seconds of ecstasy after shooting the pill, be my permanent state of mind, life would be perfect. It's all the unbearable seconds before and after the high that make me want to die. Fifteen seconds of relief from my sad reality had become my number one priority, because the escape—no matter how fleeting—was invaluable.

I thought about Jake coming to visit me, I thought about Cinco De Mayo. I had spent the night doing copious amounts of drugs and chugging countless bottles of beer. The evening was a blur, but I remember... I remember what we did.

I remember him setting the camcorder up, and crawling onto the bed with me. I remember him telling me how beautiful I was, and how he wanted to remember the moment forever. I remember feeling special, and loved. I remember him promising he would never show a soul.

Now he was going to post the tape of us on social media, if I didn't get him the money.

Tears streamed down my face as I realized that soon everyone would know the truth about me. About the things I'd done. Chuck –and all his friends and family would have a front row seat to a drug-fueled, intimate moment I'd had with another man.

I was fucked.

I couldn't let that happen. Suddenly I had an idea. I hadn't thought of it before, probably because it never in a million years was on my radar of things to do to get money. But the stakes were higher now and honestly, there wasn't a damn thing I wouldn't do to keep that video from getting out there.

I knew of a house that I could gain access to that may have some items I could borrow and pawn until I paid Jake off. Then I could return them before anyone noticed.

I picked up the phone and began dialing.

"Hello?" Chuck's mom said cheerfully.

"Heyyy! I know you guys are working today but I have a HUGE favor. Is there any way I can swing by and use your computer to reprint some of my tax stuff? I guess the accountant needs it," I lied.

"Of course, sweetheart, there's some leftover turkey in the fridge if you're hungry, make yourself at home." I squeezed my eyes shut as a knife of shame stabbed through my heart.

"Thank you, I'll talk to you later," I said, quickly hanging up.

I sat with my hands on the steering wheel for a moment, nervously tapping my foot and debating what to do. Stealing from people who had been nothing but amazing to me was a horrific thing to do. Having them find out that I'd lied to, manipulated and broken their son's heart—and had a sex tape out there that they could see if they chose, seemed worse.

I was already going to hell, there was no question of that. Now it was just a matter of how badly I was going to hurt everyone before going.

"So, you went to the parents' house?" Kelly interrupted.

"Yes. I did."

"And that's when you stole the wedding ring?"

I stared off into the distance, feeling empty, and ashamed. I could feel a knot growing in my throat as I relived this memory with Kelly.

"Hey, I'm not here to judge you. I know it's hard, but you are doing great. We are going to work through all of this I promise," she said.

I had tears in my eyes when I looked back up at her. Each time I tried to begin speaking my voice cracked.

"I didn't know it was a wedding ring. I thought he wore his wedding ring. I ... I hate that I did that. The ring was irreplaceable. I honestly want to die when I think about that," I cried.

"I think it's good for you to feel what you're feeling, it's important. The regret, the guilt, the shame associated with the things you did. The fact that you are feeling that tells me that you are making progress. You never allowed yourself to feel these emotions before, you always pushed them away and avoided them. The only way to get through it, is to go through it—and that's what you are doing," she said placing her hand on my knee.

"The things that I had taken from his parents' house, got me closer to what I needed, but I still didn't have enough. I had already gone all out and honestly at this point it was like, I didn't care. I wasn't thinking. The guilt of what I'd done to his parents was gnawing at me and I needed to get high to forget, to not feel so fucking bad."

She nodded as I continued speaking.

"I know that sounds selfish, but I literally didn't know how to cope with those feelings. Those emotions caused like, my brain to short out or something. It was so heavy, and getting high made it lighter I guess. Anyway, I didn't want to tap into the money I'd already saved, and I remembered that Chuck had gotten $300 for his birthday a few days before. I needed that money to get high, because I was starting to get sick. But since it was only him and I in the house I couldn't just take it, you know? Because he would know it was me."

"Well, couldn't you have asked him to borrow it?"

"No."

"Why is that?"

"Because he had already given me $100 the week before, and money was tight. If I asked him for more he would want to know why, and it would have been too obvious, I guess. I don't know. I wasn't thinking straight at this point. My internal setting was stuck on desperation, so I wasn't operating with common sense. I was just... I was just doing what I thought I had to do to keep my world from crumbling and it was exhausting. It would have been so much easier to just tell the fucking truth. At the time it seemed impossible, but look-ing back...If I had known how it all was going to end... I would have just told the truth."

"And how did it end, Tiffany?" she asked quietly.

I stared at the floor for a moment before slowly bringing my eyes up to hers.

"In complete fucking chaos..." I said.

## Chapter Forty-Three

Tonight, was the night.

I was meeting Jake at a local restaurant at 6:00 p.m. to give him the money I owed him. Technically, I didn't have it just yet, but, I would very soon. As I paced back and forth across my living room, Tatum, my puppy's toenails clicked against the hardwood floor as he ran beside me, excitedly.

"What the hell am I doing?" I asked him. His tail began to wag in response and I couldn't help but think how fucking wonderful it would be, to be a dog. Having no responsibility, no pressure. Just running around and pooping. I hated being human, I hated having to think and make decisions and dig myself out of the bottomless holes that I'd created. It would be so much easier to be a Goddamn dog.

I had to quit stalling, I was running out of time. I took a deep breath and bounded to the hallway closet. As I grabbed the blanket on top of the shelf, I froze.

Was I sure I wanted to do this? There was no coming back from this once it was done. I have done a lot of really messed up things in my day – but this took the cake.

I thought of what would happen if I didn't do this. I imagined the faces of everyone I'd ever known as they hit play on the video Jake would send to them. Images of that night flashed across my mind and I cringed, remembering what was on that tape.

If that tape was released, I could never show my face again. I would have to kill myself or at the very least, leave the country and change my name. My life would be over.

With a newfound determination, I ripped the blanket from the shelf and headed toward the spare bedroom.

My heart pounded as I reached into the hole in the wall of the closet for the cigar box. My fingers fumbled around until I felt the wood of the box. I reached inside and pulled out the keys to the gun safe.

Chuck kept a ton of guns in there; rifles, handguns and some automatic weapons. He never went into the gun safe unless we went shooting, and we hadn't done that in years. By the time he noticed anything was missing, I would have had plenty of time to come up with a reason they were gone. For now, however, I had to do this.

The door squeaked as I pulled it open and I could hardly catch my breath. Holy shit, I can't believe this is happening.

I quickly stretched the blanket out across the floor as if I were preparing a picnic, except this was no picnic, this was the craziest thing I had ever done in my life.

I immediately located the first two types of guns Lazarus had asked for, and placed them in the middle of the blanket before returning to the gun safe to find the third. He had specifically asked for a 9-millimeter, but I was having trouble locating it.

As I searched each gun in the case individually, I thought about the conversation I'd had with Lazarus. He said there were some guys after him and he was worried for his life. He wanted protection, and as if the universe had aligned perfectly for me to pay Jake, he messaged me and asked me if I could get him any guns.

He said he would pay me $4,000 for three of them. Now I didn't believe in God, but if there ever was a sign from heaven that I needed to see, this was it. I knew that this was what I was meant to do. Opportunities like this don't just happen, it was fate. To get my life back where it needed to be, I had to sell these guns.

There was no 9-millimeter in this safe.

I closed my eyes and sat down on the blanket feeling defeated. I didn't know how much he would give me for only two, especially when he specifically asked for a 9. I told him I had one, son of a bitch, I could have sworn we did.

Tears began streaming down my face when I realized it was over. Time had run out, and now I had no way to pay Jake. I laid down onto the blanket on the floor and stared up at the ceiling. Maybe I should just tell Chuck everything now, mentally prepare him for what was coming tonight. Tell him that our whole relationship had been a lie because I'm actually a junkie piece of trash. Let him know I wasn't strong enough to beat my demons and I'd allowed them to take over my life.

Tell him that I lied to him every day for years, and every time he ever touched me, there were narcotics floating through my veins.

I'd have to sit him down and shatter his heart and let him know that there was also a very good chance that his entire family, the entire police department and anyone else with a computer and a set of eyes was about to see a sex tape I'd made six years ago while inebriated. Maybe if I ended my life with one of these guns, I wouldn't even have to explain myself. Jake would feel too guilty to release the tape and Chuck would never have to know the whole truth about who I really am.

A frustrated scream escaped my throat as I pounded the floor with my fists. I curled up into a ball right there next to those guns and stared at the wall. I looked at the framed photo of Chuck smiling next to his mother. Neither of them deserved anything I'd done.

As I stared at the photo, I suddenly noticed something that caused me to sit straight up. His mother had her hand resting on the side of his hip, the hip where he kept his off-duty weapon.

I jumped up from the floor, startling Tatum, and sprinted to our bedroom.

I yanked the drawer of his nightstand open, and my eyes glistened with tears of relief as I stared down at the 9-millimeter handgun he kept by the bed. I knew we had one here. I slowly reached down and wrapped my fingers around the cold metal handle and pulled it up to my chest. Everything was going to be fine now. Everything was going to be okay...

"Technically you owe me another hundred, but I will let it slide," Jake said tucking the money into his wallet and placing it back into his pocket.

"Now delete the fucking video," I snapped.

"Okay, okay. Take it easy. You know, it honestly saddens me to have to get rid of this, it's actually really great," he said entering the password into his phone.

"Stop," I said.

"No, seriously, do you want to watch it together one last time? The part where you snorted the coke off my..."

"God damnit delete the fucking video right now, I am not in the mood for this shit. I just want this to be over."

"Done," he said, holding his phone up to show me that it was gone.

"Please get the hell out of my car now. And stay away from me and my boyfriend. I kept up my end of the deal, and if you fuck me over I swear to God..."

"Relax," he interrupted, "I don't want to destroy your life, Tiff, I just wanted my money. And now I have it, so we are good."

"Okay," I said, starting the car.

"Before I go," he said, reaching into his pocket, "here, for your trouble." He handed me a pill and smiled. "Talk soon," he said, slamming the door shut behind him.

The moment that door slammed, it felt as if I was finally able to drop the backpack filled with heavy rocks I'd been carrying around for months. The release of that burden was almost orgasmic. It was over. Now I could focus on getting my shit together and getting clean, that way I could put all of this behind me. After this last pill, I was done. I'd learned my lesson.

I smiled as I pulled into our neighborhood. I couldn't wait to hug Chuck, thinking that I was going to lose him at any given moment had been torturous. For the first time in a long time, I didn't have to worry. I glanced down at the clock and saw that it was almost 7:30, he should be home by now.

As I turned left onto my street, every ounce of joy I'd been feeling immediately drained and was replaced with terror. I inched closer to my home and my heart felt like it was going to stop.

Why the fuck were there three police cruisers in my driveway?

My entire body trembled as I approached the door and I listened for laughter, maybe he was having some friends over and forgot to tell me. The doorknob rattled as I wrapped my unsteady hand around it.

As I swung the door open, a man I didn't recognize was standing in the kitchen. "Are you Tiffany?" he asked.

Before I could answer I heard Chuck's voice. "Babe?" he came running around the corner -still in his uniform and seemed relieved to see me.

"Hi, whhhat's going on?" I asked, peering around the house.

"Jesus, I've been worried sick. I called you a hundred times, is your phone off?" he asked.

I pulled my phone from my purse and realized it was dead.

"Shit, Babe, I'm sorry. It's dead. I didn't..."

"It's okay, you're safe, that's all that matters," he said pulling me close for a hug.

I glanced over his shoulder at the officer and I could have sworn he shook his head before looking down at his notepad.

"What's happening right now?" I asked, just before a female officer emerged from the hallway.

"I just finished up dusting inside the gun safe, we will get these shipped off to the lab to see if we get a hit," she said.

"Thank you, Darlene, I really appreciate it," Chuck said.

I tried to hide the horror I was suddenly feeling inside.

"Tiffany, I don't want you to freak out, okay? But... Somebody broke into our house today and stole some of my guns," he said.

My eyes glazed over, and I tried my best to seem surprised. "What? Are you serious?" I asked.

"Dead serious, but don't worry, Honey. We are gonna find the Asshole that did this, and we're gonna put him away for a lonnng time."

## Chapter Forty-Four

"Miss Johnson?"

"Sorry, I was... I'm just in a bit of shock. What did you say?"

"I asked what time you left the house today."

Detective Green was sitting across the table from me, his eyebrows furrowed as he stared through my soul. I knew that I wasn't a suspect, there was no way anyone would believe that I had anything to do with this, but there was something about his unrelenting gaze that made me incredibly nervous.

I wasn't prepared for questions, I couldn't fuck this up, I'd seen enough crime shows to know that anything I said in this moment, could be used against me in the future if shit went south.

"I left around, um, 5:30. I think," I said, staring down at his notepad as he jotted something down.

"Okay. Where'd you go?"

Those piercing eyes, it was like he took a class on "How to get people to confess to murders they didn't commit."

"I met up with a friend of mine, Jake. I had an old yearbook of his, so we met up so that I could give it to him." God, that sounds so stupid.

"A yearbook?" he asked, seeming confused.

"Yes, it's his, I've had it for years, and he's been hounding me about getting it to him, so, I just met him. So, he'd leave me alone."

As he scribbled something down, I glanced back over my shoulder and noticed Chuck shaking his head while conversing with another officer. He looked devastated, confused, violated.

Guilt suddenly washed over me like an ocean wave, and I struggled to catch my breath.

"Will you please excuse me?" I said politely, realizing I hadn't taken the pill Jake gave me. That would make this so much easier. "I have to use the restroom."

"Sure. Go right ahead." He smiled, gesturing toward the hallway. It was the first time I'd seen him smile, and it was then that I was reminded that this wasn't an interrogation. He was just trying to straighten out the facts.

The moment I locked the bathroom door behind me I quickly smashed the pill into powder. I wanted more than anything to shoot it, but that would take way too long. I leaned down and quickly snorted the pill with a rolled-up dollar bill. As I wiped the remaining powder from the surface of the counter, I could hear the low murmur of voices outside the window.

I stepped a bit closer and closed my eyes to see if I could make out what they were saying.

"Yeah, apparently there's been a few break-ins in this area. Not this neighborhood specifically but two roads over a lady had her house broken into while on vacation."

"You think it's related?" a second voice asked.

"No telling. We'll see what the latent print exam says. His patrol car wasn't in the driveway, so whoever did this either waited for him to go to work, or didn't know a cop lived here. Either way, they fucked with the wrong house."

"Babe, you okay?" Chuck asked, gently tapping the door. I nearly jumped out of my skin.

"Yeah," I replied opening the door. "Just got my damn period, as if this day couldn't get any worse."

His face fell, and he stretched out his arms for a hug. I wrapped my arms around his waist and closed my eyes. "I'm so happy you weren't here when it happened, I don't know what I'd do if something would have happened to you." His voice broke and I could tell he was getting emotional.

This wasn't supposed to happen. I was supposed to give Jake the money and things were going to get better. I was going to quit doing pills. I was going to leave the past behind and dedicate myself to Chuck and our future. Instead, there's a swarm of cops with black lights and fingerprint dusters turning my damn house upside down.

They were investigating a crime that I committed.

They were looking for some unknown "bad guy" that didn't exist.

They were wasting their time and effort to catch and crucify someone, not knowing that someone was two feet away offering them cold sodas while they worked.

What kind of a monster could do something like this?

What in the hell is wrong with me?

"Detective Green has a few more questions for you, Babe. Then they are gonna call it a night," he said, looking exhausted. "Okay, Love. Don't worry, we are gonna find out who did this, okay?"

I nodded, and headed back to the table.

"Just a few more things, okay?" Detective Green asked, typing something into his cell phone before sliding it into his pocket.

"Sure. Yeah."

"So, there was no sign of forced entry, did you lock the door when you left today?"

Shit.

"Hmmm. I think so. I mean I always do, I don't see why I wouldn't have today. Then again, I am kind of scatter-brained, so forgetting to lock it wouldn't be out of the realm of possibilities," I said.

"Okay, well I need you to think hard, because it's important."

I closed my eyes and pretended to think for a moment. I was trying to buy time to figure out how the hell someone could have gotten in if the door was locked.

"I was in a rush, I remember... I remember I couldn't find my keys and then I grabbed a soda from the fridge. Let me think. I went out to the car... and then, oh! I left my cell phone inside, so I ran back in. I probably forgot to lock it after I left. I think. I'm really not sure. I'm sorry," I said sheepishly.

"Okay, no that's fine. Running back in for your phone and running out could absolutely mean you forgot. Now, do you know of anyone, or can you think of anyone, who would do something like this? Anyone who would be capable of doing something like this?" he asked.

I slowly shook my head while making it appear as if I was going through a mental rolodex of everyone I'd ever met.

"I don't. I mean we only surround ourselves with good people, hardworking people. I can't even imagine the kind of person who would have a need for guns. I mean I know people with guns but like, they get a license for them and purchase them. They go about it the right way. I don't know anyone who would burglarize a home to get them, ya know?" Except me, because I'm a piece of shit.

"I know what you mean and unfortunately it happens more often than you'd think," he said, flipping his notebook shut and tucking it into the front pocket of his shirt. "A lot of desperate people out there. I'm sure it's drug-related. We'll know soon enough."

I looked down toward the floor and nodded. I was afraid that if I made eye contact with him he'd be able to see the scene that was playing over and over in my head. Me taking the guns. Me loading them up. Me bringing them to Lazarus and laying them out on the bed. Me giving him extra boxes of ammo before walking away with the money. Me smiling as I pulled out of the driveway, because I knew the worst was over.

Me being so incredibly wrong. The worst was yet to come.

"Alright, Tiffany, I think that's it. Oh, was anything of yours missing? Jewelry, electronics, anything?" he asked, standing up from the table.

"Honestly I haven't even had a chance to look yet. I mean there wasn't much to begin with, but I can check real quick."

"No, it's okay. Check it out and if you do notice anything, let Chuck know and we will add it to the report. We are going to do a pawn search in case the piece-of-shit decides to pawn the guns, so we can have them check for anything else you may have had go missing."

"Great," I said, swallowing hard. A pawn search. FUCK.

"Well thank you for your time, Tiffany. You are very lucky, you know," he said.

"Yeah. I am. I'm glad I wasn't here."

"That's what I mean. You took Chuck's truck to meet your friend. Whoever did this, saw your car in the driveway and still chose to burglarize your home. It could have been much worse. Have a good night," he said, giving me a quick wave and walking away.

I took a deep breath as the last of the Deputies and Detectives left the house, and Chuck closed the door behind them.

"I'm gonna change and lay down," he said, walking past me to the room. His face looked like that of a little boy who'd just had his bike stolen. He was devastated. Tears began to form as the reality of what the hell just happened set in.

I changed into my pajamas and laid down in bed. I closed my eyes when I heard the water start to run in the shower. What the hell have I done? They are never going to solve this crime, because I was the one who did it. They will never think it was me, because why the hell would the cop's innocent girlfriend need a set of guns? What the hell are they gonna do? Just give up?

Chuck and I laid together in silence for a moment, my head resting on his bare chest as he stared at the ceiling.

"I'm fucking pissed," he said, interrupting the silence. "We bought this house, in this nice neighborhood. We put our blood, sweat and tears into making it our own—and someone just walks in like they own the fucking place and steals my shit. Shit I worked fucking hard for. Last week someone stole my damn money out of my wallet, and now this shit. I don't know why this is happening to us, Tiff, what kind of lesson is God trying to teach us, because honestly I don't fucking get it."

I wanted to speak up, but I couldn't find the words. I'd told enough lies and deceived enough good people for the day. So, I remained quiet.

"You know, and... like you told me not to file a report about my wallet and the money and honestly I'm wondering now if I should have. If I'd still have my guns," he said.

The wallet... I had tried to block this from my memory. I barely remembered doing what I did that day. I was on Xanax and I was desperate.

"Wait, did you tell the cops tonight about the wallet?" I asked, suddenly feeling panicked.

"You're damn right I did. I should have told them before. I mean honestly, who gets their badge and $100 stolen one week, and their house burglarized two weeks later. I must have pissed somebody off in a past life or something," he joked.

It felt like I was standing in one of those rooms. The rooms where the walls are slowly coming toward you from both sides and you know eventually they are going to meet in the middle... where you're standing.

"Anyway, the guys are gonna figure it out. I gave them my wallet for DNA analysis and they dusted the patrol car as well. We will see if the two are connected and we are gonna get this piece of shit. In the meantime, I don't want you to worry, Babe. Okay?"

"Okay," I said, suddenly more worried than I'd ever been in my life.

"I'm not going to let anything happen to you... I promise." He kissed my forehead and a tear rolled down my cheek. I wanted so desperately for those words to be the truth. But he didn't know, he couldn't know, that I wasn't the one who needed protecting.

***

"Babe, wake up, the detectives want to talk to you," Chuck said, shaking me awake. The moment my eyes popped open I instantly felt like shit. As the memories of what had happened the day before came rushing in, I was overwhelmed with anxiety.

"What the hell? I already talked to the detectives yesterday when they were here," I said from under the covers. I could feel that my hair was soaked from sweat, and my stomach was bubbling. I hadn't had a pill since the cops were here yesterday.

And I was out.

"Please, you need to get up and get dressed, they just have a couple more questions," he said.

I could feel the anger rising from the depths of my soul. I was suddenly very hot with rage. "God damn it, what is going on?" I asked, kicking off the covers and storming to the closet. "Why do they have to question me again? I already gave them all the information I have," I said, ripping a shirt off the hanger and angrily pulling it over my head.

Something was off. He wasn't responding to me. "Hello? I'm talking to you? I have work in four hours and I hardly slept last night, it would have been nice to have some kind of warning that they were coming back. Why are you being so weird?" I asked, pulling the pants up over my hips.

He didn't say a word, and I watched a single tear stream down his cheek. I froze.

The hair on the back of my neck suddenly stood up. "Are you crying?" I asked, stepping closer to him. He put his hands up to keep me at a distance.

"What the hell, Chuck?" I said. "Why aren't you respond-ing to me-"

Suddenly our bedroom door swung open with such force that it banged into the wall. A man was standing in the door-way with once hand resting on his gun, and the other holding up a badge.

"I need you to step into the living room, Miss Johnson. Now," he said, holding the door open and stepping back to make room for me. What the hell? Why was this guy talking to me like this?

I looked at Chuck and he was staring at the floor, avoiding me. As I stepped out of the bedroom and into our living room, Tatum ran toward me wagging his tail. Chuck intercepted her. I watched in shock as he scooped her up and took her to our bedroom, closing the door behind him. Why would he leave me alone out here with this guy?

When I turned back to face the man, I noticed there were five other deputies in my house. Two of them in uniform and the other three in regular clothes, with guns and badges clipped to their belts.

"Please have a seat," the man said, ushering toward the couch. "I'm Detective Kallin. I have a few questions I'd like to ask you, and if you don't mind, I'd like to do it out front on the porch. It's gorgeous outside today, we can just have a little chat."

"Okay, yeah. That sounds good," I said. I smiled at each of them. I sensed something was off, but whatever it was, I needed to seem as normal and unassuming as possible. This would be much easier if I had taken a pill this morning, but something told me these guys wouldn't wait for me to run to my dealer's real quick.

As we headed to the front door, I glanced out the window and realized both sides of my street were lined with patrol cars.

The moment I stepped onto my front porch, the world slowed down, and everything began to happen in slow motion.

The moment I saw the man in my peripheral vision standing at the side of my front door, he lunged at me, grabbing my arms and, pulling them behind my back.

I felt the heavy, cold metal of the handcuffs wrapping around my wrist and clicking tightly into place.

I opened my mouth to speak, but no words came.

"Miss Johnson, you are under arrest. You have the right to remain silent, anything you say can and will be used against you in a court of law."

## Chapter Forty-Five

I stared at the familiar eyes in the rearview mirror. They belonged to Gunnar, a friend of Chuck's that I had met back at the surprise party he had thrown me.

Those once-friendly eyes now peered straight ahead, they were cold and angry, completely different than the first time I'd seen them. Gunnar and I hadn't exchanged a single word since I'd been loaded into the back of this police cruiser, and I didn't blame him for ignoring me. After all, what could he possibly have to say? "You getting enough air back there you heartless bitch?"

I stared out the window, still in a bit of shock from this morning's events. I felt completely numb; not sad, not angry, just... numb.

My heart began pounding in my chest as we pulled up to the front of the police station. I'd been here before, quite a few times. Never in handcuffs though, never like this.

Gunnar yanked the vehicle into park and stepped out. I followed him with my eyes and realized he was coming to let me out. "Please step out of the car, Ma'am," he said, swinging the back door of the car open.

He called me Ma'am, as if I were a stranger. I slowly shook my head, and slid my way out and up onto my feet. Gunnar grabbed the chain between my handcuffs and guided me toward the entrance of the police station.

That was when I saw him.

Chuck was here too. He must have followed us. I wasn't sure if I should smile and wave or pretend I didn't see him, my gut told me to go with the latter.

When the doors of the police station swung open, I was hit with a burst of cold air. It felt as if I'd stepped into a freezer. I realized the withdrawals must be starting to set in as painful goosebumps instantly prickled up on my skin.

The moment I entered, it was as if someone hit the "pause" button on the world. Excited conversations suddenly stopped... and I was met with the glaring eyes of all the Deputies and employees inside the building. Some were holding folders, some filling out paperwork, and answering phones, while others had been having conversations amongst themselves. Everyone instantly stopped what they were doing... and stared. You could hear a pin drop.

I took a deep breath and lowered my head. Their looks of shock and disdain igniting a shame within me that I hadn't noticed before.

Gunnar led me to an elevator and it felt like hours before the car finally reached the bottom floor. I had seen Chuck out of the corner of my eye – but he darted up the stairs, apparently trying to avoid having to be enclosed in a small space with me. I certainly couldn't blame him for that.

I stared straight at the floor as the elevator carried Gunnar and I up to the 4th floor. When the elevator finally stopped, and the doors slowly opened, I gasped.

At least twenty deputies were lining either side of the hallway staring into the elevator, almost as if they were waiting for me. Gunnar gently nudged me from inside and I realized I would have to walk between the two lines of uniformed officers.

I recognized almost all of them, but the way that they were looking at me made it feel as if they were strangers. I stared at the floor and continued forward, and each cop I passed took turns calling me names under their breath and shaking their heads in disgust. I choked back the tears as I realized so many of them had been to my home, celebrated birthdays with me and now, now I was reduced to nothing but a piece of shit. Just another loser being walked to the interrogation room. I was once so close to these people and now – I am no one. I am no one. I am nothing.

The interrogation room had a television screen attached to the wall outside next to the door, I'm assuming this was for people outside to observe the interview taking place inside. I was immediately filled with dread once I realized that all these people were about to hear all my dirty secrets. Secrets I'd kept hidden for years, they were all about to be revealed and once they were, I knew that all the people outside that door would never look at me the same way again.

Upon entering the interrogation room, I observed a single table with three chairs. Gunnar led me to one of them and told me to "sit." His voice stern and robotic.

Once seated, he unlocked one of my handcuffs and I instantly breathed a sigh of relief. Thank God, the metal had rubbed the flesh of my wrists raw. My excitement was short lived, because he took the unhooked cuff and wrapped it around the metal of my chair, and clicked it shut. "Seriously?" I asked, feeling annoyed.

"Seriously," he said, mocking the frustration in my voice and rolling his eyes before exiting. I was tempted to hurl the chair at him with my good arm, but realized it was bolted to the ground.

There were no clocks in the room, but if I had to guess, I'd say an entire hour passed and I still hadn't seen a soul. My body was aching, and the cold sweats had been in full swing. It's impossible to get comfortable while handcuffed to a bolted chair in an ice-cold room while detoxing, so my frustration was at an all-time high.

"Hello?!" I yelled out to no one. "What's happening? Did you forget about me?"

Just then the door to the room swung open and I'd never been more grateful to see a set of cops.

"I'm Deputy Sherlin and this is Deputy Avalon, we have been assigned to your case," the female deputy said shutting the door behind them. She had long blonde hair that had been twisted up into clean bun, and bright blue eyes. She appeared to be younger than me and had I not seen her with a big gun on her belt, I never would have believed she was an actual cop.

After reading me my rights, Detective Avalon slid a piece of paper toward me. "If you understand your rights and are willing to speak to us, please sign here."

I reached for the pen and quickly scribbled my name onto the signature line. Somehow, in my twisted mind, I felt as if I would somehow find a way to get out of this. I had been an expert at manipulating, and knew that if I cried enough innocent tears and gave an Emmy-worthy performance, that they would believe me and send me home.

"Okay, now that we have your signature, we'd like to ask you some questions," Detective Avalon said. He was young too, he was dark skinned with a Spanish accent and there was something so kind about his big brown eyes.

I watched as he reached down into a briefcase and pulled out a stack of papers. He placed the pile on the table in front of him and looked over at me. "Do you know what these are?" he asked.

"I don't." Nice try though, copper, you aren't getting me that easy.

"Well here, let me show you."

He grabbed the first paper on the top of the stack and slid it toward me. It was a photograph.

I looked down at the picture of Chuck's drill that I had pawned, and just as the realization of what this was set in, he began flipping over photos in quick succession. Suddenly, the entire table was covered with pictures – evidence of all the things I'd been pawning in secret for months, none of which belonged to me.

"Now do you know what these are?" he asked.

Obviously, I know what these are, Asshole.

"Yes, I do."

"What are they, then?"

"Ummm, clearly, they are pictures of all the stuff I've pawned."

"Do any of these items belong to you, Miss Johnson?"

"Not really."

"What do you mean by 'not really'?"

"Well, technically, they were in my house, and they belonged to my boyfriend. We kind of share everything, so... I didn't think it was that big of a deal."

I could tell by the sudden look of disgust that had simultaneously crossed their faces, that I probably shouldn't have said that.

"Wow. Okay, well what about these then? Huh? These weren't in your house, were they?" he asked, handing me two photos of the things I'd taken from Chuck's parents' house. "You didn't live there. Therefore, technically, you burglarized their home. Now, they say that if you cooperate today, they won't press charges. However, if you aren't forthright with us, you will be charged with burglary," he said leaning back into his chair.

Jesus Christ. Burglary? Hell no.

"Are you kidding? I didn't burglarize their home. I used to live there, and they let me in," I said feeling annoyed, I felt like a child being threatened with consequences, and I didn't like it.

"I'm going to ask you some questions, and I need you to answer them truthfully," he said.

"Okay," I replied, looking over at Barbie who had been sitting there quietly. So far, she wasn't that great of a Detective.

She just sat there looking pretty. They probably had her in here to make me feel more comfortable or something.

"Okay, did you steal, and then pawn these items?"

"I pawned them, yes. But I didn't steal them. I borrowed them and was going to get them back."

"Did you know it was illegal to do that?"

"I knew it wasn't good. But I didn't know like, the charges or anything. And to be honest, I never thought Chuck would press charges even if he did find out. I thought he loved me, but instead of talking to me about it, he sent in the troops to take me away."

Just then, Detective Sherlin leaned forward in her seat and scowled at me.

"He didn't press charges you fucking idiot. While investigating the burglary at his home we did a pawn search. Just for shits and giggles we typed your name in and GUESS WHAT?! Surprise! You've been robbing him blind since back in October. Chuck had no clue until our supervisor called him into the office this morning to inform him of what had been going on, and to let him know Deputies were in route to arrest your stupid ass. He didn't have to press charges, we were investigating a crime and all roads led back to you. We had no choice, he had no choice. I had to watch Chuck breakdown into sobs today in his supervisor's office when he realized his life was a lie. So, don't sit there and question his love for you. You are the one who fucked up. So, how about you drop the attitude before I drop it for you," she said, with her eyebrows raised.

Well... Damn Barbie.

"I'm gonna take over this interview for now, I think Detective Avalon is being too generous with you," she said.

"Good cop, bad cop. I get it. Look, I'm cooperating here, okay. I am admitting I took the items and pawned them. I'm willing to pay for them or whatever. I really don't feel good though and would like to go now, please," I said, sitting up straight.

The detectives looked at each other and Detective Sherlin cracked a smile before looking back at me. "Oh my God, you are serious right now, aren't you?"

"What? What do you mean? Yes, I'm serious. I answered your questions. Chuck and I can talk about this later and I'll just give him the money. I will pick up some extra shifts at work. Now that I know he wasn't the one to press charges, I am pretty sure he will understand once we talk."

Detective Sherlin stood up from her chair and Detective Avalon followed suit. I took a deep breath, relieved that this shit was over. I needed to get to Lazarus's asap, my bones felt like they were breaking inside my skin. Shit, I didn't drive here. "Excuse me," I said, stopping the Deputies before they exited, "I'm not really sure how this works, since you guys drove me, do I have to call a cab or something or do ya'll take me back?"

Detective Sherlin leaned opened the door and I caught a glimpse of all the deputies who had been standing outside watching. Chuck's bright orange shirt stuck out like a sore thumb, and I saw he had his head lowered while another deputy sympathetically rubbed his back. "You guys seeing this?" I heard her whisper to them.

Before anyone could answer she leaned back into the room and smiled.

"Oh Honey, you just don't get it. You aren't going home, not for a long time. We aren't done here, in fact... we are just getting started," she said, slamming the door behind her.

Chapter Forty-Six

The sound of Kelly's chuckle snapped me back into the office. I had almost forgotten I was talking to my counselor. Reliving those memories verbally had brought me right back to that time. The day when my world came crashing down.

"Are you laughing?" I asked as her hand covered her mouth, attempting to conceal a smile.

"I'm sorry, it's just. My gosh, Tiffany, did you really say that?" she asked trying to keep a straight face.

"Yeah, I didn't know. I had never been in trouble before. I mean I'd seen crime shows, but I knew that you could like, call someone to bail you out. I thought that's how it worked. I had no clue how much trouble I was actually in, ya know?" I said.

"Yes. I'm sorry. It's just so funny how you were like, 'Okay guys, I'm ready to go. Thanks for your time'." She laughed.

"Stoppp. I didn't know, man!" I was laughing too at this point. I seriously thought I was going home that night. I thought Chuck and I would sit on the couch, have a good cry and work through it. Looking back on what ended up happening instead, I could see the humor in it.

Kelly glanced above my head at the clock on the wall behind me, and her face fell when she saw the time. "Okay, well I've already kept you past Marriage and Dating class, I'll talk to Felicity about that, I'm sure she'll understand. You have spoken so candidly, so honestly about everything that has happened to you and it has helped me immensely to understand your history. Usually I don't keep clients over the allotted time, however if I'm being completely honest with you, at this point I'm intrigued. You have a way of speaking, it makes me feel like I'm there with you – in the interrogation room. Why don't you pick up from where the Detectives left you in there, and we can go ahead and wrap this up," she said.

"Okay. Yeah, I mean it's basically over. The fact that I'm here tells you how it all ended, right?" I asked.

"Of course I know how it ultimately ended, but the way you tell it leads me to believe you were still defiant at this point, closed off. I want to hear about the moment you realized the jig was up, you could no longer carry the lies anymore – that's what I want to hear," she said leaning back in her chair.

I knew the exact moment she was referring to, I remember like it was yesterday.

Three hours ago, I thought I was going home. I thought I was going to leave the police station and head to my home, where I would pet my dog and kick my feet up on the coffee table in front of the couch while convincing Chuck that I should be forgiven.

I was wrong.

The sweat plastered my shirt to my back, and every joint in my body was aching. I stared across the table at Detective Sherlin and her eyes peered right back into mine. I had managed to maintain a poker face and clutch my truth tightly to my chest for hours.

They wanted me to confess to stealing the guns, but I knew they didn't have any proof, so I continued to adamantly deny that I had anything to do with it. Each time I claimed to be innocent, they left me in the room for another 45 minutes.

They would return, try a new strategy, and when I didn't give in – they'd leave again.

They took my handcuffs off at one point, thinking that perhaps if they appeared to have my comfort at heart, I would think they cared about me and would confess. That wasn't happening.

I curled up into a ball in the corner of the ice-cold room, my shirt pulled down tightly over my bare knees in hopes of generating some warmth. My withdrawals made the room unbearable to be in. It felt like I was locked in a restaurant freezer, except a camera was pointed at me and an entire police force was watching me twist in agony. I needed a fucking cigarette.

The detectives eventually returned after what seemed like a lifetime.

"I need a cigarette," I said confidently as they sat down above me at the table.

"You aren't exactly in a position to be making demands, are you, Miss Johnson?" Deputy Sherlin smiled, asserting her power. I could feel the anger rising and I clenched my fists so tightly that my knuckles turned white.

"May I please have a cigarette, Deputy Sherlin. Please." She leaned back in her chair and crossed her arms in front of her chest. She had a coy smile plastered across her face and I suddenly realized why they kept us handcuffed in here. It took every ounce of willpower in me to refrain from wrapping my hands around her fucking neck.

"I dunno," she said, looking over Deputy Avalon. "Should we give her a cigarette break?"

"Mmm...Well, I don't think she has earned it. Do you? I mean, we have spent a long time in here, Deputy Sherlin, and she refuses to tell us what happened. Maybe if she was willing to divulge some information, we would be more willing to provide her with a smoke." They were speaking as if I were a child and again, thoughts of violence bubbled to the surface.

"Listen," I began. "Give me a God damn cigarette and I'll tell you..."; before I could finish my sentence, the door to the interrogation room swung open and a small Spanish woman entered the room, placing an envelope on the table in front of Deputy Sherlin and left the room without saying a word. I looked past the woman as she exited and saw that the group of Deputies were still huddled around the TV, as if they were watching the Super Bowl, including Chuck.

"Well what do we have here?" Deputy Sherlin said, peering into the mysterious envelope. She glanced up at me with her hand wrapped around the contents of it. "Anything you want to tell us before we open our present?"

"Nope," I said, fear suddenly taking over. What the fuck was in that envelope? She pulled everything out at once and smiled as she began rifling through the pages. A smile crept across her face and she slowly turned her face up to mine, while passing the pile to Deputy Avalon. She continued staring at me, unblinking, as he looked through the pages. "Wow," he said, setting them face down on the table. I looked at him, then back to her, then back to him. The looks on their faces led me to believe that there was no way I was getting out of this unscathed. They had something on me, I just didn't know what.

Detective Avalon looked over at Barbie and nodded, and they both stood up suddenly and headed toward the door. My heart felt like it was going to exploded as my mind raced through a thousand possible scenarios. Fingerprints? Of course they had my fingerprints, I lived there.

Detective Avalon exited the room without saying a word, while Deputy Sherlin hung back for a minute, and waited for the door to close behind him. She leaned down, placing the palms of her hands on the table and put her face about an inch away from mine. Her bright blue eyes were glaring at me and I could smell the gum she'd been chewing on her breath.

"Gotcha," she whispered, before slapping her hand on the table and exiting the room.

## Chapter Forty-Seven

After what seemed like an eternity, Deputy Sherlin returned to the interrogation room with the mysterious envelope and a cigarette. She rolled the cigarette toward me before sitting down. My heart leapt at the prospect of some nicotine. It had been close to fifteen hours since I'd been arrested, and my withdrawals were in full swing.

She lit my cigarette for me and leaned back into her chair glaring at me as I sucked the sweet tobacco deep into my lungs. I closed my eyes, and truly savored the moment because I had a feeling that whatever was in this envelope, was going to be the nail in my coffin.

"Miss Johnson, I've given you ample time to be honest with me and you haven't. I've offered you a lie detector test to prove your innocence and you've denied it. I'd like to give you one last opportunity to be honest with me, because I already know the truth."

"Deputy Sherlin, I was honest with you. You pulled out the photos of me at the pawn shop and I admitted to taking the stuff, I'm not sure what else you wa—"

"**Of course you did!** You had to!" she screamed. "We've got your face, clear as day pawning all of Deputy Henlin and his parents' shit. You signed a piece of paper with your finger-print at the pawn shops stating you were the rightful owner of these items and had a right to pawn them. We have copies of your driver's license from the pawn shop. So, yeah, I can un-derstand why you admitted to those things because you didn't have a Goddamn choice. When I asked you why, you claimed you owed some drug lord money which is obviously complete bullshit. Now what I need from you is some honesty regarding the guns and the wallet. It's clear you took them. So, let's just get this over with," she growled.

I knew she was trying to scare me, but she didn't. The only thing they had on me for sure were the pawned items but that was it.

I stared across the table at her, because I had the right to remain silent, damnit. Besides, I'm not stupid, I know that the envelope is a ploy to get me to cop to the crime. There was nothing in it.

"Okay, you wanna play it that way?" Detective Sherlin asked, realizing I wasn't going to cooperate. "You want to make it difficult, that's fine. I can play, too. In fact, I wanna play a game now. Let's play 'Guess What's in The Envelope'."

I stared her in her eyes, unmoving.

She stared at me for a moment and smiled. She pulled the contents of the envelope out and laid them on the table in front of me. It appeared to be lists, and on the lists, a few areas had been highlighted.

The moment I realized what I was looking at, I sunk.

She began to speak.

"The thing about criminals is, they aren't the smartest, right?" She laughed. As if I was supposed to agree with her.

"For example; you, a girl who thinks she's smarter than everyone. A girl who shares a phone plan with her Deputy boyfriend, a girl who has spent the past two years leading a double life, a girl who sends texts to known drug dealers saying things like, 'Hey, I've got the AK 47, I can bring it by tonight' and, 'Can I get some blues, I'm desperate.' They always slip up, eventually."

I looked at the transcript of my phone records on the table in front of me. The texts between Lazarus and I were highlighted in yellow. It was all there, in writing. The details of the things I'd done in black and white. I knew that it was over. I was caught and there was no denying that I'd taken the guns. It was all right here.

"Now let's start over. I'm Deputy Sherlin, and I've got some questions about the day of November 22nd. The day before we sent eight uniformed officers to your home to dust for fingerprints and investigate a crime that you, yourself committed. The day you offered them pizza and soda as they wasted their time and resources to find a criminal, a criminal that was standing two feet away from them. Why don't you start from there," She said, leaning back into her chair and crossing her arms, knowing she had pinned me into a corner.

There was a small group of deputies – friends of mine— gathered outside the door to watch the show. It was over. Life as I knew it had come to an end. The lies I'd fought so hard to keep juggled in the air came crashing down around me. Everyone was about to know what a monster I was. I had no choice, I had to tell the truth.

I took a deep breath. Peered up at the camera in the corner of the room, and released everything. The tears, the guilt, the shame all of it came pouring out at once.

"I'm a drug addict. I've always been a drug addict. I went to rehab in 2009 and fooled everyone into thinking I was fine, that I was healed. But I wasn't, I was never fine. I was so terrified of disappointing my family and ... Chuck." My eyes fell to the floor. Chuck was watching.

"Chuck was so wonderful, the nicest guy I'd ever met and when we got together I had been clean. I thought that his profession would be enough to keep me clean. I thought that his love was all I needed but I was wrong. My addiction snuck in and tricked me into thinking I could manage it, but I couldn't. It was too strong, and things got out of hand so fast..." My voice trailed off as I sobbed and Deputy Sherlin stood up without saying a word and exited the room. I followed her with my eyes and when the door swung open I saw the crowd gathered around the interrogation room viewing the camera feed.

She returned with a box of tissues and another cigarette and I could see that her expression had softened. I'm still not sure if this was a tactic used to make me feel comfortable and open up, or whether it was her genuinely realizing I had a problem. Either way I continued speaking, because the more I said out loud, the freer I began to feel.

"Some asshole from my past was threatening to release an inappropriate video of me if I didn't pay him the money I owed him..."

"Who is he?" she interrupted.

"I'd...I'd rather not say."

"Well I need you to tell me. If there is any chance of us showing that you were being threatened I need his information."

"It doesn't matter. I did it. I owed him the money. I made the tape. I put myself in these situations. I am going to take responsibility for it and move on with my life."

"Okay, we can revisit that later. So, you were being 'threatened' and then what?"

"Honestly, I don't know. It was like, I knew that I was on a downward spiral, so nothing mattered anymore. I didn't care. I just wanted to stay high, try to get myself out of the hole I'd dug, and hopefully overdose in the process. I wanted to die, and the only reason I didn't is because I didn't want Chuck to have to come home and find my head splattered on the headboard. If it wasn't for that I'd be long gone."

"I need you to tell me about the guns. The longer that they are out there in the hands of the wrong person, the more danger people are in. You put an assault rifle in the hands of a ruthless drug dealer and we need to find them."

I paused for a moment and slowly nodded. "I don't want to get him in trouble. He will kill me."

"We already know who he is. We have your phone records, we have deputy witnesses stating that they saw Chuck's vehicle parked in front of a known dealer's house. I just need you to confirm what happened so that we can safely get the guns back into Chuck's possession. So please, tell me the truth," she said.

"When I took the things from Chuck's parent's house, it was as if I reached a new low. The guilt was worse than it usually was and I'm not sure if it's because it didn't feel as wrong taking things from my own house or what, but I couldn't handle the negative feelings, the way it made me feel. I needed to numb them, to get high, but I needed money to do that."

I paused for a moment and took a drag of my cigarette and looked up at the camera once more, wondering how Chuck was going to react to this next part.

"I needed to take the money out of his wallet, and to shift the blame from myself I... I staged a burglary in our home."

"How?"

"I broke the back door, to make it look like someone forced their way inside. I took the entire wallet, but it wasn't until I was in the car driving to Lazarus' that I realized his wallet had his ID's and credit cards and...his badge."

I could see the muscles in her jaw clench.

"I...I didn't want him to have to replace all that stuff, I felt bad..."

She scoffed, and I paused briefly. "You felt bad. Okay, continue."

I could feel my walls going back up from her reaction. I was afraid that the more I told her the angrier she would become.

"I turned my car around and hopped out, to tuck the wallet under some leaves by a tree at the end of the yard. I wanted them to find it, so they could return it to him. I wanted him to have his things back. I just… I needed the money," I said as my face flushed with embarrassment.

"And what did you use the money for?" she asked, although I had a feeling she already knew the answer.

"Drugs. I needed to not be sick, because I had less than twenty-four hours to come up with $1,000. While I was getting the drugs, I asked my guy…"

"Lazarus Bishop," she interjected.

"I asked Lazarus if he knew how I could get money. He said no at first, but as I was leaving he asked if I had any way to get a gun. I was desperate. I thought I could sell him the gun and then buy it back once I was sure that Jake was off my back. I didn't…I didn't think it all the way through."

"Clearly."

I ignored her patronizing comment and continued. "I rushed home, threw a blanket on the floor and laid a few guns on top of it. As soon as I collected the ones I didn't think he would miss, I rolled up the blanket and loaded it in the truck. Lazarus picked the ones he wanted and in exchange gave me the money I needed to pay Jake off. I paid him yesterday. You guys woke me up out of bed today. It's ironic, actually. I fought so hard to keep Chuck from finding out and my very first day of being relieved of the burden of owing Jake money, you guys show up and bring me here."

Detective Sherlin didn't say a word. She stared at me for a moment, as if trying to process everything I'd just said. I could tell she was struggling to find the words. What I had done was shocking, it was personal, it happened to someone she knew.

Just then a man dressed in full S.W.A.T. uniform burst through the door of the interrogation room and grabbed one of the empty chairs at the table. I watched Detective Sherlin exit as he slid it over to where I was and sat down, leaning forward until his face was uncomfortably close to mine.

"Are you shooting these things?" he asked menacingly.

"I've shot the AK before, but I don't think I've shot the other two..."

"Not the guns, you fucking loser. The pills, are you shooting the pills?"

"Oh. Yes. I am," I admitted.

"You do realize that you probably gave my buddy out there a disease, he's currently getting a test to check and see if your selfish ass gave him Hep. C."

The man's words made me feel filthy, like a mangy dog that nobody wanted. "I didn't give him anything, okay? I haven't been shooting up for that long and I was always careful."

"Well, you better hope so. That's all I have to say about that." He slammed the chair into the table and left the room, revealing that most of the spectators outside the door had left.

I was alone in this room, and all of my secrets had been released into the universe. I was no longer in control.

I laid on the floor in a broken heap of useless skin and bones. I was nothing but a mistake. I laid there for an hour before anyone entered the room again.

"Okay, let's go," a deputy I hadn't seen before said, motioning for me to stand up. He was careful to avoid eye contact.

"What happens now?" I asked quietly.

"Now... You go to jail," he said, as three uniformed officers walked into the room with shackles.

"And that was it." I exhaled, bringing my eyes up to Kelly. She wasn't laughing this time, instead, tears streamed down her face and I watched as her chin began to quiver.

She closed her eyes and began to slowly shake her head. "Wow, Tiffany. Wow," she said standing up to sit next to me.

"I am so sorry. I'm sorry for you, for Chuck, for his family... I'm just so sorry." She reached out to hug me, and the moment I rested my chin on her shoulder the tears escaped from my eyes. As I drew in a deep breath, it somehow felt as if I'd finally closed a book that I had been forced to read over and over, every day, for over six months.

Just as I had that day in the interrogation room, after speaking the truth to another person, I felt... free.

Now that I had emptied the two-ton suitcase of shame I'd been carrying with me all these years, it was time for me to move on and figure out why I chose to pick up the suitcase to begin with. My brain was fucked up, there's no question about that, now I needed to figure out how to fix it.

Chapter Forty-Eight

The day I finished telling my story to Kelly was a pivotal time in my journey. The moment I had stepped outside of her office and into the fresh air, I was met by a cool breeze. I closed my eyes and felt the wind dance across my skin and I couldn't help but think that it was the Universe's way of giving me hug, and letting me know that everything was going to be okay.

I spent four more months at Leap of Faith. Those months were filled with joy, defeat, happiness, frustration. Moments of wanting to run through the door, and moments of sheer bliss. There was laughter, and many, many tears. I made a few mistakes, but I never gave up.

My time at the rehab had changed me as a person, I was able to look inward, and spend time examining the real issues, without the distraction of the outside world. I knew that the time was going to pass anyway, so I chose to make every single moment count and get the most out of the program while I was there. I acquired a sponsor, and she helped walk me through the 12 Steps. Those steps saved my life, and allowed me to understand why I did all the things that I did, and other coping mechanisms and tools to use instead of turning to drugs each time I felt uncomfortable.

I attended every class – and listened intently as the instructor educated me on what I needed to do to stay clean. I focused on doing the right thing, every chance I got – even when no one was looking. I practiced honesty, and patience, both of which had been completely foreign to me prior.

Each day that passed where I didn't stick a needle in my arm, I felt more alive. Like I was a part of the world, instead of just floating through it. Like I had purpose. There were times when I wanted to give up, when I wanted to say, "Fuck this" and run out the doors; instead, I stayed. Because once I had a taste of recovery, once I belly-laughed in a room full of women, once I laid my head on my pillow at night completely at peace with myself, I knew that even my best day high, would pale in comparison to my worst day clean.

I emerged from Leap of Faith as a new creation, but my journey wasn't over just yet.

Chapter Forty-Nine

**PRESENT DAY**

The 'clunk' of my high-heeled shoes hitting the wooden floors, echoed through the hallway as I headed toward the front desk. I smiled at a woman wearing a name badge and rocking an infant as I passed her in the corridor. "Sorry," I mouthed quietly, walking on my tiptoes to keep from waking the baby.

"It's okay, you're fine," she whispered giving me a friendly smile.

A young woman with glasses and bouncy curls smiled sweetly as I approached the front desk.

"Hello, I'm Tiffany, I'm here to see the girls," I said, glancing around the office.

"Sure, just sign in here," she said, handing me a clipboard. I quickly scribbled my name and set it on the counter before heading to a seat in the waiting room.

Before I could sit, a woman emerged from the double doors to my right and held her hand out to shake mine. "Hi, you must be Tiffany," she said.

"Yes, hi." I said.

"Come on back, we are ready for you," she said, waving me toward the door. The 'clunk' of my heels was drowned out only by the sound of my heart banging around in my chest. I had done this so many times, but it never got easier on my nerves.

As I entered the room, the squeals and cries continued, but all conversation amongst the women ceased, and they all turned to face me. I smiled nervously as I passed them and headed to the empty chair at the front of the room. Once seated, the women lazily sauntered over to fill the empty seats that were facing me. The women were at all different stages of their pregnancy, some had small bumps while others looked like they were ready to explode at any second. Each of them looked exhausted, and they seemed annoyed by my presence.

Once everyone was seated, and the room fell silent, I reached into my pocket and pulled out the small, pink, worry stone my father had given me before he passed away last year. He had fought long and hard, and unlike when my mother passed, I was able to be there for him and the family as we said goodbye. My father and I had gotten sober fifteen days apart, and two months after leaving rehab, we got to walk up on stage together to collect our one-year medallions. It was one of the happiest moments of my life.

"Hello everyone, my name is Tiffany, and I'm an addict," I said.

"Hi, Tiffany," the women chorused.

"I know you guys are exhausted, and the last thing you probably want to do is sit in these shitty plastic chairs and listen to some weird lady lecture you." A few women chuckled, giving me a renewed sense of confidence.

"But if you will give me thirty minutes of your time, I promise it will be worth it." I said. As I looked at their tired faces I could tell they would rather be changing a dirty diaper than sitting here with me. I wasn't offended, because I wasn't here just for them, I was here for me.

"I spent over ten years of my life doing drugs. I lied, cheated, stole, manipulated and deceived everyone I'd ever known. I destroyed my life, and the life of those around me. I wanted to die – I tried to die, but for some reason, I couldn't even do that right."

I rubbed the stone as I cleared my throat, before continuing. "Now before I go any further, I just want to take a second and tell each and every one of you – how freaking proud I am of you." I paused for a moment to swallow back the sobs as the tears began filling my eyes.

"You all could be anywhere in the world, an alley, a trap house, the streets. But you're here, you're here in a treatment facility getting help for yourselves, and giving the babies in those rooms and inside your bellies a shot at life, man, and that's a fucking miracle. So, give yourselves a quick round of applause because you deserve it." Applause rang out through the building and the women turned to each other and smiled proudly while others wiped tears from their eyes.

"In case nobody has told you today, you guys fucking rock!" I yelled over their claps. It was like all the guilt they had felt about being in a residential treatment center for pregnant women and children had momentarily lifted.

Once the applause had settled and the women adjusted themselves in their seats, I continued.

"As far as being an addict goes, my story is no different. The only thing separating you guys and myself is that I happened to be dating a cop during my active addiction," I said.

The women let out a gasp and their eyes grew wide. A girl turned to her friend and whispered something, and I noticed a shift in the room. The women were on the edge of their seats, they were interested now.

"We can get into that later, but for now, I'd like to tell you what brings me here to Family Ties Treatment Center. After I left rehab, I moved into a Halfway House. I knew I was ready to be out in the real world, but I was also aware that I wasn't prepared to dive in head-first. I needed accountability. The halfway house rules were simple; get a job, attend one meeting a day, no drinking or using, and curfew is midnight. It was an amazing way for me to meet people in recovery, and being surrounded by strong, independent women every day really motivated me and gave me a sense of true friendship I had never experienced before.

"Shortly after moving into the halfway house I met someone. Now I don't recommend this, because it's important to focus on yourself for a while. But me being the rebel that I am figured because I had ten months clean, it was close enough to a year and would be okay. Him and I began dating and I was completely honest with him about my past, he accepted me and supported where I was in my journey. Plus, he was super-hot, so." A few of the girls chuckled and nodded.

"I found out I was pregnant in the bathroom of a halfway house." Once again, their eyes grew wide as saucers.

## Chapter Fifty

"The moment I saw the two pink lines, I collapsed into a ball on the floor and began sobbing. This was not how things were supposed to happen. He and I had only been dating for two months. I didn't have a job, a car, and only a garbage bag's worth of belongings—that's it.

"I paced the length of the small bathroom for about an hour," I continued. "Unsure of what to do, I called my sister, who basically said 'you're an idiot.' Which was completely different than I envisioned my pregnancy announcement going as I was growing up. Anyway, my sister and I spoke later that night and she convinced me to wrap the pregnancy test up in a box, with a bow, because 'how could he be upset if it's presented like a present'."

I could laugh along with the girls in the room now, but at the time I was horrified.

"So, I hopped on my bicycle, and pedaled over to his house to give him his gift. He thought it was a watch, imagine his surprise."

Laughter echoed through the room and I was no longer nervous. "What did he say?" someone in the back row asked.

"Well, he said... 'This is wonderful'. And that was about the time I started freaking out and told him 'hell no, we can't do this, we need to get an abortion'. I mean think about it, I had nothing. Nothing. I was just beginning to find out who I was, there was no way I could have a child at this point in my life, it would have been foolish."

I watched as their faces began to drop. A moment ago, they loved me, and now they looked disgusted that I would kill my unborn child.

"Listen, it would have been a huge risk for me to have a baby while jobless and homeless. What was I gonna do, have a baby in a halfway house? I was terrified. What if I relapsed?" I said, looking around pleadingly. The women couldn't even look at me, they were shaking their heads and looking away.

"I don't know about you guys," I began. "But I believe a higher power restored me to sanity, and my higher power speaks to me through my conscience and a feeling in my gut. My higher power knows what's best for me, which is why I always listen. My son was born on September 22nd, 2014. He was born on my birthday." I smiled.

Chills covered my body as the women began to cheer.

"I busted my ass, got a job, got a car, and four months after finding I was pregnant, finally moved in with my boyfriend at the time. I never gave up, even when I wanted to. The boy growing inside me was now a part of me, and I knew I would do whatever it took to give him a wonderful life."

"I am now married to the father of my son, and he is also the father of my daughter, born 16 months after my son. We acquired his other daughter from a previous relationship, full time as well. So, in the span of 2 ½ years I went from being a single woman living in a halfway house, to a married mother of three."

The women looked stunned and amused.

"I started sharing my journey on social media in hopes of inspiring others, and this past year I've acquired hundreds of thousands of followers. I'm not saying this to brag," I laughed, "I'm saying this because I receive around thirty messages a day from addicts who are still struggling. These people are begging me to help them find a way out. They are literally, dying, to get to those chairs you all are sitting in right now. Take advantage of the opportunity you all have been given." The women nodded as I spoke, and I knew my words had resonated with them. Even if only for a moment, they were reminded that it was in fact, a gift that they were here.

"So, why am I telling you all of this? I'm telling you because there was once a point in my recovery when I wanted to give up. I wanted to get high, I wanted to throw it all away. But just because I wanted to get high, doesn't mean I had to. So, I didn't, no matter how hard it got, I kept going because I knew wonderful things were waiting for me. It wasn't easy, but I knew that if I continued to fight through the weak moments, I could get my life back.

There are times now, where I will be sitting in the living room of our beautiful four-bedroom home, and I'll hear my kids giggling in the other room. In that moment, I'll think back to the times I laid in bed twisting and turning in agony from withdrawal, the times I overdosed and almost died, and I think– *Holy shit, I almost missed this.*"

"Each and every one of you sitting in here right now, has an unbelievable life waiting for you just down the road, a life better than you can dream. All you have to do, is keep walking. No matter how bumpy the road gets, or how many unexpected detours you come across, keep putting one foot in front of the other. Keep fucking walking. You know, there was a time when I couldn't go longer than five minutes without being high. But with the help of my sponsor, my higher power, friends in the fellowship and a very vivid memory of what life was like during my addiction, I have managed to put together five years in a row of abstaining from drugs and alcohol." The room was electric as everyone cheered.

"It is possible to have an amazing, fun, purposeful life after addiction. It really is. Addiction is not the end. Life is fleeting, and it will be over before you know it. You have an opportunity to say right here, and right now... That addiction, is not how my story is going to end..."

As the women stood to their feet and furiously clapped their hands, I closed my eyes and thought about my parents in Heaven. I'm sure that wherever they are, they are clapping right along with the people in this room. I thought about jail, and how desperately I wanted to die. How angry I was that they found me and saved me after my attempted suicide. Suddenly, in this moment, everything made sense. My higher power knew before I did that my work here on earth wasn't done. When I couldn't see a future for myself, He already knew I'd be standing here tonight.

As I looked out at all the hopeful, smiling faces in the room, just beginning their journey in recovery, tears of gratitude filled my eyes. I am grateful to have found recovery, grateful that I got my sister back and was able to make new, sober memories with my father before he passed. I'm grateful for the beautiful children waiting for me at home and my wonderful husband for sticking around and being an incredible father, when he could have easily ran.

I am grateful that Chuck has a beautifully forgiving heart, and that he is happy with a new love. One who will treat him with the dignity and respect he deserves.

And I am grateful that no one gave up on me. That no one wrote me off or let me die, because if they had...you wouldn't be reading this book. There is no such thing as a lost cause, and it's never too late to start over. I am living proof.

*A flicker of hope in one's heart, is capable of lighting the path to a new destiny...*

# About the Author

Tiffany Jenkins is a wife, and mother to three awesome human beings. She realized her love of writing last year when she started her blog, *"Juggling the Jenkins"*, where she writes about motherhood, addiction, marriage and adulting. Tiffany has acquired a huge social media following where her videos receive millions of views. She uses her platform to help and inspire others who are struggling with motherhood, mental health, addiction, and those who just need a good laugh. Her articles have been featured on "BLUNTmoms.com", "Themighty.com" and "Thoughtcatalog.com" and her Blog and Facebook page have been covered on several news outlets and television programs.

This year she will be celebrating five years clean and sober from drugs and alcohol. She feels that publishing a book, is a wonderful way to celebrate this milestone.

Made in the USA
Middletown, DE
12 July 2018